SOUTH AMERICA SKI GUIDE

Santiago and Mendoza to Cape Horn

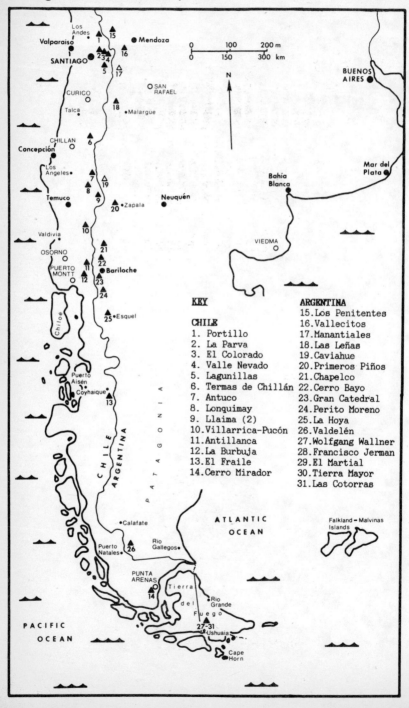

South America Ski Guide

Chris I Lizza

BRADT PUBLICATIONS, UK
HUNTER PUBLISHING, USA

First published in 1992 by Bradt Publications, 41 Nortoft Rd, Chalfont St Peter, Bucks SL9 0LA, England. Distributed in the USA by Hunter Publishing Inc., 300 Raritan Center Parkway, CN94, Edison, NJ 08810.

Copyright © 1992 Chris I Lizza

All rights reserved. No part of this publication may be reproduced, stored in a retrieval system, or transmitted in any form or by any means, electronic, mechanical, photocopying or otherwise without the written consent of the publishers.

British Library Cataloguing-in-Publication data

A catalogue record for this book is available from the British Library

Edited by Rob Rachowiecki
Maps by the author
Front cover photo: Jennifer McCoy by Brad Peatross
Back cover photo of Llaima, Chile, by the author
Typeset from the author's disc by Patti Taylor, London NW8 ORJ
Printed by Guernsey Press

To Dave, a skier's skier.

Acknowledgements

It is with great pleasure that I extend my deepest thanks and most sincere appreciation to the following people who were invaluable in their generous support, understanding, patience, and kindness beyond normal courtesy:

In Chile, I received invaluable assistance from Henry Purcell, David Purcell, and especially Marcia Weissman; David Halpert and Vern Fry; Alvaro Valdes Covarrubias; Eduardo Kuhn Sepulveda and German Klempau; Eduardo Stern and Cici; Jorge Mora Mora, my ski bro; Jose Luis Giner Izquierdo and Radoslav Drpic Garcia; Alex Gonzalez, Juan Carlos Canales, and Ricardo Mehr Schlaeger; José Luis Sanz and Walter Gebhard; Carlos Urzua, María Pia, Horacio Bovolo, Kelo Jorquera Avalos, Guillermo Leonardo Zuñiga, and Patricia who are the nicest people I've met in all my travels; Luis Ramirez; Rolando Soto and German Martinez; Ricardo Andrade; and Sra Juanita Cofre in the tourist kiosko. In Santiago, Martín Silva, Santiago Garcia, and Arturo Hammersley were generous in giving their time and whatever information I requested.

In Argentina, several devoted skiers went out of their way to help me including David Vela, Consuelo, Ricardo and all the friends of Andesport; Theresa Cano, Pedro Lauryssens, Jorge Iñarra, and Francisco Guiñazú in Mendoza; "Coco" Torres, Ricardo Williams, and "Consul" at Las Leñas; Dr Eduardo Zinni and Héctor Roaldo Giovachini; Jean Pierre Raemdonck; Pablo Roskenjer, Vicente Ojeda, Peter Somweber, and Walter Kramer in Bariloche; Heraldo Rudolph and Miguel Altamira; Arturo DeBernardi; Herman Gregory and Josefina Belforte; Gustavo and Anna Giro; and Fabio, Hernan, Andrea, Adriano and the "Bruja" who took me into their home at "the end of the world". I also wish to thank Philipo Costa, Nicolas Howard, and María Carmody; Juan Carlos Firpo and Rafael Maria Perrota

Bengolea; Sigmund Brubacher; Tito Lowenstein and Ruth; Adela Varela; and extra kisses for the secretary in the CAS who made me tea while permitting me to study in her wonderful library.

In the US, I have long enjoyed the support of Terry Palmer, Michael Day, Jean Luis Villiot, and all the great people of Precision Skis/ScottUSA in Sun Valley; Lange Ski Boots and Cordy Lawrence who keep my feet happy; Jim Kelley of HIS Travel; Michael Graber; Rick Naranjo; Ruben Macaya; John Armstrong and, most sincerely and appreciatively for his support, Dennis Agee. Don Montague, Saoirse McClory, and Petra Schepens of the South American Explorers Club have provided much needed support and enthusism to my project for which I am endebted. Special thanks to Larry Walker, Brad Peatross, Andy Johnson, and Connie who all assisted professionally with no reward. CD Ritter and Rob Rachowiecki were indispensible as careful editors. I especially would like to thank my parents, Marge, Bob, and Tib, as well as Judy and her family, for their support.

Extra special thanks are extended to Luis Nuñez and everyone at LANChile, Rob Petrinovic, Raúl Anguita, and Pilar Urzua Elers in Santiago. Finally, I wish to thank Hilary Bradt for her support, ideas, and wise vision.

ABOUT THE AUTHOR

Chris Lizza is a professional ski patrolman and chef from Mammoth Lakes, California. An ex-ski racer, Chris's professional skier credentials include seven years patrolling and one year coaching at Mammoth Mountain, a year patrolling at Crystal Mountain, Washington, and a month working with the *pisteros* at Las Leñas, Argentina.

Chris has skied extensively throughout the world. His first international ski experience came when he represented the United States in Cortina, Italy, in the olympic-style International Student Ski Championships (1977). He has since skied in Europe, Japan, and throughout the Western Hemisphere. Chris has completed four ski trips to South America, travelling the length of the Andes from Caracas to Ushuaia.

Table of contents

Acknowledgements v

PART I — GENERAL BACKGROUND INFORMATION
1. Introduction 1
2. Geography 3
   The Cordillera de Los Andes 3, Ski Regions 4, Ski Season 5, Climate and Snowfall 6, Flora and Fauna 7.
3. Development of Skiing 9
   History 10, Ski Area Operations 15, Ski Safety 17, The Future of Skiing in South America 18, A Note on Expectations 18.
4. Preparations 19
   Costs 19, Health Concerns 20, Entry Requirements 20, What to Bring 20.
5. Travelling in Chile and Argentina 21
   Lodging 21, Dining 22, Transportation 24, Money and Exchange 28, Communication 28, Medical and Rescue Services 29.
6. Crossing the Chile-Argentina Frontier 30
   Introduction 30, History 30, Santiago-Mendoza (The Uspallata Pass) 31, Puerto Montt-Bariloche 32, Tierra del Fuego 33.

PART II — CHILE 35
7. Portillo 41
8. La Parva 53
9. El Colorado, Farellones 59
10. Valle Nevado 69
11. Lagunillas 75
12. Santiago 81
13. Termas de Chillán, Chillán 93
14. Antuco, Los Angeles 103
15. Lonquimay 111
16. Llaima, Temuco 115
17. Villarrica-Pucón, Pucón 123
18. Antillanca, Osorno 133
19. La Burbuja, Puerto Montt, Puerto Varas 143
20. El Fraile, Coyhaique 151
21. Cerro Mirador, Punta Arenas 159

PART III — ARGENTINA 167
22 Los Penitentes 171
23 Vallecitos 179
24 Mendoza 185
25 Valle Manantiales 192
26 Valle de Las Leñas, San Rafael 193
27 Parque Caviahue 207
28 Primeros Piños, Zapala 209
29 Chapelco, San Martín de los Andes 215
30 Cerro Bayo, Villa La Angostura 223
31 Gran Catedral 231
32 Bariloche's Other Ski Areas 239
33 San Carlos de Bariloche 245
34 Perito Moreno, El Bolsón 252
35 La Hoya, Esquel 259
36 Valdelén, Río Turbio 267
37 Ushuaia's Ski Areas, Ushuaia 273

PART IV — THE NORTHERN ANDES AND ANTARCTICA .. 283
38 Bolivia — Chacaltaya, the World's Highest Ski Area, La Paz 284
39 Peru — Pastoruri 292
40 Ecuador — The Avenue of the Volcanoes 293
41 Colombia — Manizales and the Nevado del Ruiz .. 295
42 Venezuela — Mérida, the World's Highest Tramway ... 297
43 Antarctica — Marsh Air Force Base 299

APPENDICES
A Spanish Ski Vocabulary 300
B Ski Week Price Comparison 303
C Proposed Itineraries 305
D Buenos Aires Ski Addresses 307
E Conversion Table 308

INDEX 309

Part I

General Background Information

Chapter 1

Introduction

Why would anyone ski in South America? Simply put, for four months of the year, the world's best skiing is found in the Southern Andes. This fact is substantiated by the annual arrival of the world's top national ski teams at several of the larger resorts. But skiers of all skill levels and disciplines can enjoy the variety of excellent skiing offered in Chile and Argentina.

When most *gringos* dream of summer skiing, they consider only New Zealand where the language is familiar. The quality of skiing does not compare, however. First, there are about twice as many ski areas in South America as there are in New Zealand. And, the destination resorts of South America are far more comfortable than the best resorts of New Zealand. The most important difference, though, is the quantity and quality of the snow. It is simply unfair to compare skiing in the high Andes of South America to the slopes of the maritime-controlled climate of the South Pacific island-nation.

South American ski areas are also remarkably uncrowded. Outside the last two weeks of July when the Argentines are on holiday, skiers can travel freely to any of the resorts without advanced planning or reservations. The development boom of the last half of the 1980s resulted in slope and hotel capacities that far exceed the number of domestic skiers.

Skiing could also be an incidental excuse to travel in this scenic and untrampled part of the world. The people are extraordinarily gracious, and the countryside is beautiful and dramatic. Travel within the region is accomplished easily and economically. Outstanding food and wine is served to fit all tastes and budgets. In short, travellers can comfortably explore the region in either first class style or on a student's budget. Most importantly, Chile and Argentina are safe for travel; unlike Brazil and Peru, crimes are rarely committed against tourists.

I have divided the ski areas of South America into three groups based on their level of development. International resorts are modern complexes with complete infrastructures that offer many diversions in addition to outstanding skiing. National ski centers boast significant skiing terrain but lack some of the services well-travelled skiers may expect. The regional areas, most of which are owned and operated by a local *Club Andino*, are small and are not designed to receive international tourists. While the bigger resorts offer better skiing and services, the inconveniences encountered in reaching some of the lesser known areas are often rewarded with unique adventures and enduring friendships. The following list covers all of the South American ski areas which were in operation during the 1980s. Don't just read about it; get on a plane and go skiing this summer.

International:
Portillo
La Parva
El Colorado
Valle Nevado
Villarrica-Pucón
Valle de Las Leñas
Chapelco
Gran Catedral

National:
Termas de Chillán
Antillanca
Los Penitentes
La Hoya

Nordic:
Travesía Nórdica
Las Cotorras
Tierra Mayor
Francisco Jerman

Regional:
Lagunillas
Antuco
Lonquimay
Llaima (2)
La Burbuja
El Fraile
Cerro Mirador
Vallecitos
Primeros Piños
Valdelén
El Martial
Wolfgang Wallner
Chacaltaya
Cerro Bayo
Valle de Chall-Huaco
Piedras Blancas
Villa Arelauquen
Perito Moreno

Chapter 2

Geography

The South America Ski Guide is a rather presumptuous title for this book as skiing is developed in a relatively small part of the continent. On a land mass that is approximately 7,650km (4,750 miles) long and 5,600km (3,500 miles) across at its widest point, all skiing occurs in a narrow strip which is just 2,650km (1,650 miles) long. Excluding the tiny ski run at Chacaltaya in Bolivia, all the developed ski areas lie in a region which occupies just 23 degrees latitude of the 70 degree-long continent at the narrowest and southernmost part of the world's longest mountain range.

The Cordillera de Los Andes

The Andes, or simply the *Cordillera* as it is called by its residents, is the north-south continental divide that splits South America into very unequal halves. It is the world's second highest range behind the Asian Himalayas and boasts America's loftiest point on Cerro Aconcagua at 6,960m (22,835ft). The *Alto Cordillera* is the high-altitude portion which extends from the equator to the Valle de Las Leñas where even the lowest passes are above 3,000 meters. The range is extremely narrow and abrupt by global standards. The widest point is in Bolivia (650km, 400 miles), and the crest is never more than 300km (200 miles) from the Pacific Ocean.

The Andes can be split into three distinct geographical areas. The northern section encompasses three *cordilleras* in Colombia and runs east-west in Venezuela. The central section is broad and desolate and runs from the high *páranamos* of Ecuador, into the *puna* of Peru, through the *altiplano* of Bolivia, and to the rainless Atacama in Chile. Only the southern section, which begins at La Serena (north of Santiago), and continues to Cape Horn, is of concern to skiers.

The Andes is a geologically young range formed by the collision of the subducting Nazca plate and the overriding South American plate. Its youth is shown by the frequent volcanic activity and earthquakes for which the entire Pacific Rim is famous. There are over 2,000 volcanoes in the Andes, the most active of which are located at the northern end in Colombia and Ecuador and in southern Chile. Many of the ski resorts are located at or near active volcanoes and developed hot springs resorts.

Ski Regions

Between Aconcagua and Tierra del Fuego, the island at the southernmost end of America, the *Cordillera* takes many different forms. These are best described by dividing South America's ski areas into three main geographical clusters. From north to south, the first is the Tupungato area which clearly has the continent's best skiing. Farther south are the Lakes Regions of Chile and Argentina characterized by volcanoes in Chile and low hills in Argentina. Farthest south is the relatively undeveloped frontier of Patagonia and Tierra del Fuego which has several ski areas but few runs. Only Chacaltaya in Bolivia, and El Fraile in the middle of Archipelagic Chile, lie outside these regions.

The *Alto Cordillera*

Between Santiago and Mendoza, the *Cordillera* is high and desolate. Very little vegetation grows in these mountains, and only one difficult pass links Chile and Argentina. Tupungato is the central peak in the region, lying on the border at 6,570m (21,555ft). The area is typified by Portillo which is dwarfed by the awesome peaks that loom above the ski slopes. This region contains South America's best ski areas including Las Leñas, Penitentes, and Vallecitos in Argentina, and La Parva, El Colorado, Valle Nevado, Portillo, and Lagunillas in Chile. With summit elevations approaching 3,650m (12,000ft), this northern sector has South America's best snow, steepest slopes, and longest seasons. Skiing here combines the open, alpine terrain of Europe with the deep and dry snow of the North American West, producing world-class conditions.

The Lakes Districts

Farther south, the *Cordillera* shrinks dramatically in elevation. Conical volcanoes begin to dominate the landscape with the highest elevations deviating from the true *Cordillera*. Most lie on the west side of the border with the notable exception of Lanín near San Martín de Los Andes in Argentina, and the tops of many continue to puff steam. The mountains are skirted with a dense and ferny deciduous rain forest which gives way to an open snowfield at the 1,500m (4,900ft) level. Trout-filled lakes gather icy snowmelt and warm spring water in the valleys between the mountains. The area was perfectly described by the North American ski writer John Jay in 1947 as "a combination of New Hampshire, Norway, and Sweden."

On the Chilean side, all the ski areas are located at the base of volcanoes including, from north to south, Chillán, Antuco, Lonquimay, Llaima, Villarica-Pucón, Antillanca, and La Burbuja. In Argentina, only Caviahue is located near a volcano, while Primeros Piños, Chapelco, Cerro Bayo, Gran Catedral, Perito Moreno, and La Hoya all climb some sub-range of hills. Skiing in these areas is characterized by low elevations (up to 2,000m or 6,500ft), heavy, wet snow (sometimes rain), and interrupted seasons. The most successful of these resorts have aerial lifts to carry skiers from the warmer base below treeline to upper snowfields where skiing is generally good all season. The slopes can be vaguely compared to the smaller areas of Eastern North America but with much warmer temperatures and more skiing above treeline.

Tierra del Fuego and Patagonia

The third geographical zone includes the southern end of Patagonia and Tierra del Fuego. The *Cordillera* is at its humblest here as the rugged peaks have been eroded into rolling hills by the Patagonian winds which rip through the region each spring. Although the area is home to the world's most southerly everything, the latitudes are no more polar than Glasgow, Scotland, or Edmonton, Alberta. The winter landscape is characterized by frozen bogs and ponds, and mossy but otherwise bare trees.

Most of the ski areas are within sight of the ocean fjords and channels that dominate the region, and the normal snowline is just above the seashore. The region is best suited to nordic skiing because of the flat terrain and low elevations. Of the four alpine ski areas of the region (Cerro Mirador, Valdelén, Wolfgang Wallner, and Cerro Martial), only Mirador has more than one run. Skiing in Tierra del Fuego should be little more than an excuse to explore the unique region in the off-season when travellers enjoy substantial discounts.

Ski Season

The "normal" ski season in South America lasts from late June to early October. That definitive statement needs to be qualified however, by emphasizing that almost anything is possible. Snow is all but certain from mid-July to early September, with the heaviest snowfall in August. The best time to ski is early September when the winter storms have subsided and the slopes are least crowded. Argentine vacations are in their full, frenzied peak in the last half of July, the most crowded and expensive part of the ski season.

It is not unusual to ski outside this "normal" season. May was the traditional start, but climatic change seems to have postponed recent opening dates. On the plus side, the seasons seem to continue later than ever and a few of the areas, notably La Parva, have extended seasons into December! One of the most remarkable springs of the century is documented in the story of the Andes survivors as told in *Alive*, the story of the Andes plane crash survivors, in which the author describes heavy snowfall in the *Alto Cordillera* throughout November in 1972.

Climate and Snowfall

Each region has its own climatic patterns and snow characteristics, but hard data is only gathered and kept at the major cities. Of all the ski areas, only Portillo has a snow plot and avalanche forecaster. A study of Santiago's weather records reveals a huge variance in annual precipitation. It also shows that, in spite of sub-par years in 1988 and 1989, the decade of the 80's was one of the wettest of the century. This data is valid only for the west flank of the mountains near Santiago where storms approach loaded with moisture from the Pacific Ocean. Most systems on the drier east side spin off the Atlantic Ocean and only release their treasure in the higher elevations.

In the Lakes District, Pacific storms have no trouble crossing the *Cordillera*. They blow in strong from the Pacific Ocean and dissipate quickly over Patagonia. Fog is common in the central valley of Chile but this should not discourage skiers who are likely to find clear skies at higher elevations. The weather at lakeside ski areas like Villarrica-Pucón is characterized by increased humidity which results in significantly more, but heavier, snow. The areas closest to the international border and in the deepest parts of the rain forest, particularly Antillanca, suffer from an almost constant falling mist that may or may not turn to snow at ski lift elevations.

The landforms of Tierra del Fuego hardly effect the storms that repeatedly circle the globe from west to east all year long. Wind can be extreme in the region, but storms are rarely dramatic otherwise. A few centimeters of snow can last a long time though, in the cold temperatures and short days of 55 degrees south latitude.

Flora and Fauna

Skiers anxious to encounter new forms of plant and animal life will be happier the farther south they venture. Around Santiago and Mendoza there are no natural forests in the mountains. Low shrubs and clinging lichens provide the only greenery in the barren landscape. Massive, soaring Andean condors are the stellar aerialists of the region. They are particularly prevalent around Portillo as many scavenge at the nearby mines. Condors flying above Santiago or at other lower elevations are one of the surest signs of an approaching storm.

Both southern regions are a bird watchers dream. Pink flamingoes and black-necked swans are familiar Patagonian sights and are best observed at the Laguna Blanca near Zapala in Argentina. The flightless South American rhea is a relative of the African ostrich and Australian emu and is best seen on the plains between Punta Arenas and Puerto Natales in Chile. A wide variety of water fowl, sea birds, and songbirds migrate through the area annually.

The most interesting tree of the region is the araucaria or monkey-puzzle tree (*pehuen*) which grows in a very narrow zone between Lonquimay and Llaima in Chile, and Caviahue and Lanín in Argentina. These are the only coniferous trees growing in the mountains, and they are described in the Lonquimay chapter. Araucarias produce a 5cm-long (2in) piñon nut that is edible after roasting. In the Lakes District, the bamboo-type plant is a *colihue*, and *ñires, coligues*, and *lengas* are a few of the hardwoods which grow profusely throughout the area.

There is also a large variety of mammal life. Skiers are unlikely to spot the nocturnal hares and foxes, but their tracks are found everywhere in fresh snow. The stealthy pumas are also rarely seen, but guanacos, a wild relative of the llama, are common. At Las Leñas, the tame guanaco is the best friend of the local St Bernard dog, and the antics between these completely different creatures are hilarious. Wild boar, antelope, and red deer were introduced near Bariloche to provide meat and sport for hunters, and the region's lakes and streams are stocked with trout and salmon. Fishermen will want to stay for the opening of fishing season in November, as the region from Temuco to Ushuaia has some of the world's best fresh water fishing especially around unknown Coyhaique.

WASH & GO

First choose comfortable activewear.
Then use TX.10 Wash-in Waterproofing.
Later, wash with LOFT AUTOMATIC –
As often as you like, and still stay
warm, comfortable and DRY.
Simply brilliant waterproofing from Nikwax.

NIKWAX DURGATES WADHURST EAST SUSSEX TN5 6DF UK
TEL (0892) 783855   FAX (0892) 783748

wan•der•lust

An impulse to travel; restlessness combined with a sense of adventure.

Great Expeditions Magazine features articles on cultural discovery, independent budget travel, outdoor recreation, and destinations untouched by mass tourism. Subscribe, or request a $3 sample copy. But, be warned—it could lead to insatiable wanderlust! $18/6 issues ($24 outside North America)

Great Expeditions Magazine

Box 8000-411
Sumas, WA, 98295, USA
Phone 604-852-6170

"Great Expeditions Magazine has done it again! Overcome by others' tales of adventure in foreign lands, I am taking a leave from my job to travel in Africa for several months..."
— Peter Turner

Chapter 3

Development of Skiing

One question that curious observers will ponder is why, in such a long range of high and snowy mountains, did skiing only develop in this relatively short and sharply defined area? Why is there no skiing in Peru, and why are there no ski areas north of Portillo in Chile? Why would anyone chose a rugged valley in Tierra del Fuego to operate a cross-country touring center? Because it's there?

The answers are found in the cultural and demographic heritage of South America. First, there are no native South American settlements in areas where snow is common. Even today, Bariloche, Farellones, Río Turbio, and a few of the southern Patagonian cities are the only communities on the continent where the population actually lives amongst snow for any part of the year. The nomadic natives simply migrated to lower elevations as winter approached and they had no need to survive in or travel through the narrow belt of snow in the higher elevations of the Andes.

Another explanation cites skiing as a European sport that was developed in the Scandinavian countries before it spread to the rest of Europe and the Americas. Thus, skiing was exported to the rest of the world by dedicated British, Scandinavian, German, Swiss, French, and Austrian adventurers who brought their enthusiasm for the sport with them when they immigrated to the new world for economic or religious reasons. The Germans were particularly important to the development of skiing in South America especially around Osorno in Southern Chile and in Bariloche, where it seems every local resident in the early part of the century was named Otto. Consequently, Bariloche developed as the Argentine capital of skiing in spite of the fact that the Mendoza area is better suited to the sport. Mendoza attracted many Spanish and Italian immigrants, but they came to work the vineyards and knew nothing of snow skiing.

In Santiago, the Maipo Canyon seems to be the natural place for skiing to have developed because of its significantly easier access. Instead, Farellones became the focus of ski area development in the area because it was closer to Las Condes and Providencia, Santiago's wealthiest neighborhoods. The relatively rich skiers apparently preferred to ascend by mule rather than drive across the city to go skiing. Finally, Punta Arenas and Ushuaia will continue to develop as the focal point for nordic skiing on the continent because it is from here that equipment-laden tourist and research expeditions to Antarctica are based. Cross-country ski touring is the natural off-season activity for the tour operators.

History

South American skiing history can be broken into three main periods of development. The first begins with the end of the 19th Century when skiing was practiced by a few foreign professionals who used skis for transportation purposes.

Recreational skiing began in South America during the 1930s. While skiing in Argentina was concentrated in the Bariloche area, the sport spread quickly south from Santiago to Punta Arenas in Chile. Although Argentina is a more "European" country, skiing spread faster in Chile because of the nearness of the *Cordillera* to most Chileans.

The history of skiing in South America is the history of the ski clubs. Any attempt to study the topic proves this point, and it becomes clear that each club is interested in promoting only the histories and supremacy of their members. This section is thus the first known written work to combine the histories of all the prominent South American ski clubs. Each ski area chapter also has a short historical summary specific to that club or site. What is described below is a very brief summary of a glorious history in which many important and dedicated figures are omitted for space considerations.

The Early Pioneers, 1887-1930

The first skiing in South America was done in the Uspallata Pass between Los Andes and Mendoza. Many of the engineers and foremen who were contracted to design and build the Trans-Andean railway (connecting Buenos Aires with Valparaíso) skied the roadless route to access worksites. The first of these were the Norwegians, Elmer Rosenquist and Michel Hermundsen, who surveyed the area in 1887 and 1888. In 1889, 14 Norwegians were brought to Chile to deliver mail over the route, but this plan was scrapped after the first season (most likely due to the extreme avalanche hazard). The British brothers, John and Matthew Clark, chief engineers of the rail project, probably skied the area more than any other person between 1890 and 1910.

The first skier in the Lakes Region was the Englishman, "Ernesto" Ricketts. He skied throughout what is now the Estancia Huemul outside of Bariloche in 1911. Several names are presented in the Argentine histories like the Norwegian, "Petiso" Freed, a Sr Garten who skied around Chall-Huaco in 1923, and the Ottos Mühlenfhordt and Alberti who skied on Victoria Island in the middle of Lake Nahuel Huapi. It is not known if these pioneers skied for professional or recreational purposes. One of the more acclaimed characters is Gerard Fichback who managed the hotel at Puerto Blest. He supplied the lodge with ski trips to Puerto Frias in the winter of 1926. The ski history of the region is spotty because a lack of snow most years at the inhabited elevations made skiing unnecessary.

Ski Clubs, Universities, and the Military, 1931-1950

The first club to organize ski trips in South America was the German Excursion Club, formed in 1909 in Valparaíso and in 1924 in Santiago. Both were principally mountaineering groups, but they also skied in the Portillo area. The first true ski clubs were the Ski Club Chile which was founded on July 11 1931, and the Club Andino Bariloche (CAB) founded August 13 of the same year.

The Ski Club Chile had 87 founding members and the Canadian, "Bobby" Barrington, was the first club President. Membership in the Ski Club Chile was limited to 100 members as that was the maximum number of mules available to haul the tents and equipment up to Farellones.

The CAB was founded by a group of four *ski gauchos* who had taken to the streets of Bariloche after a snowstorm in 1930. The founding members were Juan Javier Neumeyer, Reynaldo Knapp, Emilio Frey, and the Bavarian, Otto Meiling, who would go on to become a legendary hiker, climber, and kayaker as well as Argentina's first ski instructor. Their skiing activity was focused on the Cancha de Höwencamp on Cerro Otto just outside the city.

The Club Andino de Chile was later formed in Santiago on April 8 1933 by Hermann Sattler, Francisco Carrasco, and Oscar Sanchez who were labeled "The Three Stooges" by the local press. The Club Andino chose the Maipo Canyon as their primary skiing site and built Chile's first ski hut (*refugio*) at Lo Valdés in 1934. Other branches, which later became independent, were formed throughout Chile; the Club Andino Osorno was founded by the Matthei Brothers in 1935, while 1938 saw the founding of the Club Andino Cautín in Temuco, the Club Esquí of Los Angeles, and the Club Andino de Punta Arenas on November 18.

Although skiing was not as geographically widespread in Argentina as in Chile, it was as popular in this period. The Club Argentino de Ski (CAS) was formed on November 28 1940 by Dr Antonio "Tuco" Lynch. This Club was based in Buenos Aires but concentrated its activities in Bariloche. A friendly rivalry between the CAS and the CAB soon developed, and it continues to this day.

Skiing finally began to spread in Argentina with the founding of the Club Andino Piltriquitrón in El Bolsón on April 10 1946, and the Club Andino Esquel in the early 1950s. Skiing was not organized in Mendoza until the 1952 formation of the Ski Club Mendoza, although there was some skiing activity in the Uspallata Valley and at Vallecitos in the late 1940s.

Several university clubs also helped to develop skiing in Chile although their influence was limited by a lack of funds. Many Chileans were introduced to the sport through this affiliation however, especially at the Catholic University in Santiago, at the University of Concepción, and at the University of Valparaíso.

Military forces also supported development of the sport in both countries. Their motivations were the defense of the inhospitable borders between the countries as both feared invasion by the other. This process is alleged to have begun in the 1940s when Lt Col Juan Domingo Perón requested Otto Meiling to teach some basic techniques to a few of his officers. Military paranoia helped develop lifts in the Uspallata Pass but probably inhibited many development projects in other border-sensitive areas. Advanced mountain warfare schools are presently located in Bariloche and at Río Blanco below Portillo.

Foreigners in Skiing

Many foreigners immigrated to South America to teach skiing and help develop ski areas. The most influential of these were the Austrian, Hans Nöbl, who developed skiing at Catedral for Argentina's national park service, and Andres Bossoney, the former Ski School Director at Chamonix, who not only was a great instructor but helped build lifts at Farellones, Llaima, and Antillanca. Oeltze Von Lobenthal was a German native who is recognized as Chile's first ski instructor. He worked for the Department of Tourism beginning in 1931 and was instrumental in organizing skiing in the Lo Valdés area.

An international brotherhood began to develop after favorable reports were written by such prominent skiers as Luggi Foeger and Otto Lang. Eugene DuBois reported on the state of South American

Development of skiing 13

skiing in his book *Skiing and Andes*, and the prolific British ski author Arnold Lunn wrote *Memories of America* after visiting the continent. The most entertaining of all the early accounts was written by John Jay who described his oceanic voyage to Valparaíso and adventurous skiing in Chile in a chapter of his 1947 book *Skiing the Americas*.

A North American connection was soon developed by Chilean and US skiers. The Pan American Ski Championships of 1937 attracted a team, mostly from Dartmouth University, to Farellones to compete with their Andean counterparts. The Ski Union of the Americas was developed in the 1940s by Roger Langley and Arturo Podesta to promote all aspects of the sport amongst the skiing nations of the Western Hemisphere. The Chilean ski patrol system was developed in 1942 after a delegation toured the US on an invitation extended by Ninote Dole and the National Ski Patrol.

Early Racing and Racers

Ski racing is the best documented skiing topic in the old club journals. The first great racers they describe are Curt Lindemann in Argentina and Max and Jaime Errazuríz in Chile. The first race on the continent took place in 1932 at Caracoles near Portillo, and a race was also held later that season on Cerro Otto. The first national championships were held in 1936 in Farellones and in 1941 on Catedral. Racers from Argentina and Chile as well as Bolivia, the US, and Canada were invited to ensuing national championships, and neighborly but serious rivalries developed between the ski clubs of Portillo, Farellones, Osorno, Bariloche, and Buenos Aires.

Racing was later institutionalized with the formation of the Federación Argentina de Ski y Andinismo in 1941 and the Federación de Ski y Andinismo de Chile in 1942, and both were soon associated with the FIS. The first presidents were Antonio Lynch and Arturo Podesta respectively, and the new organizations were crucial in forming inter-club communications and officiating at ski racing events. Arturo Hammersley (Chile) and Pablo Roskenjer (Argentina) were the first from their countries to serve on FIS committees and both continue to play an important role in internationalizing the sport in South America.

The First Lifts

It is very difficult to determine exactly where and when the first ski lifts in South America were operational. It is clear that most of the skiing discussed above took place without the benefit of mechanized means of ascent. Skiing progress was thus hampered due to poor equipment, difficult access to the ski runs, and the inability to take repeated runs on the unpacked snow. Thus, while the June 1941 edition of the journal of the Club Andino de Chile has an excellent article entitled *Visiting the Ski Runs of Chile*, none of the five areas described could boast any sort of ski lift.

The first ski lift on the continent was actually the train at Portillo. It carried skiers from Juncal to Caracoles in 1910, and some sort of powered rail car was later placed into skier service. The first cable tows were installed at Farellones in 1936 and at Catedral in 1939. There was a "boom" of sorts in the development of primitive *elevadores* in 1948 when Llaima and Punta Arenas added surface tows. Antillanca added their first in 1950. The first lift in Argentina outside of Bariloche appears to be a surface tow at Vallecitos built in 1954.

Although the 1955 Silla Colorado is often alleged to be the first aerial chairlift in South America, the truth is that Portillo had a single chair in the Plateau area as early as 1946! Argentina's first aerial cable lift was the Tram at Catedral which was finally inaugurated in 1950 after an 11-year delay caused by the Second World War. The first chairlifts in Argentina were built by Guiñazú of Mendoza and installed in 1964 and 1965 in Vallecitos and Bariloche respectively.

Development in the 1980s

The decade of the '80s has seen such tremendous growth in the number of ski lifts and ski areas in South America that there is now far more lift capacity than skiers on the continent. At Bariloche, the warring parties of Catedral have come together in harmonious cooperation to provide better skiing. La Parva built the continent's first triple and quad chairs, and El Colorado was quick to respond with new triple chairs of their own. Chapelco has built South America's only gondola for skiing in addition to Argentina's first quad chairlifts. Skiing has thus undergone a complete transformation from the sport for crazy adventurers to something the entire family can safely enjoy.

New areas have also opened in the last decade like Las Leñas which has finally brought to fruition the promise of skiing in the Mendoza province. Chile's Villarrica-Pucón and Valle Nevado closed the decade with massive new ski area and hotel developments of an international standard. La Hoya, Chillán, and Caviahue promise to fulfill the high expectations of the 1990s to create more variety in South American skiing. Skiers who come only to enjoy the hedonistic luxuries of these fine resorts will miss much. Be sure to reserve an extra day to visit one of the humbler but perhaps richer historical ski areas like Vallecitos, Llaima, or Lagunillas to develop a deeper understanding of what the sport means to the skiers of South America.

Ski Area Operations

South America had 31 alpine ski areas by 1990. The areas are split equally with 15 each in both Chile and Argentina and the odd one in Bolivia. In addition, there are four nordic ski centers in Argentina: three outside of Ushuaia in Tierra del Fuego, and one in Bariloche. In 1990, there were 163 major ski lifts operating in South America. If the ski centers are divided into two distinct groups called international resorts and regional areas, then the 12 resorts can be described as averaging 10 lifts each while the 19 areas average two lifts each.

Lifts are categorized by type in the chapters. The primary lift in South America is a poma-type surface tow. There are about 48 of these simple lifts on the continent with the greatest number installed at Catedral. Other common lifts include simple tows, some portable, and T-Bars (35), the classic Doppelmayr surface lifts. Skiers may also encounter a *Va et Vient* (see *Chapter 7*) or a cable/hook tow (Chacaltaya).

Chairlifts represent a more substantial investment in ski area development and as such only 16 of the areas can boast of having at least one. There are 34 double, six triple, five quad, and two single chairlifts in South America. They are crucial links at the southern ski areas, as only with an aerial lift from the base can the areas of this region assure winter-long skiing. Only La Parva, El Colorado, Valle Nevado, Chapelco and Las Leñas have triples or quads. The high cost (and low need) of high-speed detachable lifts makes them impractical in South America.

The only gondola is a new six-passenger model at Chapelco. Since 1950, Bariloche has had the only aerial tramway for skiing in South America at Catedral. The Cable Carríl, as it is known in Argentina, is also the continent's longest lift at 3,100m (10,170ft). The Marte chairlift at Las Leñas is the continent's steepest lift (48%), and it has a greater elevation gain than any other (786m, 2,579ft). Don Otto in Chillán (2,500m, 8,202ft) is the continent's longest chairlift. Valle Nevado (3,670m, 12,040ft) and La Parva (3,680m, 12,075ft) are the highest ski areas outside of Chacaltaya in Bolivia (about 5,300m, 17,390ft).

Ski areas generally operate seven days a week from 9.30am to 5.00pm. None open before 9.00am. Some of the smaller areas take a day or two off each week (eg: El Fraile), and a few are open only on weekends (eg: Lonquimay). The more limiting factor is that most of the smaller areas only operate public transportation services on weekends. A few, like Las Leñas and Valdelén, have limited night skiing on occasion.

Helicopter Skiing

There are several helicopter skiing services in South America and all are located at the major resorts. It is more developed in Chile than Argentina, and services are offered at Portillo, La Parva (Andes Powder Guides), and Valle Nevado. Several other resorts can arrange trips but do not have a regular service. The Andes Powder Guides (see Box, *Chapter 8*) can custom design a program anywhere in Chile, and their guides are the most capable on the continent. Helicopter skiing in South America is illogical though, since there is plenty of space on the uncrowded, lift-serviced slopes. A perfect example is Las Leñas which is surrounded by outstanding terrain but has so much space in lift accessed areas that there is absolutely no need to take a helicopter to find unskied snow.

Adventure Skiing

Skiers looking for out-of-bounds skiing terrain will find plenty in Chile and Argentina. The ski areas can be viewed as a mere staging area for expeditions above and beyond the lifts, and none prohibit accessing the wilderness from their boundaries. The best places for such activities are the volcanoes of Southern Chile where cheap accommodations can be enjoyed until a glorious spring day presents itself. Hiking favorites in Argentina include Cerro López near Bariloche and the Lanín and Copahue Volcanoes. Aconcagua and Ojos del Salado, the Americas' highest points, have been skied, but only the most experienced and equipped climbers should attempt descents on these rugged alpine peaks. On the other hand, anyone with basic experience and knowledge of alpine environments will greatly enjoy the relatively tame Lonquimay and Llaima volcanoes.

Nordic Skiing and Touring

Nordic skiing is still in its infancy in South America. Only in Ushuaia and Bariloche can visitors expect to find groomed or marked trails. While races have been held at several other sites in Argentina (eg: Caviahue, Chapelco), there is almost no cross-country skiing activity in Chile. This is not to say that ski touring cannot be enjoyed, however, as there are several outstanding places that can be recommended. Both Chillán and Antillanca have plans to develop a trail network, but the best nordic skiing in Chile is found between the two. The araucaria-lined slopes around the Lonquimay, Llaima, and

Antuco volcanos provide the best opportunities. Otherwise, head for Punta Arenas or Ushuaia. More specific suggestions are found in each ski area description.

Snowboarding
Every ski area in South America welcomes snowboarders. In fact, snowboarding is very popular, and proficient shredders are revered in both Argentina and Chile. The French are the established experts on the continent, especially at Las Leñas and Valle Nevado. Equipment is hard to find so bring some to sell.

Ski Safety
The risks faced on the slopes of South American ski resorts are comparable to those faced in Europe as the runs are mostly treeless and thinly populated. Although most of the major areas operate under the French system where each skier is responsible for himself, the resorts of South America are more active in marking unseen hazards and controlling reckless skiers. Only at El Colorado and Catedral is slope congestion ever a serious problem, and ski safety campaigns have begun at these areas.

All skiers should be extra cautious to avoid serious injury while skiing in South America. An injury suffered at home is an uncomfortable and expensive ordeal which is more complicated in a foreign country. It can ruin an otherwise perfect ski vacation for not only the injured skier but his entire group as well. For safety, travel and ski with a friend, and always notify the local ski patrol when leaving the ski area boundaries.

Avalanche control is much less intensive than in the US. While the risks are minimal at most areas, they can be high at some. Avalanches are of greatest concern at the northern areas around Santiago and Mendoza, but many of the Chilean volcanoes also present a hazard. Only Portillo seems to have an advanced snow studies program. Adventure seekers at Las Leñas need to be especially cautious. Many local *Mendocinos* refuse to ski at Penitentes out of fear of being caught in an avalanche there. There is no known instance of a skier being injured in an avalanche within the boundaries of a South American ski area, but the possibility always exists.

The larger hazard is on some of the roads, particularly in the Uspallata Pass through Portillo and Penitentes, and on the road from Farellones to Valle Nevado. The Uspallata Pass is often closed for avalanche safety, and travellers should be aware that they can quickly become "snowed-in" at Portillo. The cliffs above the Valle

Nevado road are controlled by their ski patrol, but motorists should avoid driving in these areas during and immediately following the large Andean storms that can bury everything on the west side.

The Future of Skiing in South America

The ambitious development of the 1980s is not expected to continue at such a brisk pace through the 1990s. This decade operations will be consolidated to determine how profitable the new ski areas will actually be. While Valle Nevado and La Hoya are likely to double in size in the next five years, Villarrica-Pucón and Portillo will improve services and marketing to consolidate their clientele. The next new ski area likely to be developed is Caviahue, while Manantiales is an exciting project for both skiers and mountaineers.

A Note on Expectations

While most reorts have a professional and responsive management, several don't. In addition, the difficult weather conditions sometimes negate efforts by the most competent administrations. Though the results may be the same, the crew at Villarrica-Pucón works hard in foul conditions to open their lifts after a humid storm, while there is never any hurry to open the chairlift at Chillán. Likewise, Portillo may seem hasty in closing some areas due to increasing avalanche danger, while at Las Leñas some hazardous areas may remain only informally closed because each skier is expected to use his own judgement.

Thus, aggressive and expectant skiers may be disappointed when things are not exactly as described or as they are accustomed to in their home countries. In addition, conditions at each area change throughout the season, and from year to year, and skiers should be aware that changes, for better or worse, will develop.

Skiers could travel to South America for hedonistic reasons (try Las Leñas or Valle Nevado), but could also use the travel opportunity to learn about South America and see what skiing in the Andes is all about. A situation which seems strange or inconveniences a visitor should be accepted as part of the adventure. Skiers who try to change procedure or complain will not have as much fun as those who simply smile in amazement at the different approaches of their Chilean and Argentine hosts.

Chapter 4

Preparations

Costs

Clearly the most difficult part of making the decision to go skiing in South America is the cost of the flight. In 1990, rates were about US$800rt from Los Angeles and Miami and £700rt from London when tickets were purchased from a wholesale travel agency. Skiers should then budget US$300-1000 per week according to lodging and dining preferences.

A good hotel room in Santiago is becoming increasingly expensive and averaged about US$40/night in 1990. Decent rooms could be found in some *residenciales* for about US$10/night, however. In the rest of Chile, prices ran about 25% cheaper for equivalent rooms. Hotel prices in Argentina were about 30% less than similar rooms in Chile in 1990 but vary greatly. Food prices are comparable in the two countries; US$15/day provides deluxe dining, but it is easy to spend only US$5/day even when building a skier's appetite. Transportation is quite economical if long distance taxi rides are avoided. Buses and trains are inexpensive and average no more than US$1 per 50km. Lift tickets average US$10 at the smaller resorts and US$18 at the larger ones. Specific prices are included in the chapters.

For extended stays, skiers can live quite well on US$1,000/month, even when travelling frequently. Prices become cheaper as the size of the group grows, and skiers travelling at least in pairs will save significantly at hotels. Single travellers can meet others, especially in Bariloche, and travel together for a time to save money. Trips to Tierra del Fuego add a substantial burden to the budget because this is the most expensive area on the continent.

Health Concerns

No special health documents or inoculations are required for foreigners entering Argentina, Bolivia, or Chile. Skiers should arrive in the top physical condition possible. Travellers journeying to South America for skiing need not concern themselves with the insect-borne diseases prevalent in tropical parts of the continent. Skiers combining a ski trip with a visit to Amazonia or other tropical environments face a different set of health precautions for which other sources should be sought.

Entry Requirements

Citizens of most countries need only a passport for entry with no visa required. Some exceptions in 1990 were for French and Mexican citizens entering Chile, and Australian and New Zealand visitors in Argentina, although these rules are being relaxed. A tourist card valid for 90 days is obtained when entering Chile and the passport stamp obtained entering Argentina is valid for a similar period of time. Multiple entries are not a problem. Customs formalities at the airports and borders are minimal and baggage checks easy for well-groomed skiers.

What to Bring

A good rule is to bring no more gear than can be carried without assistance. Good ski bags are very important (extra clothes and parkas can be stuffed inside) as is identification on each piece of luggage. Most airlines limit travellers to three bags and are not shy about charging for excess baggage.

Less-devoted skiers who prefer to travel light should at least bring ski boots as adequate skis can always be rented. Serious skiers should likewise carry their boots on the plane, as their loss would be critical. Be sure to have boots, skis, and bindings in top condition before leaving. Since ski hats, sweaters, and shirts can be purchased as souvenirs, do not bring too many of these types of items. Bring plenty of film — it is very expensive if purchased locally.

Taped copies of your favorite music make appreciated gifts to the discriminating ears of the South Americans. Other good trading articles include anything from your home ski area like pins, stickers, baseball caps, and even trail maps.

Chapter 5

Travelling in Chile and Argentina

This section will show readers how easy and enjoyable travelling and staying in Chile and Argentina can be, putting to rest all notions of South American dangers and difficulties. Travellers of every budget and taste will find something in their niche, and by travelling in the winter season, skiers enjoy a high-level service that is geared for the busier summer season.

Lodging

There is a large variety of accommodation in every town listed in this guide (except Río Turbio). Prices, addresses, and recommendations are found in each chapter. Both Argentina and Chile rate their hotels with a star system that is not comparable to the European system. Five stars is the highest, but unrated facilities should not be ignored. Budget travellers will find bargains in places that have rooms with a shared bath (*baño compartido*). All rooms at the good hotels have *baños privados* and are comfortably furnished.

In Chile, most rooms have a television, a rare privilege in all but the best hotels in Argentina. Some even receive CNN news for an informative update from the US. All hotels have their own restaurants which are usually the best in the community. Most hotels have singles, doubles, triples, and suites. Double beds can be difficult to find in the smaller towns, and couples must specifically ask for a *matrimonial*. Cohabitation of unmarried couples is rarely a problem.

Following are definitions of the types of accommodation available, although many places blur the distinctions.

Alojamiento: Any sort of lodging or bed space.
Apart-Hotel: An all-suites hotel.

Hotel: Moderate to expensive facilities of higher standards.
Motor Lodge: Roadside motel, found along Chile's Pan-American Highway.
Residencial: A boarding house, fancy or plain, usually family run and friendlier than hotels. Best in Bariloche and San Martín de Los Andes.
Hostería: A hostel with bunks and dorm rooms.
Refugio: A mountain hut or lodge usually without sleeping accommodations at ski areas but with bunks in the wilderness.
Hospedaje: Lodging in a private home. The cheapest and best way to meet local people. Difficult for equipment-laden skiers.
Bungalow, Cabaña: Cabins, usually closed in winter.
Posada: An old-fashioned inn or roadhouse that may or may not have rooms to rent.
Termas: A spa resort with natural hot springs. Prevalent along the length of the Chilean and Argentine Andes.

Dining

One of the greatest pleasures of international travel is tasting all sorts of unusual and exotic foods, and Chile and Argentina both have rich national cuisines. It is possible to eat "normal" food, but the unadventurous palate will miss some wonderful experiences. In Chile, the rule is freshly caught fish and fresh-picked fruit, and many types of both are strange to foreigners. In Argentina, everyone eats copious amounts of beef. Hamburgers and basic sandwiches are served everywhere, but pizza is the most popular food and nothing is sacred when it comes to toppings. Homemade pasta is also widely available, especially in Mendoza. The Argentines despise spicy foods, but the Chileans put hot *ají* and black pepper on just about everything. They are amazed when a foreigner sprinkles the fiery stuff on his food. Absolutely everything is safe to eat, and gastronomes should dine with confidence and abandon.

Popular beverages include coffee, tea, soft drinks, mineral water, beer, wine, and Pisco Sours. In Chile, coffee usually means instant, but a fresh brew is available at the coffee stands in Santiago. In Argentina, coffee is the strong Brazilian type served in tiny cups. It is consumed at any and every social interaction. *Café con leche* is the North American type that is popular with breakfast. Bottled mineral water is the most popular refresher in the region. It is available natural or carbonated (*sin gas, con gas*), and is served everywhere alone and with wine.

Dessert specialties include flan and ice cream. Ice cream is an addiction in South America and the variety of flavors is surpassed only by the variety of pizzas. Favorite flavors in Chile include the *lúcuma* and *chirimoya* fruits. Chocolates, candies, and jams are a specialty in the Lakes District, and all visitors bring some home. In Argentina, *dulce de leche*, a disgustingly sweet paste with the consistency of peanut butter, is spread on everything. Fresh yogurt is excellent and safe in both countries.

Both Chile and Argentina produce outstanding wines which are finally beginning to reach northern markets. They are an excellent value even when exported, and waiters (*mozos*) should be consulted for recommendations. In general, Chile produces a better white wine (*vino blanco*) and Argentina produces a better red (*vino tinto*). The wine producing regions are around Santiago and Mendoza and visits to the vineyards and wineries can be arranged.

The Pisco Sour actually comes from Peru, but it is very popular in Chile. This cocktail tastes like a strong Margarita and is sweetened with a rim of sugar on the tiny glass. Argentina produces good whiskey, but imported liquors are very expensive. The best beer in the region is Austral from Punta Arenas, but it's difficult to find.

Most restaurants maintain fresh displays of menu items in their front windows, especially in the cities. Menus are long and tedious to the uninitiated. The check (*cuenta*) must always be requested and a receipt should always be presented. Standard tipping is about 10-15% in restaurants. The best and cheapest food is found in the markets and on the streets where only ordinary caution needs to be exercised.

Following is a list of some favorite menu items from Chile and Argentina.

Typical Fare:
Barros Luco: Steak sandwich.
Churrasco: Philadelphia-style steak sandwich.
Barros Jarpa: Ham and cheese sandwich.
Completo, salchicha, pancho: Hot dog.
Papas fritas: French fries.
Lomo: Filet mignon-type steak.
   Vuelta y vuelta: rare.
   A punto: medium rare.
   Mediano: medium.
   Bien cocido: well done.
Empanadas: Chile: A thick pastry filled with meat, onions, egg, and olive (*de pino*), also cheese filled, usually baked (*al horno*), best in Santiago's Plaza de Armas. In Argentina: usually fried (*frito*) and smaller, with greater variety in fillings, best in Tucumán and Bariloche.
Chuleta de cerdo: Pork chop.
Trucha: Trout, best in Bariloche and San Martín.

Chilean Specialties:
Congrio: Conger eel, white meat, found everywhere.
Corvina: White sea bass.
Albacora: Swordfish.
Locos: Small abalones.
Choros: One of several types of mussels.
Centolla: King crab from Tierra del Fuego, out of season in winter.
Mariscos: Shellfish.
Parrillada: Mixed grill served over a fire, meat or fish, minimum two people.
Ensalada Chilena: A refreshing salad of peeled tomatoes, onions, parsley, garlic, oil and seasonings.
Cazuela de Ave: Outstanding broth with ¼ chicken and fresh vegetables.
Pastel de Choclo: Incredible meat-corn meal pie, served springtime in Chile.
Ají: Chilean hot sauce, a cross between Tabasco and Mexican salsa.

Argentine Specialties:
Milanesa: Thin but huge breaded steak, a favorite found everywhere.
Suprema de Pollo: Breaded tender chicken filet, many styles.
Asado: A large and festive Argentine backyard barbecue in which many strange parts of a cow are roasted. If invited, drop everything and go.

Breakfast is continental-style although eggs are available in better hotels. In Argentina, *media lunas* (croissant-type rolls) accompany juice and coffee, while in Chile, the universal starch is a flaky, puck-shaped roll. Lunch begins at about 1.30pm and can include anything from a sandwich to a steak. *Once* is the late afternoon tea served around 5.00pm that is supposed to hold starved skiers until the 10.00pm dinner hour. The evening meal is a prolonged social event from which no one leaves hungry.

Transportation

Travelling throughout Chile and Argentina is made easy by a wide variety of economical options. Since few can afford automobiles or the gasoline to run them, mass transit is much better developed than it is in the US and comparable to European transportation networks. When travelling, most passengers stare blankly into space or socialize with others, especially on trains where it's easy to stroll up and down the aisles. Kids are given free rein to terrorize other passengers and will forever badger anyone who offers attention.

By Plane

All flights from the US are overnight and arrive early in the morning at either Buenos Aires or Santiago. This schedule gives skiers ample time to reach the ski resorts on their first day in either country. Because Santiago is much closer to all the South American ski areas, it is a better destination than Buenos Aires. It is not difficult to ski a world-class resort the day after leaving home. Most flights from North America originate or pass through Miami and have at least one other stop before arriving in Santiago. Since Chile is on New York time through the winter season, there is no jet-lag or time change when coming from any eastern US city.

The national airlines in Chile are LANChile and Ladeco. They have practically the same prices but slightly varying routes. Both service Miami, New York, and most South American capitals, but only LAN has flights from Los Angeles, Montreal, Madrid, Tahiti, and Easter Island.

The two main airlines in Argentina are Aerolíneas Argentinas and Austral. Only Aerolíneas has international destinations including seven European, five North American, and a dozen Latin American cities in addition to a trans-polar route from Sydney and Auckland. LADE is the airline of the Argentine Air Force that flies to just about every destination in the country. Their flights are always booked, but there are many no shows. To assure a seat, arrive at the airport several hours in advance and stand by the ticket window to be the first on the stand-by list. The extremely low prices — often lower than bus fares — make the inconvenience worthwhile. TAN is a recommended regional airline that flies small 20-passenger planes to every ski destination in Argentina (and Temuco and Puerto Montt) from their hub in sunny Neuquen. Prices fluctuate widely for all flights in Argentina, and the prices listed in the chapters should not be taken as gospel.

By Train

Both Chile and Argentina have good rail networks. In Argentina, all routes converge on Buenos Aires where different stations cope with the differently-gauged lines. Railroads once ran the length of Chile but now run only between Santiago and Puerto Montt. It is the best way to see the country, and skiers should at least ride the train to Chillán. Prices are slightly higher than buses, and the trips are a bit slower. It is a more relaxing mode of travel though, especially in Argentina where some roads, especially highways to Buenos Aires, are very poor.

Five classes are normally available from cabins (*departamento*) to berths (*cama*, upper and lower), seats (*salón*), tourist (*turista*), and first class(*primer clase*). The last two should be avoided. The price difference justifies the added comfort and security of the airplane-style seats of the *salón*. "No smoking" cars are designated for some classes. Service on the trains is excellent, and most have a dining car and a bar car that may have a small and noisy cinema. Magazines and snacks are available on the train or at the stations.

By Bus

Buses are the most inexpensive and convenient forms of travel. The long distance buses are very comfortable with beverage bars and video movies, in English, on the longer routes. In the last few years smoking has become illegal on all buses in both countries. Stops are made in big cities and at special restaurants on the longer hauls. Almost every city has a central bus terminal with the best at Buenos Aires and Mendoza.

On popular overnight runs, a luxury class is offered (*servicio de lujo*) in addition to the normal service. For about US$5 more, passengers enjoy fewer stops, wider seats (3 across), and better food. Some routes even have a bed (*cama*) class where passengers can stretch out.

Taxis, *Colectivos*, *Remises*

From the airport, train station, or bus terminal, a taxi is usually the best means of transport. They are widely available and very inexpensive in most cities and are identified by black bodies and yellow tops. Never get in a taxi without a meter unless a price is set beforehand. Prices are generally increased by as much as 50% on Sundays, holidays, and in the wee hours of the morning. Most drivers are very friendly and helpful especially to riders who make an attempt at the language. Know your destination before boarding, but be open to the driver's suggestions. Tipping is not mandatory but appreciated. At some line-ups, especially at Santiago's train station, drivers set their own absurd rates. In such cases, travellers should walk a half-block and hail another.

Colectivos are the black cars with large signs attached to the roof or windshield that indicate by a number or name their particular route. Some are for inner-city travel while others run between towns. They are especially economical and are popular with the locals. A standard fare of about US$0.40 is charged to any destination on their set route in cities. They are hailed with a simple wave and have no regular stops. Ask at the hotel or a tourist office to learn which *colectivos* are best for your destination. A *colectivo* is most economical for single travellers while large groups will be better off sharing a taxi.

A *remise* is a special type of taxi more prevalent in Argentina. They are generally larger and nicer cars that are unmarked and unmetered. *Remises* can be more or less expensive than taxis depending on the particular town or city. They are best arranged with your hotel and do not generally have fixed waiting stations. Most taxis and *remises* are radio controlled in the cities.

Driving

Renting a car may be a viable and convenient alternative when hauling ski equipment around the continent. It is probably the best mode of transport for larger groups and offers a great degree of freedom. Avis has the best network in Argentina. In Chile, Hertz has the most offices but is easily the most expensive. Renters must be at least 25 years old, have a major credit card, and possess an International Drivers License. The License is available at auto clubs in home countries and is inexpensive. Auto Club benefits are reciprocated in both Chile (*Automovil Club de Chile*) and Argentina (ACA), and membership is very beneficial in this far-away land. Be sure the vehicle has tire chains for snow.

Driving is very difficult in the cities and should be avoided. Highway driving is, on the other hand, encouraged. Chile's Pan American Highway is an outstanding artery through the middle of the country with well-developed services all along the route. Several spur roads are also in excellent condition, and the roads between Coyhaique and Aisén, and Punta Arenas and Puerto Natales, are excellent.

In Argentina, the poor roads and long distances between Mendoza, Bariloche, and Buenos Aires make driving impractical. A tour of the southern ski areas alone is viable, however, and cars are more economically rented in Neuquén than Bariloche. Driving in Tierra del Fuego is discouraged as the roads are tortuous.

Some roads have expensive tolls. Police checkpoints are becoming less routine in both countries, but a few are still maintained. Driving after dark is not recommended. Gas prices fluctuate dramatically and are generally twice the price of US fuels and slightly less than prices in Europe. Most South American drivers become *muy macho* when they get behind the wheel of a car (auto racing is the continent's second favorite spectator sport), and accidents are common. Be particularly careful on the Farellones road.

Ferries

Ferries become an option in the fjords south of Puerto Montt. Many are modern and comfortable and reservations can be made in Santiago and other major cites. See *Chapter 19* for more details.

Money and Exchange

Money is easily exchanged in the larger cities, and efficient exchange houses are found in the commercial centers. The bigger hotels and international airports have exchange services but their rates are inferior. Most of the street vendors take customers to an exchange house and receive a commission. Never exchange cash on the street. Receipts will always be given clearly showing the rate. Bargain only with the street vendors and only after observing the current rates displayed in the windows of the exchange houses. Money can be exchanged even on Sundays in Santiago but is limited to weekdays and perhaps Saturday morning in the smaller towns. Be sure to plan ahead to avoid being caught short.

The exchange game is difficult to gauge when travelling for the first time especially in Argentina with its high inflation. Huge amounts of cash are often exchanged in the cities. Solitary gentlemen with paper sacks filled with tens of thousands of cash dollars are routinely trading money at the exchange houses. In Argentina, exchange only what is immediately needed as the rates change on an hourly basis. Travellers checks are safer, but their exchange is more difficult and commissions are larger. Since travel is so safe, cash is recommended for ease of exchange. Passports are required as identification at all exchange facilities.

A neck pouch is a comfortable way to securely carry cash, a spare credit card, passports, and plane tickets home. The following credit cards are widely accepted: American Express, Visa, Master Card, Diner's. A stack of US$5 bills is very handy in getting out of jams when the supply of local currency runs dry.

Communication

A little Spanish will go a long way in South America. Skiers who spend some time studying the language before arriving will have greater freedom to enjoy all of the country's offerings. Pronunciations are different from Mexican or Spanish. Chileans drop the "s" at the ends of words, and Argentines slur the "ll" sound. Even within Argentina, regional dialects vary greatly and travellers can become easily confused.

The Chileans and Argentines actually call their language *Castellano*, and both countries have many of their own words.

Argentine males are often called "*Che*" or "*Flaco*" but the terms are not limited to fellow countrymen. A favorite Argentine slang word is "*quilombo*" which is a tongue-in-cheek description of a typically Argentine foul-up. Many local expressions and words are presented in the text to demonstrate how easily the language can be understood.

To communicate with friends at home, mail letters from the central post office (*Correo Central*) in each city. Telephone calls should be made from offices conveniently located in the center of each city. Rates are reasonable, but do not call internationally from hotels as huge surcharges are added. Chile's telephone system is one of the best in the world, but Argentina's leaves much to be desired.

Medical and Rescue Services

There are competent, professional ski patrols at all the major resorts of South America. Most use exclusively professional patrollers, but some, notably El Colorado where it seems there are as many patrollers as skiers on weekends, use volunteers as well. Most are trained by international specialists, but some are trained locally.

All the major areas have medical clinics at the base with a doctor either present or on-call. Most also have an ambulance standing-by, and a helicopter is available to transport the most serious injuries. Skier's insurance is included in many of the ski packages and is available separately at the major ski areas.

The best hospitals are located in the capital cities of each country, and the most serious cases will be flown back to Santiago or Buenos Aires for treatment. Bariloche, Mendoza, and Osorno also have modern hospitals. Good health care is available in all the other cities, and efficient networks operate to evacuate more serious cases to better hospitals if needed.

There is a good rescue organization in Chile called the *Cuerpo de Socorro Andino* or Andean Aid Corps. They are based in Santiago, but will be called upon to undertake rescue operations in other parts of Chile as well. The *Carabineros* of Chile also may assume some rescue operations. In Argentina, there is no known rescue organization, and outside assistance is especially tenuous in the winter season when no one is supposed to be climbing around in the mountains. In Mendoza, services can only be expected in the summer climbing season, while in Bariloche, the Club Andino could assist in response to a backcountry emergency.

Chapter 6

Crossing the Chile-Argentina Frontier

Introduction

There are only three places in the region where skiers can cross the border between Argentina and Chile. All other border crossings in the area are minor and closed in the winter. Travellers should have no fear about crossing and recrossing the frontier. The customs formalities are neither excessively slow nor inconvenient, and the searches are minimal for well-dressed foreigners.

All customs stations are open until 8.00pm at the absolute latest, and attempts to cross after nightfall will be rebuffed. The guards are professional and friendly and can assist hitchhikers and other stranded travellers. Cigarettes make the best gifts, but any sort of bribe would be a serious insult. Don't forget the 1hr time difference between Chile and Argentina.

History

Although relations have become amiable to the point of near economic integration, Chile and Argentina have had several border disputes. The original treaties were signed in 1881 and 1893, but the border was closed as recently as 1978. The actual border between the nations does not necessarily follow the crest of the high Andes but is determined by the watershed. There has not always been agreement on this distinction however, and the countries have nearly gone to war several times.

The latest dispute centered on the oil-rich area of Tierra del Fuego. The Argentine military, looking for an international conflict around which the fractured nation could unite, decided it could not accept the 1977 arbitration decision of Queen Elizabeth II in confirming the current borders of the area. In contention was an area called "The Hammer," consisting of the islands of Lennox, Picton and Nueva which lie east of Chile's Isla Navarina. Argentina claimed that no treaty ever intended to give Chile an Atlantic shore, and the border should thus run due north from Cape Horn to the Beagle Channel. Another dispute centered on the exact course of the Beagle Channel, an important part of the southern border.

International mediation efforts were successful at averting war, and Argentina's military leaders eventually got the war they were looking for in 1982 at the Malvinas (Falklands). The Argentine side of Tierra del Fuego is still administered from Buenos Aires but is due to become a self-governing province sometime in the next few years. Some insecurity remains however, as Chilean territory must be crossed if travelling overland between the Argentine mainland and their portion of Tierra del Fuego. Transportation in the area is complicated by politics, but the new democratic leaderships of Patricio Aylwin and Carlos Menem are likely to lead new cooperative efforts in the frontier areas of Chile and Argentina.

Santiago — Mendoza, The Uspallata Pass

The Uspallata (oos-pie-*yah*-tah) Pass is the main route between Buenos Aires and Valparaíso and is the most important for trade between the two countries. The historical importance of this pass in the development of both countries and skiing in South America is discussed in other sections of this guide, especially in *Chapter 3*.

Although the Chilean side is almost completely undeveloped (except for Portillo and Río Blanco which serves the La Andina copper mine), the Argentine side is of some interest to tourists. From the top, travellers pass four tiny but interesting settlements. The first, Las Cuevas, is a small military post that is being converted to the Argentine customs checkpoint. Several kilometers down is Puente del Inca, the staging point for expeditions to the base of Aconcagua. There is a natural rock arch over the Mendoza River here that gives the village its name.

A few kilometers lower is Los Penitentes which has the most complete tourist infrastructure in the Uspallata Valley. Below this is Punta de Vacas, and eventually the village of Uspallata is reached at the intersection of the two roads to Mendoza. The northern route is more scenic, but the road is much rougher. It passes through the closed hot springs resort of Villavicencio where mineral water is bottled. The southern route passes through Potrerillos and Luján de Cuyo before arriving at Mendoza.

The actual border is crossed through a 4km-long tunnel at the top of the pass. On the Chilean side, the road has tight switchbacks on the initial descent from the Los Libertadores customs station from which Portillo is viewed. The Juncal River is followed until it becomes the Río Blanco and then the Aconcagua River. This flows into the city of Los Andes at the bottom of the pass and feeds the rich farms of the Aconcagua Valley.

The entire road is well paved but is in constant peril of avalanches on both sides during the winter season. High snowbanks form sheer walls on the sides of the road especially where avalanches have rumbled down their timeless paths. The pass is closed for an average of 30 days/year, and chains are required and needed near the top most of the winter season. When it is open, the traffic is one-directional with ascents allowed in the morning and descents permitted in the afternoon. Thus, do not try to ascend either side in the afternoon or evening hours.

Transportation

There is quite a variety of overland transportation between Santiago and Mendoza. The cities are linked by a few flights, and a large number of road transportation services are available. Since all of these are based in the same area of the Santiago and Mendoza bus terminals, it is easy to shop around to get the best price. There are several auto transport companies (eg: Chi-Arg, US$16, 2½hr) which provide fast service, but the drivers and vehicles can be unsafe (I nearly perished!). They feature hotel pick-up and drop-off though. Several bus services also cover the route (eg: TAS Choapa, US$12, 4hr) and their service is excellent and safe. All road services depart from the cities' bus terminals around 8.30am.

Puerto Montt — Bariloche

There are two routes between Puerto Montt/Osorno in Chile and Bariloche in Argentina. Very little commerce crosses here in spite of prominent geographical and cultural similarities, but the route is very popular with tourists. The traditional route uses several ferries to cross the mountains via long, pristine lakes, but the Puyehue Pass is now a more popular and important route. The only air connections between Chile and Argentina south of Santiago are the twice-weekly flights between Temuco and Neuquén and Puerto Montt and Bariloche with TAN of Argentina.

The Puyehue Pass

The Puyehue Pass road runs from Osorno to Bariloche and is now paved for almost all of its 160km (100 miles). Most of the tortuous

Crossing the Chile-Argentina frontier

section along the northeast shore of Lake Nahuel Huapi was paved in the spring of 1990. The drive is detailed in *Chapters 18* and *30*. At least four bus companies cross each day (eg: Bus Norte, US$20, 7hr) and all leave Bariloche and Puerto Montt at 8.00 or 8.30am. The price is the same if leaving from or destined for Osorno or Puerto Montt in Chile. The Chilean customs house is set beautifully alongside the Río Gol-Gol.

The *Cruz de Lagos*

The *Cruz de Lagos* is one of the most scenic trips in all of South America. While the ferries are full in the summer months, the winter trips are rarely booked and less expensive. Passengers cross the Nahuel Huapi National Park in Argentina and the Vicente Pérez Rosales National Park in Chile.

The journey begins, if coming from Bariloche, with a lakeside bus trip from the city to Puerto Pañuelo, the main port for Lake Nahuel Huapi. A ferry then crosses the long lake to Puerto Blest from where a bus takes passengers a few kilometers to Puerto Alegre on Lake Frias. The next ferry heads south to Puerto Frias from which the Pérez Rosales Pass is crossed in another bus to Peulla in Chile. The final ferry then crosses All Saints Lake beneath the Osorno Volcano and docks at Petrohue. From there, the fourth and final bus carries passengers along the southern shore of Lake Llanquihue to Puerto Montt. Although this sounds very complicated, there is plenty of personnel to transfer luggage items and the buses and ferries are comfortable. The ferries do not carry vehicles.

From April 1 until August 31, the trip lasts two days with a leisurely night spent in the nice hotel at Peulla (US$132 all included). From September 1 until March 31 a quicker day-long trip is added (US$36). The relatively small price differential from the Puyehue Pass bus services makes this a preferred option for spring skiers. Even when the weather is poor, often enough in the winter, the journey will be an unforgettable part of any South American ski adventure.

Tierra del Fuego

Travel connections are so difficult in this part of the world that only the most durable travellers should attempt a winter visit. Maintain flexible schedules and be prepared for every contingency when travelling on Tierra del Fuego. With nordic skis, any delay can be made bearable with ski adventures.

Punta Arenas-Ushuaia

There are two ways to make this "so close, yet sooo... far" connection. The easiest route is to take one of the daily buses to Río Gallegos in Argentina (eg: Ghisoni, US$10, 6hr), then fly Aerolíneas (daily, US$30) or LADE to Ushuaia.

Hardier travellers can ride the twice-weekly ferry (US$3, 2½hr) across the Strait of Magellan to Porvenir. The ferry has a tiny indoor passenger lobby which fills quickly. There is some room in the hallways but overall indoor space is limited to perhaps 20 uncomfortable bench seats. Everyone smokes inside, but it's bitterly cold outside. Get a seat early, dress in your warmest ski clothes, and travel with a friend in case you have to get up.

The pristine inlet of the Porvenir landing is a welcome first sight of Tierra del Fuego. Porvenir is a small town with many Czechoslovakian immigrants. It would be a nice hike, or possibly ski, to the bus terminal, but distance and lack of directional signs in the town make a taxi mandatory (US$2). The bus terminal is a safe place to deposit luggage while eating a hot, nutritious family-style lunch at a house a few doors down from the terminal. The Río Grande bus (Senkovic, US$12, 8hr) leaves at about 1.00pm in coordination with the ferry.

The trip from the west end of the island to the east coast is rather miserable. The bus's windows are caked with mud, and the early nightfall limits nocturnal vistas to the bright flames of the distant oil platforms. The road is in serious disrepair, and the average speed is probably 20kph (12mph). Despite the late hour of arrival, Río Grande is a lively oasis of civilization. The **Frederico Ibarra Hotel** (Sgl:US$31, Dbl:US$40), located on the Plaza de Armas, has a complete bar and a beautiful young crowd of well-dressed locals that astounds travellers at the end of the grueling day.

From Río Grande, skiers can rise early for the bus to Ushuaia (Los Carlos, US$10, 5hr), or sleep-in and catch the LADE flight (US$20, 30min) which leaves at about 1.00pm (don't forget the time change). Both trips provide spectacular scenery. The Río Grande-Ushuaia road is better than the Porvenir road and passes two nordic ski centers a few kilometers before Ushuaia.

Puerto Natales-Río Turbio

This is much simpler than the crossing described above because the distance is quite short (34km, 21 miles) and the service frequent (4-5/day, US$2, 1hr). The beauty of this crossing is that the ski area is at the Argentine customs house making the regular bus service a skiers' bus as well. Ski gear could be deposited at the customs house in order to visit the town unencumbered. Ski after dark (the run is lit) and catch the last bus (8.15pm) from Valdelén back.

Part II

CHILE

Geography

Chile is often described as the string bean of South America or, by more poetic observers, the teardrop from Peru. The country is 4,329km long (2,690 miles) and averages 180km (112 miles) in width. Chile's eastern border is defined by the watershed of the *Cordillera de Los Andes* and the western border by the frigid Pacific Ocean. To the south, the tip of Chile curves east to the Atlantic Ocean and the sailors' bane of Cape Horn. The northern frontier is located in the Atacama Desert, the world's most nitrate-rich but parched land. Chile also possesses the Pacific islands of the Juan Fernandez Archipelago and the archaeologically famous Easter Island, locally called La Isla de Pascua, or *Rapa Nui*, its native name.

The country is best described in comparison with the west coast of North America and, by turning Chile upside down and widening it a bit, the geographic similarities are startling. In the north, the Atacama is a drier and more desolate area than either the Mojave or Sonora deserts of California and Arizona.

Farther south, a Central Valley parts a rolling coastal range and rugged mountains to the east. While the east slope of the mountains are dry and productive only with irrigation, the forested western flank slopes into a flat central valley which has an abundant water supply, fertile alluvial soils, and a benevolent Mediterranean climate. A wide variety of fruits grow profusely, and the Maipo Valley, like California's Napa Valley, produces some of the world's best wines. Along the coast, beautiful beaches and a bountiful fishery promote relaxing vacations and a varied diet for the ocean-oriented population.

Continuing south, volcanoes begin to dominate the landscape much as the Cascades do in the US Pacific Northwest. Chile's southern volcanoes rise in a land of clear, trout-filled lakes and dense, ferny forests. The parallel continues through Puerto Montt and Chiloé, the geographic Vancouver and Victoria of South America. The mainland then breaks up, becoming an archipelago of inhospitable and sparsely populated islands covered with slow-growth forests. They are most easily reached by boat which can easily access the dramatic ocean fjords. The Pacific-destined glaciers of the Alaskan panhandle are matched by those of Chile's Magallanes region.

The mirror image of the western coasts of North America and Chile concludes with the anomalies of Hawaii and Easter Island, both located far from the mainland and supporting isolated South Pacific populations and cultures.

History

Before the first Europeans arrived in Chile, the Mapuche, or Araucano, tribe was firmly established in most of the region. Their heaviest concentration was around what is now Temuco, and they inhabited most of the land between the Chillán and Antillanca volcanoes. The Mapuches resisted domination by the Inca empire through fierce defense of their territories. The only remaining Inca influences in Chile are a few place names and sacrificial mummies discovered high in the *Cordillera*.

The first *conquistador* to explore Chile seriously was Pedro de Valdivia. Under the direction of the Viceroyalty of Peru, Valdivia founded not only Santiago but also many of the southern cities which were attacked repeatedly by the Mapuches. Valdivia's exploits ended abruptly when he was captured and killed by the Mapuches in 1554.

Chile continued as an adjunct of Spanish Peru for the next two and a half centuries until the illegitimate son of an Irishman began to sow the seeds of an independence revolution. Bernardo O'Higgins was born in Chillán to a Chilean mother, Isabel Riquelme, and was educated in Lima and London. From his congressional seat, O'Higgins is largely credited with carrying the independence movement to the people of Chile. In 1810, he was the commanding general of the revolutionary forces, but it was not until 1817, with the help of the Argentine liberator José de San Martín, that the decisive battles were won. On February 12 1818, O'Higgins declared the independence of Chile and was appointed its first President. He eventually returned to Lima in mild disgrace after being accused of becoming too autocratic.

Throughout the next 80 years, Chile was run by the landed aristocracy who had more or less dictatorial powers throughout the period. The War of the Pacific was fought against Peru and Bolivia from 1879 to 1883. The victorious Chileans, who actually occupied Lima, were rewarded with the nitrate-rich Atacama desert which had been shared by Bolivia and Peru. The landed elite and their President, José Manuel Balmaceda, were overthrown in 1891 with a naval revolt led by Jorge Montt. The legislative body then possessed Chile's constitutional authority until 1973.

Economics

Chile is the largest copper producer in the world with proven reserves that account for 25% of the world's supply. Although Chile produced 40% of the global output of copper in 1860, it now provides between 15 and 20 percent. Most is produced at the huge open pit mine at Chuquicamata and in the underground mine of El Teniente. There are also important mines yielding gold, silver, coal, nitrates, molybdenum, iodine, lithium, rhenium, and boron in various parts of the Andes foothills. About half of Chile's oil needs come from their Patagonian territories.

The Pinochet years brought a broad diversification in the economy of Chile. Although their major trading partner is still the US, Chile enjoyed a US$2 billion trade surplus with Japan in 1989. The most important new export products coming from Chile include fresh fruit, fresh and processed fish and fish products, wood, lumber, and wood furniture, and on a smaller scale, wine, which is now widely available in the US. Annual inflation held under 20% and the annual growth rate was 5-6% through the final years of the 1980s. The exchange rate fluctuated around 300 pesos(C$)/dollar in 1990.

Foreign investment is also on the rise and is likely to continue its brisk pace through the 1990s. One of the biggest success stories is the Chilean Telephone Company (CTC) which was purchased by the Australian investor Alan Bond in the late 1980s. After building the continent's best communications network, the CTC became the first South American company to be listed on the New York Stock Exchange in 1990. The Japanese are investing in industry, and the Europeans are participating in development projects like Santiago's Metro and Valle Nevado.

Demographics

Chile has about 13 million habitants. 20% are of European heritage, and 75% have mixed *mestizo* blood. From 1850 to 1940, when over 60,000 Germans settled in the country, immigrants from throughout Western and Eastern Europe colonized the southern frontiers of the Lakes District. About 80% of the population is Roman Catholic, although many are now turning to the Christian evangelical sects.

Much to the dismay of the central government which emphasizes agricultural production, Chile has become one of South America's most urban societies. Some 84% of Chileans now live in cities. Santiago, Concepción, and Valparaíso account for 63% of the population.

The Chilean people are renowned as the most polite, inviting, and honest on the continent. Some writers have gone so far as to suggest that Chileans are the British of South America. What really sets them apart is their eternal optimism. Perhaps this is due to the catastrophic earthquakes, volcanic eruptions, and tidal waves that have besieged the country throughout history and forced the Chileans to work together to rebuild their society again and again. A brief glimpse at their recent political history does not support this unity theory however.

Modern Politics

After a century of rule by the elitist land barons, Arturo Alessandri became Chile's first leftist President in 1920. He began a second term in 1932 but had become more conservative as had his son, Jorge, who served as President from 1958 to 1964.

These formative years of the democracy were characterized by extreme factionalism. In a twelve month period in 1932, six individuals actually served as President of the weak government. Chile was so democratic that the proliferation of uncompromising political parties and newspapers were destroying the foundations that allowed them to flourish. The one unique property of the Chilean system was that the military was always relegated to civilian rule in contrast to Argentina, Brazil, Bolivia, Paraguay, Venezuela, etc, where the military has always felt free to intervene in politics.

Eduardo Frei, the standard-bearer of the Christian Democrats, ruled Chile from 1964 until 1970. The following election was won by Salvador Allende, an avowed Marxist who was a Senator in Chile's Congress. With weak candidates from the center and right, Allende won the popular vote with 36.2% of the ballots. His three-year tenure came to be known as the "Thousand Days of the UP" (his party was called the *Unidad Popular*). In the uncooperative atmosphere of the "negative majority," nothing could get passed in Congress, and Allende was forced to rule more and more by decree to forward his programs.

Allende was overthrown in 1973 in a bloody *coup d'etat* led by General Augusto Pinochet. The Presidential Palace was heavily bombed, but Allende allegededly took his own life. Some blame the US government for the *coup*, accusing Richard Nixon and Henry

Kissinger of protecting the interests of the US-owned Kennecot and Anaconda copper companies. The generally accepted theory is that US intervention was but one of many causes that led to the military takeover with roughly the same footing as the uncontrolled spread of violence in the country, the high polarization and sensationalism in the media, the uncontrolled attack on private property, continuing labor strikes, deflated copper prices, runaway inflation, an extremely active black market, and overzealous military officers.

The Pinochet years were extreme on the opposite end of the political spectrum. Military rule and oppression became the new standard. Political opponents were taken and shot in the national stadium, thousands were forced to flee the country in exile, others simply disappeared without a trace or explanation. Chile's human rights record was hideous throughout the Pinochet period, and the US was forced to halt all trade and aid as a result.

In October of 1988, Pinochet succumbed to international pressure and held a national plebescite in which Chileans were to vote *sí* to continue with the dictator for another eight years or *no* to hold a general election in which Pinochet could not be a candidate. Despite unfair campaign practices, the "yes" vote was soundly defeated.

The ensuing 1989 presidential election was won by the Christian Democrat, Patricio Aylwin, who took office in March of 1990. His ability to bring the factions together in the defeat of the plebescite made him the most logical choice to the cautious voters. Aylwin's abilities to form coalitions in the highly divisive political spectrum is the key to his success. He has continued to develop the pro-business, free market policies of his predecessor and has vowed not to seek reelection at the end of his term. Should he stumble, Pinochet, a Senator-for-Life and Chief of the Armed Forces, remains a fairly popular option to the businessmen of Chile. The families of the 220 remaining *desparecidos*, or disappeared ones, can't understand why.

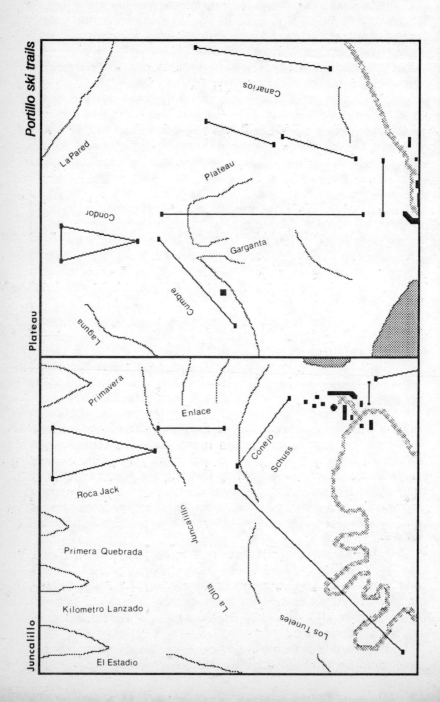

Chapter 7

Portillo

Ski Area Facts and Figures

Elevation: Top: 3,348m; 10,984ft.
            Bottom: 2,512m; 8,241ft.
Vertical Drop: 836m; 2,743ft.
Season: Early June to Mid October.
Lifts: 11:
            3 Double Chairs, 2 *Va et Vients*, 6 Poma Lifts
Runs: 23:
            20% Beginner, 30% Intermediate, 20% Advanced, 30% Expert
Ticket Prices, 1990:
    US$19 Adults Full Day, US$17 Youths 6-21, US$8 Children under 6.

Introduction

Portillo probably provides the most comfortable and relaxed ski experience in South America. With nearly all the guests lodged together in the grand Hotel Portillo, you really get to know your fellow skiers, and most people who frequent Portillo tell you they return year after year for this congenial atmosphere. Since the resort is owned and operated by a North American family, communication for English speakers is easier here than at any other South American ski area.

Portillo's greatest asset is, however, outside. Crisp, sparkling days are the rule with Andean condors soaring in the crystalline blue skies and skiers floating in thigh-deep styrofoam-snow between pointy, shadowed rock outcroppings. When the glassy Laguna del Inca isn't frozen, it perfectly reflects this pristine scene as if the spectacular sight needed repeating.

Portillo seems small on arrival because the ski area is split by the hotel complex and because the lifts don't even approach the surrounding 4,300m (14,000ft) summits. The highest lift-serviced points on both sides are about half way up steep avalanche chutes, and are reached by Portillo's own lift, the *Va et Vient* (see Box). The best skiing is found by sneaking over ridges and around corners on a high traverse from the top of these tow lifts. It is here, in the snow pillows, wind pack, and corn deposits of Portillo's upper slopes, that Portillo justly earns praise from skiers around the world.

History

Skiing in South America began in the Portillo area when English and Scandinavian railroad engineers surveyed the Pass in late 1800s (see *Chapter 3*). Recreational skiing began in 1910 with the completion of the railway. Skiers used the twice-weekly Trans-Andean train for access. They could unload at top of the Paso del Bermejo near the statue of *Cristo Redentor* (Christ the Redeemer) at the Chile-Argentina border, or at the Caracoles station near the present day hotel. The train remained the only way to reach Portillo until 1968 when the international road from Santiago to Mendoza was completed.

Skiing was here to stay only after the completion of the Hotel Portillo in July, 1949. Throughout the seven-year construction period, the hotel was utilized as a *refugio* by skiers, and a gas-powered rail car was enlisted to transport skiers. The main run began at the summit at Cristo Redentor and descended to the station at Juncal below the hotel site. The hotel was connected to Portillo's own train station via a tunnelled walkway.

The hotel was originally financed by a private company called Hoteles de la Cordillera, SA, but it had to be completed by the federal government because of the high cost of the ambitious project. The hotel and ski area were initially operated by HONSA, the government hotel company, and marketed by Ferrocarriles del Estado, the federally operated train system who transported everyone to the area in those early days.

The Hotel Portillo had all the finest comforts of its day. Richard Joseph, writing in *Esquire* in 1947 described "...central heating, stall showers, private sun porches, a movie theater, night club, library, music rooms, and... an infirmary. They also keep a herd of six cows for fresh milk, right on the spot." Portillo was the unrivalled place to see and be seen on the continent by the wealthy of both North and South America. John Jay, the eminent North American ski writer of the period, concluded that Portillo "...promises to be the St Moritz of South America," after his 1946 trip.

The first conventional ski lifts in Portillo were built in 1946. They accessed the Plateau area with a single chairlift to the top of

Garganta and a smaller platter tow from the top of the chairlift to the top of Plateau. Remnants of these early lifts can be seen in the area around Tío Bob's restaurant.

The Modern Era

In 1961, Portillo was sold as part of a nationwide privatization program. The purchaser was an investment group of North Americans led by Robert W Purcell who promised dramatic changes and new investment at the stagnating ski resort. While 11 new lifts were eventually built, the most important projects undertaken by the new owners were the successful bid for the FIS World Championships of 1966, and the introduction of Bob's nephew, a graduate of the Cornell School of Hotel and Restaurant Management, as General Manager.

Henry Purcell, who actually negotiated the purchase of the historic resort, understood that the World Championships would provided the forum and media spotlight that Portillo needed: "If we could do it, people would realize there's skiing in South America." The concept of the modern World Cup ski racing circuit was born in the hotel at the conclusion of the successful event.

Henry continues, with the assistance of his brother David, to manage Portillo in his calm, deliberate manner. He is widely respected and admired by the ski industry, the media, and his loyal employees. In addition, Henry has used his self-imposed "sentence" in Portillo to become an outstanding powder skier as well as one of the most knowledgeable and professional snow physics and avalanche control experts on the continent.

Racing History

The first ski race in Chile took place at Caracoles in 1931. More local races organized by the Ski Club Chile were held in the area throughout the 1940s and 1950s. In the 1966 FIS World Championships, the French maintained their ski racing dominance with Jean Claude Killy and Marielle Goitschel winning the combined golds. With Annie Famose winning the slalom, and Guy Perillat prevailing in the giant slalom, France took all but one gold medal. Only Carlo Senoner of Italy prevented the sweep by winning the men's slalom.

Portillo has also been a favorite site of speed skiers. In the three trials held here, a new world record has been set at each. In 1963, Dick Dorworth and CB Vaughn shared the record at 171.428kph (106.523mph). Steve McKinney, the original extreme skier from Squaw Valley, was the first to break the 200km barrier with his mark of 200.222kph (124.416mph) here in 1978. Most recently the record was broken by Michael Prufer of Monaco in 1987 with a speed of 217.680kph (135.264mph).

Geography

Portillo sits in the heart of the southern Andes a mere 40km (25 miles) from the base of Cerro Aconcagua, the highest point in the Americas. Portillo translates to "narrow pass" which aptly describes the main crossing point between Chile and Argentina. The pass was first crossed by mules and horses and later by the Trans-Andean international train, reputed to be one of the most spectacular rail journeys in the world. Once the international road was built, the train service became uneconomical and obsolete and was closed in the mid-1970s.

The pass is of great strategic importance and has been a site of contention between Chile and Argentina. The statue of Christ the Redeemer was dedicated on March 13 1904 at the border at 3,854m (12,644ft) to commemorate the lasting peace that was finally negotiated by the diplomatic offices of Britain's King Edward VII.

The hotel was built at 2,890m (9,480ft), 1km below the Chilean customs station at Los Libertadores and 6km from the Argentine border. It is 69km (43 miles) from the bottom of the pass at Los Andes and 149km (93 miles) from Santiago.

Storms approach from the southern Pacific Ocean. Suddenly cooled by the extreme elevation and unable to penetrate the Andean barrier, the heavy clouds dump loads of snow throughout the area. The weather conditions are either clear and sunny or storming and snowing with few days finding a compromise. The high altitude dryness insures light snow and no rain. Portillo will operate weekends outside of the normal season if snow conditions permit.

The landscape of the region is completely treeless and has a barren, lifeless appearance. The Laguna del Inca is one of the very few lakes in this remote region of the Andes. The lake is so named because the Inca Illi Yunqui is said to have buried his princess there after she was tragically killed on a hunting trip. According to the legend, at that moment the lake's water "turned emerald, dyed by the color of the eyes that the son of the Sun could no longer awaken." It is also said that on certain still winter nights you can hear the low moans of the heartbroken Inca.

Skiing Tips

Portillo's slopes are split into two unintegrated halves. To access the Juncalillo (west) side, you need to skate over to the base of the Conejo double chair. The Plateau chair on the east side provides the easiest and quickest access to skiing though. It loads just a few meters from the hotel and ascends to the top of a wide bench under foreboding cliffs.

THE VA ET VIENT

The *Va et Vient* is a lift unique to Portillo. Designed by Jean Pomagalski, the name translates in French to "Come and Go," and Portillo's slopes are blessed with two of these bizarre creations. Roca Jack, South America's most famous ski lift, pulls five skiers at a time while Condor hauls four skiers to the highest point of the ski area. Portillo's *Va et Vient* solved an access problem that plagued the area in the early years, when skiers could only salivate at skiing the powdery runout zones that these lifts now climb. A conventional lift with lift towers was not the solution as unloading areas could not be constructed on the steep alluvial deposits, and no lift tower could withstand the destructive avalanches that regularly pour down these chutes. To solve the problem, Jean Pomagalski noted that because the Andes are a young mountain range, erosionary forces have had little impact on the shape of the slopes. Thus, lower slopes have a concave rather than convex shape. Jean figured that if he could match a cable sag to this concavity, a surface lift could succeed.

The lift is a cross between a conventional tramway and a towerless cable tow but has three bullwheels. One is mounted at the bottom on a regular lift tower; the other two are attached to wires anchored in rocks high in the chute. These upper bullwheels are then kept suspended in the air by the tautness of the haul rope which describes a triangle and can run in either direction. Two tow bars with platter seats are attached to the haul rope, and an operator starts and stops the lift at designated points. When an avalanche hits the lift, the cable drops and is buried. After the storm, a crew locates the cable and cuts it. It is then repaired or replaced, and the cable is reinstalled. This entire process can be completed within 48 hours after the offending storm. To load, simply pull the tow bar down with the attached rope and place a platter between your legs like a regular poma lift. Be sure that the bar is balanced and not weighted with an extra skier on one side or the other. When everyone is settled with poles, skis, hands, and the rope in their proper positions, take a deep breath and hang on! The ascent is a true thrill due to the extreme speed, the slope steepness, and the sometimes rough track. Just as your skis seem pointed impossibly vertical up the mountain, the lift suddenly stops. Here, a prearranged unloading sequence should have been negotiated. Wait after the stop for slack in the system to lower the load back down the slope. Only then can each skier carefully, in a balanced order, unload without losing significant elevation. In spite of their difficulties, the *Va et Vient* provide access to some of the best powder skiing in the world and have helped make Portillo a world-class ski resort.

The recommended way to ski Portillo is to start on the Juncalillo side in the morning. It is possible to watch the sunrise from a bunk in the Inca Lodge as the light descends the east-facing slope and eventually reaches the Roca Jack, the first run to soften in the early morning sun. After lunch, explore the Plateau side as it softens and warms.

The best beginner run is Canarios. It is close enough to the hotel for security but far enough away that less successful efforts are not visible to the critical sundeck crowd. Intermediates will find their greatest pleasure on Juncalillo which rolls over shelves and through valleys. The Los Túneles section of the run passes over two long tunnels which the government had to build over the road because the ski run "was here first." Powder and corn snow are handily tested on the sides of this run before venturing out to some of the more advanced runs.

The clear favorite at Portillo for advanced skiers is the Roca Jack. In the heart of winter, the Roca Jack is surrounded by feathery new snow. On a good spring day, the north side will have glittering corn snow, the middle slushy bumps, and the south side firm, dry wind pack. Another recommended advanced run is Garganta, a steep chute that opens into a wide bowl north of the Plateau chair. Expert skiers will need a full week to explore Portillo's vertical secrets. The greatest opportunities lie to the south of the Roca Jack. A high traverse left (away from the lake) leads to a series of four major ridges where numerous possibilities of varying width and pitch await. Skiers who are lulled into believing there's no more untracked powder simply are not looking hard enough.

Good moguls are most often found on Plateau, and pay-per-run courses and public races are often set in a dual format under the lower end of the chairlift. Roca Jack is the FIS homologated downhill run, and Plateau is certified for slalom and GS races.

Adventure Skiing

Portillo is the only resort on the continent with an active avalanche warning system administered by a resident snow physics expert. There is a flagpost in front of the hotel's pool on which the current danger level is indicated with either a red, yellow, or blue flag (explained on a large board in the hotel). In addition, rope and sign closures are often painstakingly set for skiers' protection, an uncommon service in South America.

Many of the local skiers seem to favor the steep hikes in the chutes above the *Va et Vients*. While a great view of Aconcagua can be had from above the Roca Jack, there are better places to ski that don't require so much exertion for so few turns. The best examples are the lake descents from the *Va et Vients*. Of the two, Condor provides a slightly longer vertical drop, drier snow (especially in the morning), and greater variety. Conditions are optimum when the lake is frozen and someone has already "broken trail" back to the lifts. On the Roca Jack side, return to Conejo via a traverse across the face of the last knoll above the lake surface.

Another excellent option is the Cancha del Tren. This can be spotted and the route planned by looking right while riding the Juncalillo chairlift. It is the obvious snowfield that fans out to the road with the old railroad tunnel crossing the middle. Access this run with a high traverse from the Condor lift to a point below the border checkpoint where the highway is crossed. At the bottom, cross the road again to return to the Juncalillo chair.

Nordic Skiing

Because of its high elevation and steep terrain, Portillo is not a good place for cross-country skiing. Avalanches frequently threaten the few flat places where nordic skiing might be appropriate. The only terrain really apt for this activity is the frozen lake surface or possibly around the Los Libertadores customs station.

Skier Services

Ski School

Some of the greatest skiers in the world have taught at Portillo, and the list of past directors is impressive. Emile Allais, Stein Erickson, Othmar Schneider, and Pepi Steigler all served full terms as Portillo's Ski School Director. The current Director is Jimmy Ackerson, a Vermont native who also heads the ski school at Heavenly Valley, California.

The ski school is staffed mainly by bilingual North Americans most of whom are on college breaks of varying durations. There are also many instructors from Latin and European countries, but Portillo is unsurpassed on the continent for the number of *gringos* on its staff. All instructors are fully certified and have extensive teaching experience.

The Ski School offers special racing and powder clinics as well as a full line of collective and private lessons. A video service films the classes and then shows them with analysis in the evenings. Private video service is also available. Prices range from US$12 for a half-day group lesson to US$32 for a one-hour private. Weekly rates are also available.

Medical Facilities

Portillo has an all-professional ski patrol of about 12 Chileans who handle first aid and trail maintenance. It is the only patrol in South America using the North American standard Cascade toboggan. Without question, Portillo has the safest and most professional snow safety program south of Texas.

The medical clinic is located inside the lodge near the slope access exit. It is staffed by two doctors and two nurses and is equipped to handle any emergency. The helicopter is always at the disposal of any serious medical emergency.

Helicopter Skiing

Portillo has heli-skiing available any time the Andean weather permits. From Portillo, five valleys of untouched snow can be accessed for heli-skiing. Rates are from US$700 per hour of helicopter flight time with four or five skiers.

Unique to Portillo is a one run program to the statue of Christ the Redeemer on the border with Argentina. For US$40, skiers are flown to the site at the top of the pass and are led down by a guide after a brief visit. Flight time is about 12 minutes and the descent is a tame traverse back to the ski area. This excursion is thus appropriate for skiers of lower intermediate ability or sightseers without skis. Information and sign-ups are at the ski school desk.

Base Facilities

When they check in, hotel guests receive a pass valid throughout the length of their stay. Day skiers can purchase a lift ticket in the booth set up just left of the hotel. Only hotel guests are guaranteed a lift ticket. Assuming full operation, Portillo will sell no more than 300 additional tickets to day skiers. If operations are limited by conditions, no tickets may be sold to the public. Lifts operate daily from 9.00am to 5.00pm.

Hotel guests have ski and boot storage facilities on the ground floor of the hotel. Boot storage is across the hall from the rental shop while the ski room is at the exit to the slopes. Walking with ski boots in the hotel is prohibited. Day use skiers have no special facilities for changing, but the restrooms on the ground floor are adequate.

The rental and repair shop is located on the ground floor of the hotel near the main slope access. They maintain a large stock of Atomic rental skis which rent for US$7. A full package rented for US$16.50 for adults and US$12 for kids in 1990.

Dining

There are three dining facilities at Portillo. The main dining room dominates the second floor and seats about 500 people. It is rich with tradition and maintains an air of respectable formality. Breakfast is reserved, lunch leisurely, and dinner special. Although dinner jackets are no longer required for gentlemen, most patrons still bring formal dress especially for the dinner event. The most desirable tables sit up against the huge picture windows with a great view of the lake. Be sure to try the tap water, the best (and safest) in South America.

Inca Lodge guests, day visitors, and the skiing employees eat in the self-service cafeteria located on the first floor past the lobby. The cafeteria serves a basic but satisfying menu four times a day.

Tío Bob's is the slopeside dining facility located at the top of Garganta. The views are spectacular, and on a hot spring afternoon, Tio Bob's sundeck is popular with the regulars who know that this is the best place for lunch. It rarely gets crowded because hotel guests have their lunch in the main dining room. The menu consists of meats broiled over an open flame and a nice salad bar. Fresh fruit and Chilean wine complete this Andean experience.

To experience a bit of what Chile is really like, try an evening at **La Posada**, a small pub maintained for Portillo's employees across the highway from the hotel complex. It is especially recommended in mid-September when the Chileans celebrate their independence with *chicha*, a homemade wine, and the *cueca* dance which the men practice dutifully amongst themselves or with any lady bold enough to join them.

The Hotel

The **Hotel Portillo** is one of Chile's modern architectural treasures. Completed in 1949, it was designed by the Chilean architect Martín Lira who also designed the Grand Hotel Pucón. The odd, arc shape was intended to create a convex face to provide guests with a broader view of the encompassing scenery.

Although the hotel was completed in 1949, it is no crumbling remnant of a building. The lodge has continually grown with a heated swimming pool and modern gym being the latest additions. A four-year remodelization project has left all the rooms in the old hotel fully redecorated. Lake-view rooms are somewhat more expensive than the backside rooms which merely have a view of snow-capped Andean peaks.

The first floor houses the main street entrance to the lobby, the transportation desk, the sport shop, the cafeteria, the video viewing theater, and the day care facility. All important notices of upcoming events are posted next to the elevator in the lobby. The second floor houses the main dining room, a very comfortable lounge area where *onces* and cocktails are served, the bar which can supply you with backgammon, chess, or domino equipment, a card room, and hotel rooms.

On the ground floor is the parquet-floored gym where soccer, basketball, and volleyball are played with vigor, the game room with ping-pong and pool tables, video games, and a snack bar, and Portillo's famous disco where a different sort of entertainment continues into the ridiculous hours of the morning. The sauna and outdoor swimming pool are also accessed here and are open only to adults 18 and older.

Other facilities on the ground floor include the ski school desk, the ski rental and repair shop, the ski and boot rooms, an aerobics room, the medical clinic, and, of course, the beauty parlor. There is also a small ice skating rink in front of the hotel. Ask at the sport shop for skates.

The **Octagon** is a less expensive bunk facility with 60 beds, private baths, and a nice deck to enjoy the views. The budget skier will delight in the **Inca Lodge**, an economic alternative at an otherwise pricey ski resort. There are six beds to a room and all residents share a common bath. The seven chalets are generally rented on a seasonal basis. There are a total of 482 beds in the complex.

Prices for accommodations vary greatly depending on location. A sampling of ski-week prices is presented in Appendix B. Stays of less than a week are also available.

Getting There

Portillo can be reached from Mendoza, Argentina or Santiago, Chile. From either direction, head for the top of the well-travelled Trans-Andean pass and stop when the lifts are in sight. Although the road is the best maintained mountain pass in South America, it is closed an average of 30 days each winter. Road closure is due more often to avalanche danger than snow on the road. The authorities are especially cautious since a 1984 avalanche at the Los Libertadores customs station killed several stranded travellers. See *Chapter 6* for a detailed description of this route.

The Hotel Portillo maintains a posting of current road conditions and an excellent warning system if closure is imminent (located behind the front desk). If the road closes, it may be possible to arrive or escape on the helicopter if time is limited, but be prepared for delays.

From Santiago
Via Private Auto:
Santiago-Los Andes: Highway 57, 88km (55 miles), 1 hour.
Los Andes-Portillo: Highway 67, 69km (43 miles), 1½ hours.
Via Portillo Bus:
Tourservice or Sportstours Travel Agencies will pick up guests at their hotels at 8.00am: 3hrs, skiing by noon, US$25. Arrange through Portillo office in Santiago.
Via Mendoza Auto or Bus:
Arrange at Santiago bus terminal, international area. Many companies, bargain for best price. Buses drop you off on the highway 50 meters downhill from hotel. Car:US$16, 2½hrs; Bus:US$12, 4hrs.
Via Helicopter:
Arrange at Portillo office in Santiago, 35 minutes.

From Mendoza
Via Private Auto:
Mendoza-Luján de Cuyo: Highway 40, 19km (12 miles), 15min.
Luján de Cuyo-Uspallata: Highway 7, 86km (53 miles), 1hr.
Uspallata-Los Penitentes: Highway 7, 67km (42 miles), 1hr.
Los Penitentes-Las Cuevas(customs): 17km (11 miles), 15min.
Las Cuevas-Los Libertadores(customs): 10km (6 miles), 10min.
Los Libertadores-Portillo: 1km.
Via Santiago Auto or Bus:
Arrange at Mendoza bus terminal, international area. See above.

Further Information and Reservations
In Santiago:
Hotel Portillo, Roger de Flor 2911, Santiago. Tel: 231-3411, FAX: 231-7164, Telex: 440370 PORTI CZ
At the Hotel:
International Road, Km 16, Portillo. Tel: 243-3007, FAX: 243-3007, Telex: 441361 PORTI CZ

La Parva ski trails

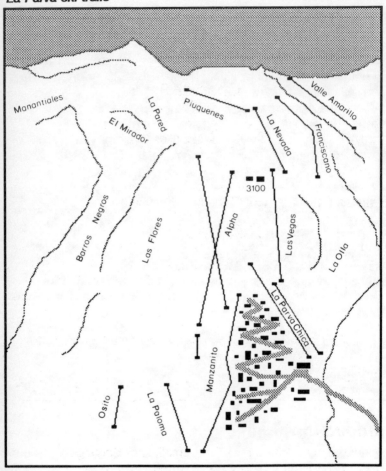

Chapter 8

La Parva

Ski Area Facts and Figures

Elevation: Top: 3,630m; 11,909ft.
            Bottom: 2,670m; 8,759ft.
Vertical Drop: 960m; 3,150ft.
Season: Early June to Mid November.
Lifts: 13:
            1 Quad Chair, 1 Triple Chair, 1 Double Chair, 10 Poma Lifts
Runs: 20:
            15% Beginner, 55% Intermediate, 20% Advanced, 10% Expert
Ticket Prices, 1990:
  US$20 Adults Full Day, US$18 Youths 7-23, Seniors, Adults Half Day.

Introduction

La Parva is the northernmost and smallest of Santiago's three ski resorts. The village climbs parallel to the lower slopes but has no hotels or other tourist services. La Parva is reminiscent of a small village in the European Alps but is really Chile's answer to Aspen. The ski area is like a private club for Chile's wealthy families, most of whom maintain a second (or third) home in the village. Like Aspen Highlands, the ski area is positioned atop a long ridge. With the completion in 1990 of the Las Tortolas chairlift, skiers are able to traverse easily into Valle Nevado in addition to El Colorado.

History

The ski area was developed in 1952 by European entrepreneurs who originally set out to create a private club at La Parva. Within 10 years, two double chairlifts and a surface lift were in operation, but economic concerns forced a sale of the resort in 1962. The buyers were led by the North American, Robert Purcell, who had bought Portillo a year earlier.

The Purcell period was marked by a greater commercialization of the ski resort. Eventually led by David Purcell, Robert's nephew and Henry's younger brother, the next 25 years saw the construction of 10 new lifts including Chile's first quad chairlift. La Parva thrived with the wealthy weekend market but suffered from stiff mid-week competition with its neighbor, El Colorado, whose more familiar atmosphere and steeper slopes attracted the greater majority of Santiago's die-hard skiers.

In 1989 a local investment group purchased the resort. They hope to make La Parva more of a tourist destination by developing a hotel complex of international standards and combining with Valle Nevado to make a common lift ticket. A chairlift was constructed in 1990 in the Valle Amarillo giving easy access to Valle Nevado's Camino Alto.

Geography

La Parva's lifts ascend a narrow, rolling slope between the valley which separates it from the cone of El Colorado and the flat, featureless, and snowy plain to the north. The ski area was the highest ski area in Chile until Valle Nevado accessed the Tres Puntas ridge in 1989. With four lifts above 3,100m (10,170ft), La Parva has had several late seasons, with closing dates in mid-December in 1983 and 1984. Under poor snow conditions, the area operates from the 3,100m level which is reached via the quad chair. La Parva translates to "The Haystack" which is the name of the peak that overlooks the ski area.

Skiing Tips

As mentioned earlier, the ski area has a longitudinal orientation. Many runs will thus be accessed with more than one lift. The advanced local skiers shun the comfortable chairlifts for the speedier and less crowded poma lifts which seem to shoot off in every direction on the mountain.

Beginners can ski undisturbed at the northern base of the ski area below the village. Intermediates seem to enjoy the super-wide Las Flores bowl which boasts a consistent drop for long, cruising, GS turns. Advanced skiers should try the south-facing bowl under the return traverse from the new Las Tortolas chairlift. This is probably La Parva's best mogul and powder area. Experts are advised to venture out on the Manantiales traverse and ski the Mirador and Pared areas which then feed into the Super-G terrain of Barros

La Parva

Negros. Be sure not to pass the access road back to the lifts from Barros Negros. It is easy to miss because the gully's high walls blind skiers to the rest of the ski area.

Racing

La Parva has one of the best junior racing programs in Chile. Members of the Ski Club La Parva hone their technique on one of La Parva's four FIS homologated runs, the most at any area in Chile. Slalom training is done on the steep Las Vegas runs, and visiting junior racers may be able to arrange a training program with the Chileans. The downhill course starts high on Piuquenes and then follows Barros Negros into Las Flores. Speed skiing races are held in the Manantiales area on the far north side of the ski area.

Adventure Skiing

The most distinctive chute of any South American ski area taunts skiers from its high perch north of the ski area. La Chiminea is a perfectly shaped chute and is something of a rite of passage for the local youths. The typically firm windpack snow surface is sunken below high rock walls. La Chiminea is accessed by hiking a short and easy ridge left of the top of the Piuquenes poma. Ascend this ridge until high enough to traverse on a flat above a multitude of corniced chutes which loom over the Manantiales road.

Past La Chiminea is a steep, south-facing wall called La Cara. Another option is to head right from the corniced plateau mentioned above and continue up the ridge. There are two big bowl systems in this area, the farthest of which is called Galerias del Pintor. This can feed inattentive skiers into Valle Nevado. Check at the restaurant at 3,100m for more information or to tie in with locals headed for the area.

Skier Services

La Parva has a full staff of bilingual ski instructors from a variety of countries. Lessons start at US$20 for a 1hr private. There is also a well-trained ski patrol at the ski resort. The Andes Powder Guides helicopter skiing company is based at the ski area as well (see Box).

Base Facilities

Tickets can be purchased on the slope side of the main base facility at the bottom of the Enlace and La Parva Chica poma lifts. This is the first structure found when driving into the village. Inside the lodge is a cafeteria and a very informative color computer which provides current data about La Parva (in English too). There is also a ticket annex near the base of the Las Flores chairlift. Multiple day tickets can be purchased at a discount.

The ski area's rental shop is located on the left side of the lodge access path and they have a well-maintained stock of intermediate gear. There are no locker facilities so change in Santiago and boot-up in your vehicle.

ANDES POWDER GUIDES

The Andes Powder Guides is the only independent helicopter skiing service in South America. The company operates from La Parva and serves an immense area between Portillo and the Cajón del Maipo. This includes about seven distinct ranges west of the main Cordillera de Los Andes. Their favorite area is the Cordón de Los Españoles, offering a wide variety of slopes for different levels of skiers.

The company is run by Robert Petrinovic, an Americanized Chilean who teaches skiing at Vail during the off-season. Rob has extensive patrol experience in Vermont and Utah, and has skied much of the local backcountry with his partner, Jorge "Yoyo" Tiska. Rob and Yoyo have developed a safe and successful program that is comparable to many of the heli-ski operations in North America.

Andes Powder Guides uses Aerospatiale Alouette 3 helicopters, widely recognized in the industry as the best high altitude equipment available. The helicopters can carry six people, but only five skiers are taken to provide an extra margin of safety. Andes Powder Guides prides itself on developing customized programs. Whatever the ski abilities or ambitions of your group, Rob will find the best snow and terrain for your party.

A minimum of four people are needed to form a group. Half and full-day programs are available. Rob can also arrange accommodation and transport in the Santiago and Farellones areas. Rates average about US$200 for a half day of skiing, depending on the ambitions of the skiers. Less expensive trips can be arranged. For example, trips to the top of La Parva Peak and the Lengua run require very little flight time because the run ends in La Parva.

For further information, write Andes Powder Guides, Casilla 48, Correo San Enrique, Las Condes, Santiago, Chile, or FAX 772-758 or call (09) 221-6752, or stop by the Tres Mil Cien ("3,100") restaurant at the midpoint of the La Parva ski area.

Dining

Tres Mil Cien ("3,100") is the mid-mountain restaurant at La Parva. It is centrally located at the top of Alpha and below the upper poma lifts. English is spoken by the Canadian owners who have had the concession here for several years. The *andescuchos* (shish kebabs) are hugely popular (US$4) and the hamburgers are possibly the best in Chile (US$3). Meals are enjoyed outside on the large wooden sundeck or in a new dining room. Tres Mil Cien also serves as the informal headquarters of the Andes Powder Guides heli-ski operation.

There is also a good cafeteria at the base of the ski resort serving a variety of food including salads, pizzas, and assorted sandwiches. Prices run from US$3 for a burger to US$10 for a large pizza.

The Hotel

There is no hotel facility in La Parva but the ski area does own a condominium complex which has rooms for four and six people. Guests can cook their own meals in their rooms (buy food in Santiago before coming up), or enjoy the international restaurant. La Parva village has some 4,200 beds in total and some of the homes can be rented. Call Rob Petrinovic at Andes Powder Guides to arrange this type of lodging. Otherwise, stay in Farellones or Santiago.

Further Information and Reservations
Centro de Ski La Parva
2874 San Sebastian, Santiago, Chile. Tel: 233-2476, FAX: 231-3233.

Chile: Tupungato Region

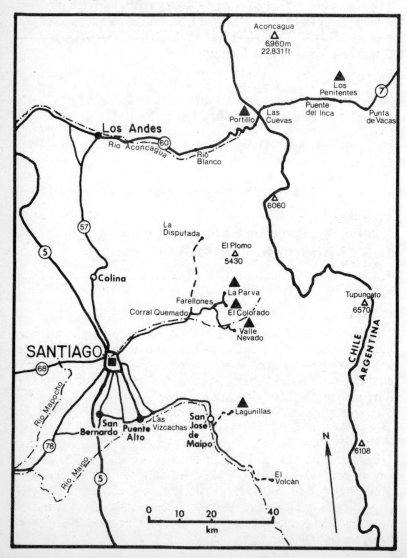

Chapter 9

El Colorado

Ski Area Facts and Figures
Elevation: Top: 3,333m; 10,935ft.
Bottom: 2,430m; 7,972ft.
Vertical Drop: 903m; 2,963ft.
Season: Late June to mid-October.
Lifts: 16:
3 Triple Chairs, 1 Double Chair, 11 T-Bars, 1 Surface Tow
Runs: 25:
40% Beginner, 20% Intermediate, 30% Advanced, 10% Expert
Ticket Prices, 1990:
  Weekends: US$18 Adults Full Day, US$17 Youths 7-21, US$8 Children 6 and under.
  Weekdays: US$13 Adults Full Day, US$12 Youths, US$5 Children.

Introduction

El Colorado is Chile's biggest and most popular ski area with nearly twice the number of lifts as its nearest competitor. It has the best ski runs in Chile with plenty of space for beginners and challenging terrain for experts, and is exceeded in size on the continent only by Cerro Catedral at Bariloche in Argentina. El Colorado is like Mammoth Mountain in California. Both are real skiers' mountains and receive plenty of snow; both are popular with the young, local skiers who spread over the vast and sunny slopes on winter weekends.

There are two base areas at the ski resort. The first, on the eastern edge of the town of Farellones, is used by beginner skiers, tobogganists, and non-skiing visitors. Villa Colorado is the more modern base area several kilometers past Farellones. It is here, at the main base lodge called El Parador, that most of El Colorado's skiers begin their day.

History

El Colorado is Chile's second oldest ski resort. Chile's first ski lifts were built around the Farellones base. But long before any lifts were built, and even before there was a road to the area, people were enjoying the snow of the Farellones area.

Skiing at Farellones was first organized with the formation on July 11 1931 of the Ski Club Chile. Their weekend skiing experience began on Saturday with a drive up the La Disputada mine road to a point named Corral Quemado. At 7.00am Sunday morning, they would load the mule train for a four-hour ride up to Farellones. The main run was called La Gran Bajada. It ran through the existing village between the hotels Farellones and Posada.

Until 1935 when the first *refugio* was finished, club members stayed in tents which were erected on the exposed and snow covered terrain. In 1937, the Refugio Ski Club Chile boasted 90 beds with hot running water, a kitchen, and a bathroom. Various groups constructed several other lodges and cabins, the most notable of which was operated by Francisco "Pancho" Guerrero.

The first lift cable tow was installed in 1936 in an area just above the Posada hotel. Development was fostered by Agustín Edwards, a local banker and ski enthusiast who assumed the club presidency in 1937. In 1939, the Farellones road was completed and the area saw the installation of its second lift, El Gancho, which reached the 2,500m level near the top of today's Novicios T-Bars.

In 1946, Clifton Ledtherbee, a Bostonian who had worked for many years in the North American ski industry, arrived in Chile. He promptly purchased the Yerba Loca and Portrero Grande ranches which consisted of some 5,000hc (12,350ac) on and around the cone of El Colorado. He formed a new company to engage in the development of the area as a commercial ski center. The new enterprise, called Andariveles de la Cordillera, SA or ANDECOR, built its first lift in the area adjacent to the Ski Club's Hotel Tupungato in 1949. It was named Embudo for the long funnel chute nearby. In 1955, the Silla Colorado was erected to access El Colorado's summit. Previously, the top was skied perhaps once a year on the long *Dieciocho* (Sept 18) holiday.

In the mid 1960s, three T-Bars were constructed in anticipation of the 1966 FIS World Championships in Portillo which were sure to attract a number of foreign skiers to El Colorado's slopes as well. The 1970s saw further expansion with five new T-Bars accessing new areas of the mountain. More chairlifts were not constructed until the mid '80s when heavy crowds and increased competition motivated the company to build Chile's first triple chairs.

Geography

El Colorado is a red, cone-shaped mountain with south-facing slopes. It is bordered on the south by Farellones village, on the west by La Parva, on the north by Valle Nevado, and on the east by a long cliff-band that stretches from Cono Este to the base of the Embudo lift.

The western slopes that face La Parva are exposed to the prevailing winds and are thus undeveloped and usually rocky. The deepest snow is found in the Cono Este area which lies in the lee of the mountain. Excellent views of the surrounding ski areas and Santiago's smog blanket can be enjoyed from the upper slopes.

Skiing Tips

Most skiers will stay above the base lodge at Villa Colorado. Below this point the trails are mostly rated beginner except adjacent to the Embudo lift where slalom training courses are often set. The Silla Colorado is the only lift to reach the summit and often closes in inclement weather conditions. The double-grip chairs bounce radically over each of the 23 erector-towers, but it seems to run almost as fast as the modern triple chairs that parallel it.

Beginner skiers will find the best trails alongside the Los Zorros T-Bars although Colorado Chico, Pinguino, and the Novicios Farellones lifts provide plenty of alternatives. The El Condor runs are wide, groomed trails with a consistent pitch which will appeal to intermediate skiers. Advanced skiers should try the Cono Este run for a long and steep pitch with a broad view of Valle Nevado.

Expert skiers will find more excitement at El Colorado than at any of the neighboring resorts. Two areas should be investigated. The first is low on the mountain, just above the lowest beginner lifts. Here, the narrow and vertical Corredores chutes and walls are lined side by side between the Embudo lift and the chute called Falsoembudo (false funnel). Access this cliff area from the top of either the Embudo lift for the lower, shorter drops, or from Zorros for longer runs and Falsoembudo. If the snow is too thin at those lower elevations, explore the chutes to the skiers' right of Cono Este. Do not go too far right as these chutes soon fade into unskiable cliffs.

Good moguls are found at the top of Cornisa although they are often interrupted with traverse trails and human obstacles. The best powder at El Colorado is found in the late opening but sheltered Cono Este which also closes early (4.00pm).

Racing

A great deal of racing and other competitive events take place at El Colorado. Promotional and recreational races often close the

El Colorado ski trails

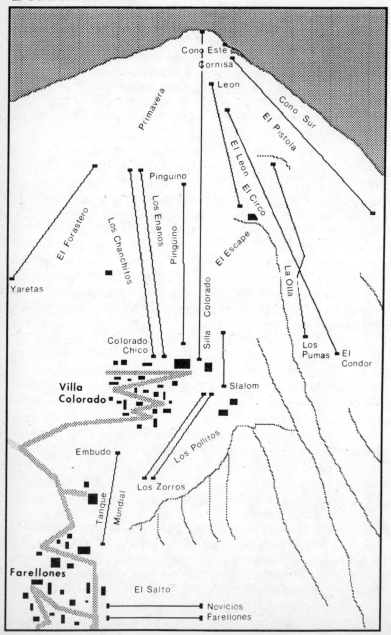

Pinguino run in front of the main lodge. A speed skiing course is designated on the east facing slope above the Yaretas T-Bar. El Cono is a certified slalom hill, and Los Pumas is homologated for GS races.

Adventure Skiing

There is less backcountry access from El Colorado's lifts than at either of its neighbors. An area which could be explored is the long cliff area between Cono Este and the Embudo lift. This region can be thoroughly scouted from Valle Nevado's access road where a car could be parked for escape. The chutes and bowls are controlled by helicopter by Valle Nevado's avalanche protection team since many of the snowfields threaten the road.

Skier Services

Ski School

El Colorado's ski school is headed by José "Pepo" Hanff who has taught skiing for nearly fifty years at a variety of ski resorts in Europe and South America. A former Chilean national team coach who studied at the University of Grenoble, Pepo takes special pride in his children's program. The *Mini-Escuela* is tailored for kids aged 4-12. With a special lift designed for youngsters, this program is one of the best and safest in Chile.

Medical Facilities

El Colorado is committed to the safety of its guests, and reckless skiers are likely to be disciplined by one of the Patrullas de Chile who seem to be everywhere on crowded weekends. Trails are well-maintained with appropriate signage and tower padding. There is also a small group of professional patrollers at El Colorado. First aid clinics are located at both base areas.

Base Facilities

Tickets can be purchased at either base area. In Farellones, the ticket booth is the only structure on the slope side of the parking lot. Up at the main lodge, tickets can be purchased at the outdoor ticket windows on the slope side of the top level of the main lodge. Many of the hotels in Farellones also sell tickets. Lift hours are 9.00am to 5.00pm with several of the upper lifts closing earlier.

A good basket-check facility will guard your belongings for a nominal charge while skiing. It is located downstairs in the main lodge by the large and clean toilet facilities. Be extremely careful about leaving your skis unattended in the Farellones-El Colorado area. If they were to disappear anywhere in Chile, it would be here.

Rental shops are everywhere. For beginner skiers looking for a bargain, rent from one of the booths in the Farellones parking lot. More modern equipment can be rented in the efficient facility on the second floor of the **El Parador** base lodge.

Dining

At the base of the Leon triple chair is the slopeside dining facility called **El Mirador del Puma**. There is an indoor facility for about 100, but everyone crowds onto the outdoor sundeck which can accommodate about 200 diners. Sandwiches, burgers, and yogurt can be purchased inside. On the outdoor grill, US$4 *fierrazos* (shish kebabs) sizzle in front of the long lines of bronzed, Vuarnet-covered faces.

The base lodge has an excellent cafeteria with many choices of entrees from their steam tables. A more formal option is in the round dining room of the Apart-Hotel where a long menu of steaks, chops, sandwiches, and many other typical Chilean dishes are available. **La Marmita de Pericles** is a friendly fondue hut with a full bar on the south side of the road just west of the main lodge.

Other ski-in options include the modest but homey restaurant of the **Hotel Tupungato**, the highest structure (blue) on the skier's right side of the Embudo ski lift. The restaurant in the **Hotel Farellones** is also convenient. Finally, for a more economical snack, try the food booths in the Farellones parking lot.

The Hotel

The small, slopeside **Colorado Apart-Hotel** is the reasonably priced condominium complex owned by the ski resort. Plans are available for two to seven people with three meal plan options. All units have fireplaces and balconies. Rooms are normally rented by the week only and, due to the limited number of rooms, reservations are seriously recommended. The resort also operates a very helpful lodging referral service in the main ski lodge.

Further Information and Reservations
Centro de Ski El Colorado
Edificio Omnium, 4900 Avda. Apoquindo, Loc.47-48, Santiago, Chile.
Tel: 246-3344, FAX: 220-7738. Ski Report: 220-9501

FARELLONES

Farellones is the name of the small, scattered village that is the service community for the La Parva, El Colorado, and Valle Nevado ski areas. Farellones, which translates as "cliff bands," is also the name of the lower part of the El Colorado ski area. La Parva, Villa Colorado, and Valle Nevado are the proper names of the villages located at the bases of these resorts, and all services offered at each are listed with their respective ski resorts.

The village of Farellones is perched at the top of a broad plateau. It encompasses the area from the fork of the Valle Nevado road to the final split of the road to La Parva and El Colorado, a distance of about 4km. The center of the town is around the Hotel Farellones at the base of El Colorado's Embudo lift.

Skiing in Farellones

Farellones is at the center of the best skiing in South America. Three of the continent's largest and most modern ski area developments are within a 15 minute radius of the village. Elevations range from 2,500m (8,202ft) in Farellones village to 3,670m (12,040ft) at the top of Tres Puntas in Valle Nevado, and all the resorts are south-facing. These elevations are sufficient to provide excellent snow cover even though the latitude compares with Phoenix, Atlanta, Osaka, and Beirut. The ski season begins in early June and continues through most of October.

Each ski area, although similar in many ways, serves its own skier market, and the locals are fiercely loyal to their favorite. El Colorado is the ski area of the middle and upper-middle classes and is the most popular of the three. La Parva is for the wealthier upper class. The ski area is practically a club for the rich, second home owners who exert strict controls over their village. Valle Nevado is a destination resort of international order out of reach to most Chileans. Rich Argentines, Brazilians, Mexicans, North Americans, and Europeans form the bulk of their market.

The *Centro Cordillera de Las Condes*

In spite of a high concentration of ski lifts around Farellones, there is no common lift ticket for the area. Ski connections are simple between all three resorts. The new Las Tortolas chairlift at La Parva completed the logistical puzzle in 1990. The three together would create a great ski center with 10 chairlifts and 25 surface lifts (not including the ongoing development at Valle Nevado).

Unfortunately, few expect to see a common lift ticket in the near future. Since each serves a distinct market, the ski areas really are not in direct competition with each other. Valle Nevado and La Parva may nevertheless begin a ticket exchange for their international guests only. That is, foreign tourists staying at either resort's hotel would be able to obtain tickets to both ski areas. This plan would likely exclude budget travellers who are staying in less expensive accommodations in Santiago or Farellones and would probably include ski-week guests only.

Nordic Skiing and Mountaineering

There is no organized nordic skiing in the Farellones or Santiago regions nor are there any shops which rent nordic equipment (although a few sell nordic gear). There are, however, some nordic and ski mountaineering activities in the area. For good maps and information about backcountry areas, check at the Hotel Tupungato. They organize summer expeditions to most of the higher summits in the area. Check also with the Andes Powder Guides people for ideas at the Tres Mil Cien ("3,100") restaurant on the slopes of La Parva.

The best areas for nordic touring in the region are probably around Manantiales at La Parva, and along the ridges west of the summit of Lagunillas around Cerro La Cruz and Tinajas Peak. To escape all mechanical lifts, proceed up the Cajón de Maipo past the Lagunillas road to Lo Valdés. The German Club has a *refugio* at the site which was one of the first ski runs in Chile. Avalanche danger in the region can be extreme so bring good equipment and common sense.

Transportation

The road to Farellones is fully paved and well-maintained but narrow and precipitous. On weekends, traffic is allowed uphill only from 8.00am to 2.00pm and downhill only from 4.00pm to 8.00pm. Chains are often required near the top. The route follows the Mapocho River up a canyon until the turnoff to the La Disputada mine at Corral Quemado from where a series of switchbacks climbs a near vertical wall. The locals drive like maniacs on the steep switchbacks, and there is usually at least one major accident every weekend with or without ice on the road.

There are several transport options to Farellones and the ski areas. El Colorado and Valle Nevado have their own mini-bus services and there are several other private operators. All leave at 8.30am from the Edificio Omnium except for Valle Nevado's which leaves from the Ski Service sport shop. The drivers are safe and

El Colorado

polite, and the passengers young and enthusiastic. Most stop at a convenience store on the way up and will play a favorite cassette.

Several of Santiago's main hotels have their own service to the ski areas in season, but these are generally inconvenient to serious skiers looking for a full day of skiing. With a big enough group however, private transportation can be the most economical. Hitchhiking from the start of the Farellones road is a good option only for non-skiers or others with little equipment.

Once in Farellones, transportation is difficult. All of the hotels access the runs of El Colorado except La Posada which runs buses to El Colorado and La Parva. Their location is ideal to hitch to Valle Nevado, too.

From Santiago
Via Private Auto:
Follow O'Higgins to Providencia to Apoquindo to Las Condes to Camino a Farellones: 52km (32 miles), 1½hr, paved, carry chains.
Via Bus:
Many from Edificio Omnium: 4900 Apoquindo, all resorts, 8.30am, US$7rt, 1½hr.
Ski Service: 4251 Apoquindo, to Valle Nevado, 9.00am, US$7rt, 1½hr.

From Farellones
To La Parva:
Left at intersection: 6km (4 miles), 5min, paved.
To El Colorado:
Right at intersection: 7km (4 miles), 5min, paved.
To Valle Nevado:
Right before Farellones: 15km (9 miles), 15min, paved.

Lodging

Most of the private homes in the town are owned by families or groups of families from Santiago. Others are operated as private clubs closed to all but members. Private houses can be rented at times, and some of the clubs' *refugios* are open to the public albeit at a higher rate than members. There are also several good hotels with reasonable rates but no outstanding, international-class hotels except at Valle Nevado. The only restaurants in the village are located in the hotels.

Some skiers will prefer to stay in Santiago to enjoy the capital city's cultural attractions. This is a viable and recommended option

as there is excellent daily transport to each of the three ski resorts.
Tupungato, alongside Tanque run; res and info: 4750 Candelaria Goyenechea, Santiago, Tel:211-7341. Daily prices: 6 person apt:US$33 each, 6 person cabin:US$53 each, 4-bunk room:US$19 each, prices include breakfast and dinner; 9 person cabin:US$60, 4 person cabin:US$50, no meals. Ski classes, rentals and tickets available, transportation to/from Santiago. Operated by Santiago Garcia and Ski Club de Chile, very homey, historical, interesting memorabilia, weather station, good food, recommended.
La Posada de Farellones, at entrance to Farellones on left; information: 4900 Apoquindo, Loc 43, Santiago, Tel:246-0660. Weekly prices: Sgl:US$238-623, Dbl:US$161-462 each w/private bath and 2 meals, US$126-210 each w/shared bath and 2 meals; free transport to La Parva and El Colorado, gas station, rustic, cozy, busy bar w/live music, great food, 2km from ski slopes.
Farellones, at base of Embudo lift; information: 251 Teatinos, Of 603, Tel:721-887, FAX: 56-2-698-1474. Daily prices: Sgl:US$45-95, Dbl:US$80-220, Suite:US$165-285, including breakfast, and lunch or dinner. Central location, multi-level structure, good bar and restaurant.
Refugio Manquimavida, near Tupungato; information: 4248 Alonso de Cordova, Santiago, Tel:220-6879 or 09-362-2612. No prices available. 50 person capacity, newer, Gustavo Latorre speaks English.
Refugio Aleman Andino, on Los Condores adjacent to ski run; information: 1789 Fuente Oveja, Santiago, or 2735 El Arrayán, Tel:211-9310 or 232-4338. Owned by Club Aleman Andino, small but good, lessons, rentals, and tickets available, German spoken.

Other Lodging
Edificio Monteblanco: Cecilia Wilson, Tel: 273-1568, slopeside condos.
Ski Total: 4900 Apoquindo, Loc 32-3, Tel: 246-0156, offers a full range of lodging referrals.
La Marmita de Pericles: 102 La Paloma, near El Colorado main lodge, 8 apartments.
Andes Powder Guides: Casilla 48, Correo San Enrique, Las Condes, Santiago, Tel: 09-221-6752, FAX: 772-758, can assist especially for private homes in La Parva or Farellones.

Chapter 10

Valle Nevado

Ski Area Facts and Figures
Elevation: Top: 3,670m; 12,040ft.
Bottom: 2,880m; 9,450ft.
Vertical Drop: 790m; 2,590ft.
Season: June 15 to October 15.
Lifts: 8:
1 Quad Chair, 1 Triple Chair, 1 Double Chair, 5 Poma Lifts
Runs: 21:
15% Beginner, 40% Intermediate, 30% Advanced, 15% Expert
Ticket Prices, 1990:
  Weekends: US$21 Adults Full Day, US$19 Youths 12-21 Full Day;
  Weekdays: US$12.50 Adults Half Day, US$10 Youths Half Day.

Introduction

Valle Nevado is the finest destination ski resort in Chile. Unlike Las Leñas where lodges are spread about ample grounds, Valle Nevado resembles a compact Whistler Village with everything operated by the same proficient management. Inaugurated in 1988, Valle Nevado already boasts three first class hotels, six outstanding restaurants, and eight modern ski lifts.

The wood-finished hotel complex is perched on a ridge above the plunging Ballicas canyon. When viewed from El Colorado to the west, the huge structure is dwarfed by the towering Cordón del Cepo in the background. Current slope development closely resembles that of neighboring La Parva but with more advanced terrain. With some 30 additional lifts planned, Valle Nevado should soon surpass even the best resorts of North America in terms of both skiing terrain and quality of service.

Valle Nevado ski trails

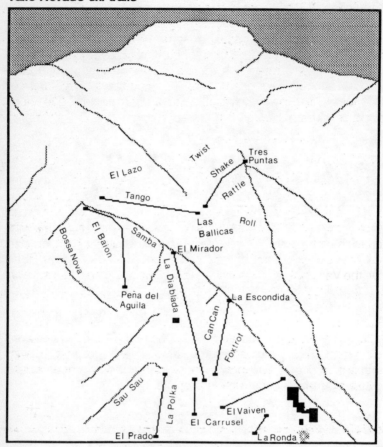

The Valle Nevado Story

The resort at Valle Nevado is the brain child of Eduardo Stern, a Chilean architect whose college thesis was a plan for a ski area at Valle Nevado. The unassuming student earned a scholarship for study in France and worked with CIE in developing Les Arcs. He now serves as Project Director, Chief Architect, and Executive Vice-President of Valle Nevado.

With the completion of Les Arcs, CIE sought a new site for an even better resort, this time in the southern hemisphere. After an exhaustive worldwide search, they sided with Sr Stern and his scheme, but the oil crisis and recession of the 70s put the project on the back burner for several years. Finally, in 1986, Spie Batignolles was contacted. This French construction company had been involved in many of Chile's most important development projects including Santiago's Metro subway. Valle Nevado would be the diversifying multinational's first investment in international tourism, and they own a 90% share in the project.

With expert planning and secure financing, the project got under way in 1987. By the 1990 season, some US$60 million had been invested in the project. This includes 14km of paved road and a complete infrastructure to service a population of 1,300. Development plans through 1994 call for an additional investment of US$90 million to fully integrate the resort with about 2,000 more guest beds spread through five more hotels.

Geography

Valle Nevado, or "Snowy Valley," is the name given to the area to the south of the rounded and glaciated El Plomo peak (5,430m, 17,815ft). It is bordered on its east side by deep canyons and on its west side by the La Parva and El Colorado ski areas. The name was given to the area by ranchers who migrated through the region with herds of livestock. In late spring when other valleys had lost their snow, the Valle Nevado was still white. This is because it faces south and is protected from the northern and northwestern winds that can devour more exposed snowfields.

Plans call for lifts to extend to the distant base of El Plomo at over 4,000m (13,125ft). Valle Nevado will be the highest modern ski area in the world. The ski season is set from June 15 to Oct 15 with operations forced to end not because of the lack of snow, but to prioritize off-season construction projects.

Skiing Tips

With 700 beds and a limit of 400 cars daily (the gate at Farellones closes after this), long lift lines should be rare but are found on the upper lifts on sunny weekend days. The ski area can be separated into two zones with the first encompassing the rolling intermediate terrain between the hotel complex and El Colorado's Cono Este T-Bar. The second zone is above this valley and begins at the top of the quad chair. It is characterized by more advanced runs on typical alpine terrain of exposed ridges and snow-filled bowls.

Beginners should utilize the El Prado chairlift below the hotel where they can enjoy skiing the winding trail called El Cuando. The long, rolling, and groomed descents on either side of the El Mirador quad chairlift will appeal to most intermediate skiers. Advanced skiers appreciate Shake, the often-mogulled slope to the immediate left of the Tres Puntas poma lift. On the right side, Rattle, Roll, and the chutes between them will challenge the most adept skiers. Another good expert area is the bowl called Bossa Nova.

Adventure Skiing

The only area for adventure skiing within a reasonable distance to the lifts is the La Parva peak which could be accessed from the top of the Peña del Aguila lift. There are other areas farther back which will someday be lift accessed and are now serviced by helicopter. None is worth a hiking effort. The most desirable extreme terrain plunges into the deep Ballicas canyon from the hotel complex. Most of these east-facing chutes feed into cliffs which become unskiable. Difficult escape from the bottom of the canyon and extreme avalanche hazard deters adventure skiers. Most avalanche control at the ski area is undertaken to protect the access road from Farellones.

Helicopter Skiing

Valle Nevado has the best helicopter skiing program of any ski resort in South America. Flight time and cost is kept at a minimum because the terrain used is so close to the ski area. For example, one program picks up skiers near the top of Tres Puntas where they enjoy a fifteen minute ride to the top of El Plomo. No return trip is needed as the lengthy run ends at the ski area. Rates begin at US$50 per run with helicopter time costing US$670/hr. Programs are available for all levels of skiers and all limits of credit.

Skier Services

There is a group of 40 ski instructors at Valle Nevado. Most are bilingual and many teach in the northern hemisphere in the Chilean summer. Monoski, snowboard, parasail, and hang gliding lessons are available in addition to regular alpine classes. Rates range from US$14 for a two hour group lesson to US$34 for an hour-long private. Lessons are significantly cheaper when purchased as a package upon arrival.

Valle Nevado has 25 professional ski patrollers. They bring injured guests to the resort's fully-equipped and staffed medical clinic which is affiliated with the Clinica Las Condes in Santiago. The helicopter is always at the disposition of any medical emergency.

Base Facilities

The ticket window is located at the left corner of the lodge complex at the end of the parking lot. A large variety of multi-day packages are available. For example, after seven tickets, prices drop to US$10 each day for adults. Half-day tickets are available weekdays only and cost US$10. Ticket sales are limited and could sell out on weekends, so arrive early if coming for the day. Lift hours are 9.00am to 5.00pm, but the upper lifts open later and close earlier.

There are no public storage or changing facilities for day skiers at Valle Nevado. The rental shop is located in the middle of the parking lot in front of the lodge. Superior equipment is available for US$20/day and US$12 for additional days. A standard set-up runs US$14 for a day and US$10 for kids.

Dining

Valle Nevado is surpassed only by Cerro Catedral at Bariloche for dining options. Slopeside is the **Jazz Grill** which serves US$3-4 hamburgers and sandwiches and a complete "Meal-of-the-Day" for US$10. It is located at the midpoint of the quad chair and has indoor seating and a north-facing sundeck.

At the base, most skiers eat at the **Slalom Grill** which has a simple sandwich menu. The **Café de La Plaza** features a fantastic outdoor buffet with cold salads and shellfish and a grill of sausages and chops.

Fancier fare is found first at **Le Monde** in the **Puerta del Sol** hotel. Fondues and other alpine-type items are available in **Le Montagnard**. Finally, the finest in French sauté cuisine is offerred in the elegant **La Fourchette D'Or**. The best thing about staying at Valle Nevado is that guests can dine at any of these fine restaurants as part of the ski-week package.

The Hotel

In 1990, three distinctive lodging options were available at Valle Nevado. The first is the **Hotel Valle Nevado**, a pricy facility for couples. Ask for a room on the west side to view the slopes or the east side for a view over the seemingly bottomless Ballicas canyon. The newer **Hotel Puerta del Sol** is geared towards family groups. Rooms here face towards Santiago or El Plomo.

The **Mirador del Inca** lodge provides a condominium option for guests. Studio, one bedroom, and two bedroom floor plans are available, and all include maid service. Packages can include two meals, or food can be cooked in the fully-stocked kitchen facility. Buy supplies in Santiago as prices in the resort's mini-market are inflated.

All rooms at Valle Nevado include a mini-bar, color TV with CNN reception, personal safes, international telephone service, and outdoor sundecks. Both hotels have their own gym, jacuzzi, and sauna. Cocktail bars, card rooms, and comfortable lounges seem to exist around every corner. Particularly relaxing is the "Tropical Room" which is filled with leafy ferns, wicker furniture, and a small aviary with several species of songbirds. Guests of the hotel or the condominium are allowed to use any of the facilities in the resort without an additional fee.

The resort publishes a list of activities each week detailing entertainment at the three piano bars, the two daily movies showing in the 180-seat theater, and the daily specials at the restaurants. Valle Nevado also operates their own radio station. Once a week there's a dinner with night skiing at the Jazz Grill. Aerobics, massages, a swimming pool, and two discos complete the list of "extra ski-icular" activities.

Other facilities at the complex include a day care for 2-6 year-olds, a mini-market, a drug store, a bank/exchange shop, a travel and tour agency, a sport shop, a boutique, and a hair salon. The exhibit room had a fascinating display of an Inca mummy found in 1954 on El Plomo.

Further Information and Reservations
Valle Nevado
441 Gertrudis Echeñique, Santiago, Chile. Tel: 480-839, 484-995, FAX: 487-525, Telex: 341527 VANESA CK

Chapter 11

Lagunillas

Ski Area Facts and Figures

Elevation: Top: 2,480m; 8,137ft.
           Bottom: 2,130m; 6,988ft.
Vertical Drop: 350m; 1,150ft.
Season: Early July to Late September.
Lifts: 3:
       1 T-Bar, 2 Pomas
Runs: 12:
      20% Beginner, 60% Intermediate, 20% Advanced
Ticket Prices, 1990:
   Weekends: US$13 Adults Full Day, US$10 Students, US$4 Children under 7.
   Weekdays: US$ 8 Adults Full Day, US$ 6 Students, US$3 Children.

Introduction

The main pass east into the mountains from Santiago follows another major river, the Maipo, from the south side of the city. This road leads up the Cajón del Maipo, one of Chile's most fertile valleys. The alluvial soils that fill the bottom of this glacial canyon produce South America's finest wines. It is in this easily accessed canyon where Chile's early ski clubs first came.

After skiing the mega-resorts around Farellones, Lagunillas may seem a bit insignificant. The quaint town of San José de Maipo and the unpretentious Chilean ski center at Lagunillas provide a less filtered glimpse of South American life though. At Lagunillas, the sport of skiing is undertaken at more of a local than international level. The Club Andino's motto sums up this difference: "Under our roof lives the love of the mountain."

THE LEGEND OF LA LOLA

The Club Andino of Chile prides itself on its mountaineering tradition and legend. One example of this is the story of La Lola which the Club has kept alive throughout the years. The legend says that sometime around the turn of the century, on "a dark and stormy night...," a mule driver was killed. His grieved widow set out into the mountains in search of her mate. Hooded with white, flowing robes, she still wanders the *Cordillera*, searching. The wispy figure sometimes appears to distressed mountaineers or mule drivers on inclement evenings.

The Club used to have a unique race in honor of the legend in which hooded, pole-less skiers attempted to emulate the mourning widow in style and skiing prowess. A competitor was eventually chosen by a skeptic judge. This winner then had to personify the widow's spirit over the coming year. In its day, it was quite the event, and the Club is trying to revive the traditional race but these efforts have been frustrated in recent years by uncooperative weather.

History

Lagunillas is owned and operated by the Club Andino de Chile, Santiago. The club was founded on April 8 1933 when its founder, Hermánn Sattler, a nationalized Chilean from Germany, organized a meeting to form the club. His newspaper ad attracted only two others, a Castilian immigrant named Francisco Carrasco, and Oscar Santelices, a native Chilean. These "three stooges," as they named themselves, quickly built a strong membership.

The Club Andino began their activities at Lagunillas upon the completion of their first *refugio* in 1934. They obtained the land for the ski area from a Chilean writer named Eduardo Barrios without cost in 1934. The new *refugio* was expanded in 1938 to a three level hut for 80 members. This lodge, like so many others in the earlier South American ski areas, was destroyed by fire in 1951. It was Chile's Independence Day, and the lodge was full of festive members and guests. A two-story *refugio* was completed in 1956 to replace the old lodge, and no smoking is allowed.

Geography

Lagunillas is located 18km (11 miles) up a subsidiary valley from the canyon of the Maipo River. By air, it is about the same distance from downtown Santiago as Farellones, but the trip is much easier and prettier, at least until San José de Maipo is passed.

The ski area faces south in a broad saddle between the hills of

Lagunillas

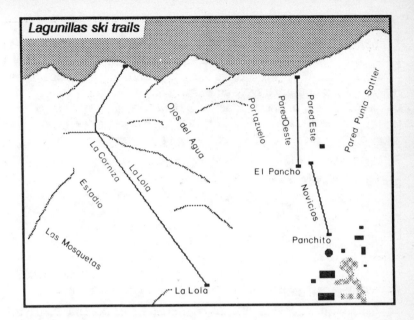

Punta Sattler and Cerro La Cruz. The highest mountain in the region is the Cerro San Lorenzo; at 3,902m (12,802ft) it dominates the view while coming up the Maipo Valley.

Skiing Tips

Run suggestions include the right side of the Panchito lift for beginners and the Pared Oeste off El Pancho for intermediate skiers. There is a short but corniced bowl on the west side of the La Lola T-Bar to excite and challenge advanced skiers.

Adventure Skiing

Punta Sattler offers the only good terrain for adventure seekers within a reasonable distance to Lagunillas. Begin hiking from the top of El Pancho and expect to spend up to an hour in the ascent. There is great avalanche danger on the south-facing canyons of this treeless hill. This hazard is evidenced by a house constructed in the run-out zone which also crosses the Lagunillas access road. People still live in the lower level, but the second story was taken out several years ago. A lesser avalanche hazard exists in the Estadio bowl west of La Lola.

Nordic Skiing

There is a designated nordic skiing area west of the alpine slopes under the Tinajas summit, but the entire region has plenty of easy, rolling terrain. But, the ridges all have barbed-wire fence lines making cross-country travel somewhat difficult. For other ideas, seek out Ian Farmer, a British teacher at The Bothy, a *refugio* of the *Centro de Educación al Aire Libre (CEAL)* located a few kilometers short of the ski area on the north side of the road.

Skier Services

Instruction and patrol services are basic at Lagunillas. Good instructors can be found for entry-level skiers, and some may be bilingual. The ski patrol is made up of volunteer members of the Patrullas de Chile who have a small facility at the base.

Base Facilities

Tickets are purchased in the small booth at the base of the Panchito lift. Hours are from 9.30am to 5.30pm but will vary depending on the crowd. Be sure to check at the office in Santiago if concerned about operations.

There are no good storage facilities at the ski area but there are several corners where belongings could be safely stashed. Two ski rental facilities, called El Gringo and El Checito, rent rudimentary equipment; both are located on the right (east) side of the parking lot.

Dining

There are at least three good places to eat at Lagunillas. **La Francisca** is a small cafeteria which is the highest building at the base area. The **Rotunda Sol y Nieve** is the smaller round structure behind the ticket booth at the bottom of Panchito. Both serve a basic selection of hamburgers, sandwiches, and beverages. A more formal meal is found at the club's *refugio* which has a modern kitchen and a nice dining room with a fireplace.

The Hotel

The comfortable *refugio* of the Club Andino de Chile has two double rooms, 16 rooms for four, and a large dorm-bunk room. All are located in three wings on the second floor and share common bathroom facilities. Downstairs is a warm lounge, a bright dining room, and a recreation room. The lodge is constructed of rock and wood and is filled with ski memorabilia from around the world. It is located directly across from the base of the La Lola T-Bar for ski-in and ski-out convenience. Check in the Santiago office for more information and prices.

Other Lodging

The Chilean sports organizing body *DIGEDER* also maintains a *refugio* at Lagunillas which is usually filled with assorted dignitaries. San José de Maipo has no hotels of international standard. Other options might be found in the Maipo Valley though. Otherwise stay in Santiago and make it a day trip. Try **El Campito** located just 2km past the Lagunillas turn-off for a great steak in a beautiful garden setting.

Getting There

The Club Andino has no regular public transportation service to Lagunillas, and it can be very difficult for a foreigner to escape Santiago in a rental car without circling it a few times. Follow Vespucio to Las Vizcachas and then follow the signs to San José de Maipo. Several *rotundas* need to be negotiated to complete this part of the journey so get a good map and navigator and have patience. The route is safe and paved. From central Santiago to San José is about 45km (28 miles).

From San José de Maipo, it is 1km to the turn-off to Lagunillas on the left (north) side of the road. Then, it is 17 rough, unpaved kilometers (11 miles) to the ski area. When required, the Club Andino contracts with the municipality of San José to plow the road. Often it will not be cleared for several days or perhaps weeks after a major storm, so check at the Santiago office before going up. The total trip from Santiago is about 63km (39 miles) and should take about 1½hr. Arrival at Lagunillas is confirmed upon sighting the giant steel statue of a *Christo Huaso*, which looks like a Rastafarian Jesus with open arms spread in generous welcome.

Further Information
Club Andino De Chile
Apoquindo 5681, Loc 5, Caracol VIP's, Las Condes, Santiago, Chile.
Tel: 211-2687

Chile

CENTRAL SANTIAGO

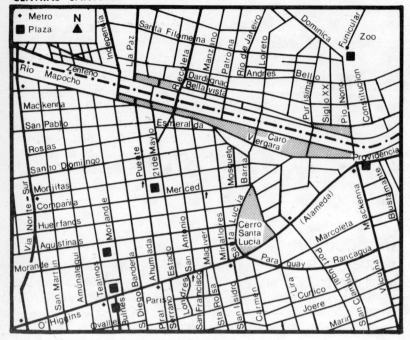

ANDES POWDER GUIDES

Customized Ski Vacations
For Skiers, By Skiers

- Airport Transfers
- Guide Service
- Lodging
- Heli Skiing

Casilla 48
Correo San Enrique
Santiago, CHILE
Tel/Fax: (56)-(2)-772-758

Owned and Operated by North Americans

Chapter 12

Santiago

Introduction

Santiago presents itself as a city big enough to be interesting but small enough to remain inviting. It is a city for those who hate the coldness of cities, a city that even skiers who have forsaken urban blight for rural tranquility can enjoy. Santiago's downtown area is easily explored by foot, and the modern suburbs are quickly and cheaply reached with an immaculate subway train. Most importantly, Santiago is safer than most cities in North America and Europe. Unlike Lima and Rio de Janeiro, violent South American cities where trouble seems to lurk around every corner, all parts of Santiago invite probing street hikes. The city compares to Salt Lake City, Utah, as a modern metropolis surrounded by snow-capped mountains with the country's best skiing a short drive away.

Santiago is Chile's capital and largest city. It is the fifth-largest city in South America with a population of around five million including the surrounding suburbs. This number represents about 40% of Chile's population. Santiago accounts for about 40% of the country's GNP with some 54% of the nation's industrial output produced in the metropolitan area.

History

Santiago was founded by Pedro de Valdivia on February 12 1541. He named the site *Santiago de Nuevo Extremo* after Spain's patron, St James. On some old maps, the city is identified as "St Iago." It is also commonly referred to as *Santiago de Chile* to distinguish it from the multitude of other Santiagos that exist throughout the Spanish-speaking world.

Soon after its founding, the city was attacked and destroyed by a band of Indians led by the *Cacique*, Michimalongo, who is not to be confused with the Italian renaissance artist. Initially, it was not the most important city in Chile. Santiago was merely one of nine cities that Valdivia founded as he travelled throughout Southern Chile. As the southern cities came under increasing attacks by the Mapuches, the European population moved to Santiago which was better fortified and farther from the Indians' principle territories. Earthquakes later took a gruesome toll, and destructive events in 1647 and 1730 completely wiped out the city.

Santiago began a period of planned reconstruction in 1872 when Benjamin Vicuña MacKenna was appointed Mayor. His administration completed plans to create a public park in the fort at Cerro Santa Lucía and to construct a main boulevard (Alameda) over the old channel of the redirected Mapocho River.

Geography

Santiago is one of the most southerly capitals in the world, but its latitude is comparable to Los Angeles, Rabat, and Osaka in the Northern Hemisphere. Positioned between Chile's desert north and forested south, Santiago is centrally located between the Pacific coast and the crest of the Andes. Some of the world's best skiing and nicest beaches are both within an hour and a half drive of the capital.

The city is crossed east-west by the Mapocho River which runs furiously in the spring but dries in the summer. The elevation at the Plaza de Armas is 543m (1,781ft) with the top of the San Cristobal Hill overlooking the city from 880m (2,887ft) above sea level.

Santiago's climate has been compared to San Francisco's, but this parallel is accurate in the winter months only. Summers are hot, dry, and smoggy in Santiago, while winters are cool and wet with storms temporarily but frequently cleansing the skies. Temperatures on clear winter evenings approach freezing, but 20C (70F) days are not uncommon. Downtown Santiago receives about 350mm (14in) of rain each year and sees snow accumulation about once a century with July 13 (Friday?) 1948 the last known episode.

Smog (*contaminación*) is a major problem and issue in the city. Santiago was reported to have higher smog levels in 1989 than either Los Angeles or Mexico City. The major culprits in the complex smog-producing equation are the diesel-burning buses that provide the primary source of transportation for the bulk of the urban population. As the city is surrounded by mountains of staggering height, the contaminants have no escape except into the strained lungs of the suffering *Santiaguinos*.

Programs for mitigation have included impounding older buses that don't meet new federal standards, and banning cars on certain days from the downtown and/or the entire metropolitan areas based on license plate numbers. Optimism for the future derives from planned expansion of the electric-powered Metro system. Another plan would mix a copper additive into all diesel fuel to reduce emissions by raising the combustion temperatures of the gas. Santiago Garcia and David Purcell, who have about 80 years of observation between them, agree that the smog has an increasing impact on snow levels and depths around Farellones. With lung disease a growing problem among the population, look for drastic measures to be enacted in the near future in an attempt to control Chile's most profound growing pain.

The City

Santiago's main boulevard is the **Avenida Libertador General Bernardo O'Higgins**, shortened to "Alameda" by the locals. From the Alameda, the pedestrian street called **Ahumada** leads to Santiago's Plaza de Armas. Don't miss the political satirists, clowns, singers, bands, and yes, Hare Krishnas, that enthrall large crowds on Ahumada around 10.00pm nightly. Evenings on the Ahumada offer a public street scene that reflects the mood and character of the city better (and safer) than any other city in the world.

The **Plaza de Armas** is an open city block in the geographic center of what can be considered central Santiago. Artists dominate the southwest corner producing portraits and landscapes to the enjoyment of appreciative locals. Circling clockwise, Santiago's main Cathedral is discovered. The front steps are a popular protest site, and the dark and spacious interior is well worth a visit. On the north side of the Plaza is the pink **Correo Central** or main Post Office. Next to the Post Office is the Natural History Museum and municipal offices.

The east side of the Plaza contains the Portal Bulnes with dozens of luggage vendors. Remember this place after discovering that you have accumulated way too much stuff to fit in the bags you brought. Circling to the south side of the Plaza are restaurants and food stalls which sell cheap *empanadas* and pastries. In the middle of this block is the legendary deli, cafeteria, and restaurant of **Chez Henry**. The Plaza features live music on Thursday and Sunday but has a festive air about it every day.

Ahumada becomes **Puente** for four blocks to the Mapocho River and the Parque Forestal. The nearby Central Market is ideal to investigate the wide variety of strange sea creatures and fruit which are common fare to Chileans. Interesting exhibits are often on display in the vacant steel rail station alongside the river.

THE AHUMADA

Ascending the loaded escalator from the bright tunnels of the city's spotless Metro subway, one is suddenly confronted with the myriad of urban stimulations of Santiago. The **Paseo Ahumada**, a pedestrian mall which is the heart of the city and indeed of the nation, emerges as a human menagerie of rushed business people, desperate vendors and public entertainers.

A dirty, ragged kid dances a little jig rhythmically beat on a drum strapped to his back with a string tied around his ankle. Vendors peddle everything from posters, panties, and pens to candy bars, leather wallets, and live tarantulas. One repeatedly tosses a parachuted GI Joe in the air and dives between the passers-by to keep it from being trampled upon landing. Others roll dice for huddling gamblers who nervously place their coins despite ridiculous odds. Money changers peruse the crowd while maintaining a constant baritone chatter of "cambio, cambio, cambio...," until a tourist mistakingly makes eye contact to elicit a tenoric "dólares?"

The most intense part of this urban circus is three blocks farther at the intersection with Huerfanos, Santiago's other pedestrian mall. To escape, browse at one of the two kiosks which display recent issues of the world's best newspapers and magazines. Or, duck into the **Café do Brasíl** or **Café Caribe** for a full-flavored *café cortado* with huddled businessmen in trenchcoats. Better yet, prevail another block to the Plaza de Armas where an empanada and beer can be peacefully enjoyed on a shaded park bench while surveying the continuing drama of life in Chile's capital city.

The park heads east to Bellavista, Santiago's neighborhood of artists, musicians, and intellectuals. **Antonio Lopez de Bello** boasts interesting hippie art and several outstanding Italian restaurants. **Pio Nono** leads to the funicular on Cerro San Cristobal. The city zoo is located at the funicular's midpoint, and only the uphill cars stop for passengers. The zoo is worth a visit to see local fauna such as pumas, condors, and pudu. The funicular continues to the summit of the wooded Cerro San Cristobal where a large statue of the Virgin Mary continually blesses all *Santiaguinos* with open arms. Chile's only gondola traverses the summit ridge before descending into the Providencia shopping district.

Providencia is the Beverly Hills of Santiago, and modern malls and shops line the streets. Continuing east is Las Condes, and then El Arrayán is reached. This hilly area is in the foothills below Farellones and suffers greatly from the city's thick smog.

Santiago

The city is encircled by the **Avenida Americo Vespucio**. The Metro provides convenient transportation all along the Alameda up to Vespucio in the east. Buses and *colectivos* take over from there. Taxis in the city are also plentiful and cheap.

Things to Do

To get a fair taste for Santiago, a visitor needs to stay at least three days. Good diversions include brushing up on video game skills in the seven-cent arcades. Dollar movie theaters, many with classic decor, abound on **Huerfanos**, and sweet popcorn is sold in front. Explore Cerro Santa Lucía and the labyrinth of steep paths and stairs that wind around the walls of the several forts that were erected on the hill.

Shopping in Santiago is done in the tiny, highly specialized shops of the inner *galerías* and *caracoles* of the city's high-rises. Each mall specializes in a particular product or service. A good introduction to the system is to stroll through the five block long *galería* between Teatinos and San Antonio a half block south of and paralleling Huerfanos.

For evening entertainment, check the daily listings in the *El Mercurio* newspaper. Events at the Teatro Municipal are stiffly formal but worth the experience to see the classic interior of the theater. Ballet is especially popular in Chile. Rock and jazz concerts are held in the National Stadium with top international stars appearing every month. Jazz is clearly the most popular music among Chile's listeners. Check flyers on Pio Nono for the less commercial entertainment in the cafes of Bellavista.

For a day excursion, take a bus to Valparaíso (US$3rt) and then find a way to Viña del Mar. There are all types of connections and it's relatively quiet in the winter season. For a unique travel adventure, fly to Easter Island which is Chile's Hawaii. At *Hanga Roa*, as the inhabitants call it, you can see the famous "Moai" statues and observe the Polynesian customs practiced proudly by the 2,000 remaining natives.

Transportation

From Outside Chile

Via Air:
Aeroflot: Moscow, Luxembourg, Shannon, Havana, weekly.
Aerolíneas Argentinas: Buenos Aires, daily; via Mendoza 2/wk.
Air France: Paris, Rio, Buenos Aires, 3/wk.
Alitalia: Milan, Rome, Rio, Buenos Aires, weekly.
American: Miami, Buenos Aires, daily; New York, Miami, Panama, Lima, 3/wk.
Canadian Airlines: Hong Kong, Tokyo, Vancouver, Montreal, Toronto, 2/wk; Buenos Aires, 1/wk.
Iberia: Madrid, Las Palmas, Buenos Aires, 1/wk.
KLM: Amsterdam, Rio, Sao Paulo, Buenos Aires, 2/wk.
Ladeco: Service from Miami, New York, Asuncion, Buenos Aires, Bogota, Guayaquil, Mendoza, Rio, Sao Paulo.
LANChile: Service from Los Angeles, Miami, Montreal, New York, Madrid, Caracas, La Paz, Lima, Mexico City, Montevideo, Panama City, Rio, Sao Paulo, Papeete.
Lufthansa: Frankfurt, Sao Paulo, weekly; via Rio, weekly.
Swissair: Zurich, Geneva, Rio, Sao Paulo, Buenos Aires, weekly.
Varig: Rio, Sao Paulo, 5/wk; Rio, Puerto Alegre, 1/wk.

Via Bus:
Direct international connections from, Buenos Aires, La Paz, Lima, and other South American capitals at Terminal de Buses.

From Inside Chile
See specific Chapters.

From Mendoza
See *Chapter 6*.

Hotels

Deluxe:
Carrera: 180 Teatinos, Sgl:US$100-140, Dbl:US$110-150, Suite:US$190-360, best location in Santiago, businessmen's favorite.
Plaza San Francisco (Kempinski): 816 O'Higgins, Sgl:US$150, Dbl:US$165, Suite:US$200-580, newest, ultra luxurious.
Crowne Plaza (Holiday Inn): 136 O'Higgins, Sgl:US$148-165, Dbl:US$165-181, also Suites, Penthouses, tennis courts, helicopter pad, large shopping gallery, inconvenient location.
San Cristobal (Sheraton): 1742 Santa Maria, Sgl:US$135, Dbl:US$145, taxi dependent location at base of Cerro San Cristobal, a resort hotel, tennis courts, skiers' favorite, reservations needed.

Santiago

First Class:
Tupahue: 477 San Antonio, Sgl:US$75, Dbl:US$85, Suite:US$120, great location, new lobby very friendly and helpful, recommended.
Hostal del Parque: 294 Merced, Sgl:US$80-104, Dbl:US$92-126, Penthouse:US$179, near US Consulate, good location on park facing Mapocho River, walking distance to downtown and Bellavista, small.
Galerías: 65 San Antonio, Sgl:US$85, Dbl:US$95, Suite:130-150, located in commercial hub, pool, modern.

Moderate:
Ritz: 248 Estado, Sgl:US$30, Dbl:US$40, Suite:US$69, best value, 6th floor balconies, big rooms, recommended.
Riviera: 106 Miraflores, Sgl:US$36, Dbl:US$41, small, 1 block from Metro and Cerro Santa Lucia, some rooms very noisy.
Foresta: 353 Subercaseaux, Sgl:US$38, Dbl:US$60, beautifully furnished, garden dining room on top, great Jazz Bar, recommended.
City: 1063 Compañia, Sgl:US$32, Dbl:US$50, Suite:US$59, very central, nice restaurant, classy.

Budget:
España: 510 Morande, Sgl:US$12-15, Dbl:US$16-19, large rooms, cold, noisy.
Cervantes: 631 Morande, Sgl:US$17, Dbl:US$18-21, good value.
Sao Paulo: 357 San Antonio, Sgl:US$17-19, Dbl:US$18-23, great location, run down, difficult to get in.

Residenciales:
Londres: 54 Londres, Sgl:US$6, Dbl:US$8, English spoken, good location in old house, highly recommended, popular.
Familiar: 81 Principe de Gales (off Moneda), Sgl:US$12-13, Dbl:US$23-27, at end of closed street, hard to find but worth trying.
Huerfanos: 1373 Huerfanos, Of 803, Sgl:US$17, Dbl:US$23, good location on one floor of large building.

Providencia:
Principado: 24 MacKenna, Sgl:US$31-40, Dbl:US$40, 1 block from Metro Baquedano, closest to Bellavista, modern, comfortable.
Orly: 27 Valdivia, Sgl:US$25-34, Dbl:US$45, old world style, quiet location near Metro Valdivia, recommended.
Hostal El Golf: 2981 Roger de Flor, Dbl:US$40, next to Portillo office in nice neighborhood, 8 rooms, overpriced.

RESTAURANTS
Tourist Oriented:
Enoteca: on Cerro San Cristobal, wine tasting and wine museum,

good food and views.
Los Adobes de Argomedo: Argomedo w/Lira (outside of the city), good beef and typical Chilean fare, *Cueca* and other floor shows.
Giratorio: 2250 11 de Septiembre, rotating rooftop restaurant with views of city and mountains, nice bar, expensive.

Italian:
Le Due Torre: 258 San Antonio, elegent, expensive, locals' favorite.
La Divina Comida: 215 Purísima, just off Bello, excellent, popular, make reservations.
Ristorante Da Renato Di Vittoria: 183 Fernández, off 11 de Septiembre between Los Leones and Suecia, homey, excellent.

Typical:
Chez Henry: 962 Portal Concha (S side of Plaza), huge menu, spotless kitchen, 3 dining areas, best in Chile, not to be missed.
Bar Nacional: 1151 Huerfanos, 317 Bandera, dining downstairs, smaller and less expensive than Chez Henry, recommended.

Budget:
Marco Polo: on Alemeda in Plaza, good Cazuela de Ave, quick service, clean.
Empanadas and beer deals in front of Chez Henry on Plaza.
Venezia: Pio Nono w/Andres Bello, in back for good, cheap food, live music, eclectic crowd.

Sandwiches and Beer:
Geo Pub: 138 Encomenderos, very popular especially evenings.
Red Pub: 29 Suecia, American style sandwiches, salads, and juices.
Lomit's: 1980 Providencia, less expensive, informal, fast.

Vegetarian:
El Huerto: 54 Orrego Luco (off Providencia by Valdivia), popular with *gringos*, live music, recommended.
El Vegetariano: 827 Huerfanos, good *empanadas*, salads and juices, expensive.
El Naturista: Los Leones w/Pio X, good, basic menu, live music.

Important Addresses

Foreign Exchange:
131 Ahumada, many offices (eg. Laser Tour, Loc 5), walk in briskly to avoid agents at entrance.
1000 block Agustinas between Ahumada and Bandera (eg. Viajes Austral Tours: 1022 Agustinas, Of.204), compare rates in windows here before exchanging anywhere, very professional.
Intersection Ahumada and Huerfanos from solicitors, arrange good rate before following, browse at newsstands for effective delay

Santiago

tactics, safe and fun.
Intercam Turismo: 39 Andres de Fuenzalida, Providencia, less hectic than downtown.
American Express: 1360 Agustinas, exchange travellers checks for any currency, credit card advances.
Bank of America: 1465 Agustinas.

Post Office:
Correo Central: 1137 Catedral, northwest corner of Plaza de Armas, many mail-related vendors at entrance, *Poste Restante.*

Telephones:
Entel: 1133 Huerfanos, best for international calls, rates in window.
CTC: 1151 Moneda, 760 Monjitas, 2155 11 de Septiembre, Loc.166, also in six Metro stations.

Consulates:
Argentina: 41 MacKenna, 222-8977.
Australia: 420 Gertrudis Echeñique, 228-6065.
Brazil: 225 MacIver, 398-867.
Bolivia: 2796 Santa Maria, 232-8180.
Canada: 11 Ahumada, 696-0550.
France: 65 Condell, 225-1030.
Germany: 785 Agustinas, 693-5031.
Great Britain: 177 La Concepción, 223-9166.
Italy: 843 Triana, 225-9439.
Japan: 2653 Providencia, 232-1807.
New Zealand: 3516 Isadora Goyenechea, 487-071
United States: 230 Merced, 710-133.

Hospitals:
Clinica Las Condes: 441 Lo Fontecilla, 211-1002.
Clinica Alemana: 5951 Vitacura, 229-9515.

Tourist Offices:
Sernatur: 1550 Providencia, 698-2151.

Travel Agents:
Sportstour, Tour Service: 333 Teatinos, 696-3100.
Festival Tours: 949 O'Higgins, Of 603, 696-4924.

Airlines:
Aerolíneas Argentinas: 82 Tenderini, 394-585.
Air France: 1136 Agustinas, 698-2421.
Alitalia: 949 O'Higgins, Of 1003, 698-3336.
American: 1199 Huerfanos, 713-004.
British Airways: 669 Huerfanos, Of 502, 333-973.
Canadian Airlines: 669 Huerfanos, Loc 9, 393-058.
KLM: 802 Agustinas, 398-001.

Ladeco: 210 Valdivia, 251-7204; 107 O'Higgins, 395-053.
LANChile: 640 Agustinas, 632-3211.
Lufthansa: 970 Moneda, 17th Floor, 722-686.
Swissair: 10 Estado, 15th Floor, 337-014.
Varig: 156 Miraflores, 395-976.

Car Rentals:
Auto Club de Chile: 122 Marchant Pereira, 274-4167.
Avis: 334 La Concepción, 495-757; also Sheraton, Crowne Plaza, Plaza San Francisco.
Budget: 4900 Apoquindo, Loc 96, 246-0888.
Dollar: 3455 Isidora Goyenechea, 231-4084.
First: 1429 Andres Bello, 09-221-5475.
Hertz: 1469 Costanera, 225-9328.
National: 212 La Concepción, 223-2416; 6360 Apoquindo, 212-1524.

Bus Terminal:
Estación Alameda: Pullman Bus and Tur Bus, 3712 O'Higgins w/ direct access into terminal from Metro Universidad de Chile.
Terminal de Buses Santiago: 3878 O'Higgins, 1 block from Est Alameda, many other companies to Mendoza and other destinations.
Tour Express: 1523 Moneda, 717-380, every half hour fm 6.30am to 9.30pm for airport, US$2.

Train Station:
Estación Central: 3322 Alameda, 91-682.
Ticket Agency: Galería Hotel Libertador, Loc 21, 398-247.

Ferry Offices:
Navimag: 178 Miraflores, 12th Floor, 696-3211.

Newstands:
Intersection of Ahumada w/ Huerfanos, 2 kiosks, excellent selections of magazines and newspapers from Americas and Europe.
Deluxe hotels.

Books:
Altamira: 669 Huerfanos, Loc 1; 2124 Providencia, Loc 64, English selection of books and dated magazines.
Books and Bits: 4727 Apoquindo, English, mostly introductory readers, some novels.
Eduardo Albers: 820 Merced, Loc 7; 2671 11 de Septiembre, English and German, excellent selection of novels.
Française: 337 Esyado, Loc 22; 187 Santa Magdalena, all French, very good.
Inglesa: 669 Huerfanos, Loc 11; 47 Valdivia, all English, very good selection.
Iven's: 730 Moneda, English, mostly magazines, helpful owner.

Santiago

Cinemas:
Many on Huerfanos, check *El Mercurio* for listings.

Arts and Crafts:
CEMA: 351 Portugal.
Across O'Higgins from Cerro Santa Lucia.
On Lopez de Bello between Pio Nono and Purisima.
1277 Compaña.
3410 O'Higgins, around central train station.

Marketplaces:
Mercado Central: Balmaceda between Puente (Alameda) and 21 de Mayo (Estado).
10 de Julio between MacKenna and Portugal.

Ski Shops:
Panda Deportes: 2217 Providencia, Paseo Las Palmas, 232-1840, rude.
Ski Service: 4251 Apoquindo, 482-790, large selection, nordic gear.
Ski Total: 4900 Apoquindo, Locs.32-33, 246-0156, good rentals and repair, lodging and transportation services.
Ski Wind: 55 Holanda, 231-7325, basic repairs and equipment.
Sparta: 12,250 Las Condes, 471-047, 5 other locations, nationwide.

Ski Area Offices:
El Colorado: 4900 Apoquindo, Loc 47-48, 246-3344, Ski Report: 220-9501.
La Parva: 2874 San Sebastián, 233-2476.
Portillo: 2911 Roger de Flor, 231-3411.
Club Andino de Chile (Lagunillas): 5681 Apoquindo, Loc 5, 211-2687.
Termas de Chillán: 2237 Apoquindo, Loc 41, 251-2685.
Valle Nevado: 441 Gertrudis Echeñique, 480-839.
Villarica-Pucón: 3144 Napolean, 232-1787.

Other Ski Related Addresses:
Andes Powder Guides: call cellular phone 09-221-6752.
Cuerpo de Socorro Andino (Mountain Rescue): 329 Ricardo Cummings, 699-4764, Emergency: 136.
Federación de Ski de Chile: 40 Vicuña MacKenna, 222-8733.
Hotelsa (Coyhaique): 53 Las Urbinas, Of 42, 232-6825.
La Posada de Farellones: 4900 Apoquindo, Loc 43, 246-0660.
Operadores Penitentes: 1022 Agustinas, Of 702, 717-559.
Patrullas de Ski de Chile: 713 Huerfanos, Of 608, 33-2757.
Ski Club Chile (Hotel Tupungato, Farellones): 4750 Candelaria Goyenchea, 211-7341.
Termas de Puyehue (Antillanca): 2902 Vitacura, Of 1404, 231-3417.

92   Chile

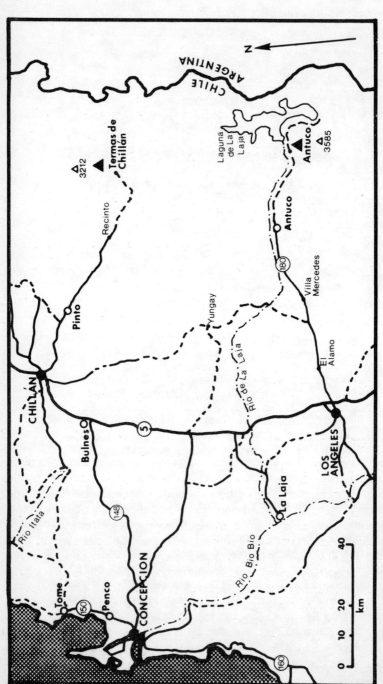

Chile: Chillán to Los Angeles

Chapter 13

Termas de Chillán

Ski Area Facts and Figures

Elevation: Top: 2,500m; 8,200ft.
　　　　　　Bottom: 1,800m; 5,900ft.
Vertical Drop: 700m; 2,300ft.
Season: Late June to Early October.
Lifts: 6:
　　　　1 Double Chair, 2 T-Bars, 3 Pomas
Runs: 15:
　　　　20% Beginner, 30% Intermediate, 30% Advanced, 20% Expert
Ticket Prices, 1990:
　Weekends: US$15 Adults Full Day, US$10 Children under 12;
　Weekdays: US$10 Adults Full Day, US$ 6.50 Children.

Introduction

Any ski trip to Chile's southern volcanoes begins at the Termas de Chillán. The legendary hot springs resort is best reached on the scenic "skiers' train," a six hour ride in a comfortable coach from Santiago through Chile's heartland. It is the only ski resort in South America with hot springs at the base lodge, and thus, like Pucón, Chillán was a summer resort first and a ski mountain second.

As a ski area, Chillán is blessed by optimal geography and topography. Everyone lauds the potential for skiing here. As early as 1945, the *Revista Andina* of Santiago declared that "Chillán could be the most complete winter resort in America." At about the same time, a couple of visiting French ski instructors reported "the best and most fascinating runs in the world are found in the springs and snows of Chillán." Even Arturo Hammersley, the most important figure in Chilean skiing, believes that the future of skiing in Chile lies at Chillán.

Termas de Chillán ski trails

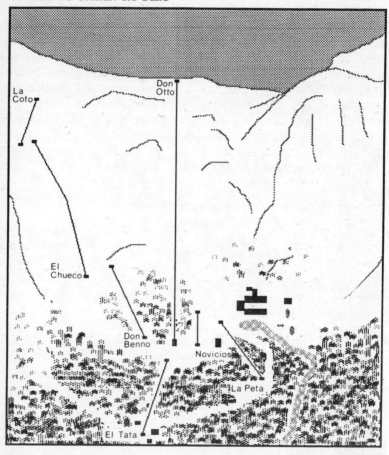

The mountain boasts the longest chairlift on the continent, is consistently covered with deep snow over a lengthy season, and has great runs to challenge any skier. For a foreign skier seeking unique adventure, its greatest treasure is the huge bowl on the east side of the ski area called Pirigallo. Here, the advanced skier can descend a steep, powdery bowl through a primitive land of steaming fumaroles and flowing mud for a true fire and ice ski encounter.

History

The existence of the hot springs has been known since the early 18th Century when a Spanish monk publicized the curative and therapeutic effects of the waters. The Termas were popular with the Spanish forces operating in the region through the latter part of the century. The site was commercialized in 1830, and a variety of

Termas de Chillán

lodges, cabins, and tents have since occupied the geothermic setting.

The region has been skied extensively by members of ski clubs from Concepción and Chillán since the 1930s. These early activities were centered in a more accessible and less challenging area several kilometers below the current lifts called Shangri La. In order to promote skiing, the municipal government of Chillán, which owns the property at the Termas, gave a 25-year lease to a private entity in 1978. The modern ski era was inaugurated in 1984 with the completion of Chillán's first aerial chairlift. The hotel company Somontur now has the difficult task of creating the resort that so many others claim nature has provided.

Geography

The Termas de Chillán sit near the southern end of the *Alto Cordillera* at the base of the first of Chile's many southern volcanoes. The mountain actually has two summits. The one further west is called the Nevado de Chillán and has the higher summit at 3,212m (10,538ft). The ski area is built on the slopes below the active Volcán Chillán which reaches 2,950m (9,678ft).

Storms can come from the northwest or southwest with plenty of moisture laden clouds from the Pacific. The snow is always heavy and wet making powder skiing more difficult than in the higher resorts around Santiago.

Skiing Tips

The Don Otto chairlift is the longest on the continent at 2,500m (8,200ft). The season is prolonged because the chairlift can be loaded at Tower 15 for good skiing after the snow disappears at the base. It is a 21 minute ride to the summit or nine minutes from the midpoint loading ramp. The chairlift is a bit antiquated, and maintenance problems often force it to close for short periods.

The ski area can be divided into four sections with the first comprising the beginner areas below the hotel, the second encompassing the runs on either side of the chairlift, the third being the west side near the T-Bars and upper poma, and the fourth containing the adventure ski areas of Pirigallo. A fifth area might be defined as the 9km (5.6 mile) run called Tres Marías which ends below the hotel at the site of the new villa.

Beginners will be happiest on the pretty tree-lined run right (east) of the Peta poma. The poma track, however, can be very difficult as it is poorly maintained and a fall will leave skiers in the midst of a thick forest with no easy escape. Intermediate skiers will prefer the groomed slopes of the west side. When skiing this area, ride the Novicios poma to return to the lodge.

Advanced skiers will discover many leg-burning bowls on both sides of the chairlift. The snow off-piste in this area can be wind packed, crusty, soft, heavy, or all four. Conditions are very dependent on slope orientation. The ski patrollers often close much of the area to all skiing due to the challenging conditions. Some days the chair will remain closed in the mornings for grooming to provide a safer means of descent.

Expert skiers will discover one of the best bowls in all of Chile at Chillán. Pirigallo is reminiscent of a small Tuckerman's Ravine and is reached with a high traverse right (east) from the top of the chairlift. The south-facing bowl is really a series of 10 finger chutes between ridgelines which dissect the slope. When descending, the faint scent of sulfur will begin to overwhelm already stressed lungs as skiers become engulfed in clouds of the noxious steam at the bottom end of the bowl. Be sure to scout the run from the hotel before riding the chair.

Racing

Chillán has a FIS homologated downhill course from the top of the chairlift. In addition, foreign race teams have come here to train after discovering that other areas don't have sufficient snow for their needs. Slalom and GS training courses are often set by the Don Benno T-Bar, and Chillán has produced some of Chile's better racers. Speed skiing events have been held on Condor.

Adventure Skiing

Extreme skiers will look to the two summits for extra adventure. Either can be reached in less than two hours from the top of the chairlift. The face of the Nevado summit is covered with a small glacier but has tamer runs in general. The Volcán has a greater variety of steeper chutes, snowy bowls, and exciting sidewalls. A third option is the Shangri La run, a 14km (8.7 mile) trail to the historical ski site in the valley below the Termas. Ask a ski instructor for directions or guide service and to arrange a pick-up.

There is some serious avalanche hazard at Chillán, the most obvious being in the Pirigallo area. Be sure to allow this area to settle for a time after a storm. Other areas of concern are the east-facing ridgelines which support large and weak cornices. The ridge just west of the Chueco poma is especially hazardous, but the patrollers do some control work in this area.

Nordic Skiing

Like the other southern volcanoes, Chillán has excellent terrain for nordic touring. There is ample open space west of the ski area on, around, and below the Nevado summit. Tamer surroundings can be enjoyed below treeline in the area where the new villa is being developed below the hotel. At times, trails are maintained and cross-country events have been held.

Skier Services

The ski school specializes in teaching novice skiers and has instructors that speak English and French. Rates begin at US$18 for a one-hour, one-skier private lesson and US$21 for two skiers. There is a professional ski patrol staff of local origin who are well-trained by the Patrullas de Chile. These employees enjoy socializing in uniform in the hotel evenings and are good sources of information. Doctors are on hand to service the spa facilities as well as ski accidents.

Base Facilities

Tickets are normally purchased in the cafeteria by the Novicios poma but are sold at the ski rental desk in the hotel during slack periods when the cafeteria is closed. Tickets are not included with nightly stays but are included in ski weeks.

There is a good storage and changing area at the hotel's slope exit. Boots are not allowed in the hotel past this area, so leave footwear in the boot rack. If staying overnight, bring ski boots into the warm hotel room to dry as the storage area is not heated.

The equipment rental area is also located at the hotel's slope access door. They have a full selection of entry-level equipment (US$14/day), and the staff is very helpful.

Dining

There are two dining facilities when the resort is in full operation. The slopeside cafeteria adjacent to the Novicios poma offers a wide selection of hot sandwiches, but desserts are the specialty here.

The hotel's dining room is a more formal affair. Breakfast is a buffet of Chilean fruit, yogurt, and pastries with egg dishes available on request. Lunch and dinner are even more leisurely with live band music setting the mood. The *cocineros* cook some of the best steaks anywhere. Friday evenings are special with an erupting *Volcán Chillán* served for dessert under dimmed lights. The soupy ice cream oozing under the liqueur-fed flames is a fitting symbolic representation of the ski experience at Chillán.

The Hotel

The sprawling hotel complex has 108 rooms for about 350 guests. It fills quickly on weekends during the season, so be sure to make reservations in July and August. The hotel has a cocktail bar, a drinking lounge with fireplace, a TV/video theater, a card room, a game room with ping pong, billiards and video games, a complete sport shop, a day care center, the ski rental/storage room, and the hot spring facilities. It is decorated with period photos of the site at the turn of the century, which, if the captions are to be believed, indicate that it snowed here in the hot summer months of January and April 100 years ago.

The spa facilities are split between the east end of the hotel and the new bath house/gym which is separate from the main complex. In the hotel are the sulfur baths and medical/massage facilities. The new bathhouse has a gym with modern exercise equipment and four beautifully tiered and landscaped swimming pools of which two are maintained for winter use.

Following is a list of services connected with the spa facility and their alleged benefits:

Sulfur bath: Muscle relaxant, smooths skin, improves circulation.
Iron bath: Relaxes nerves, improves strength.
Scotch shower: Reactivates skin cells, stimulates muscles.
Hydro massage: Relaxes muscles and nerves, induces perspiration.
Mud therapy: Smooths, rejuvenates, strengthens, and heals skin.
Steam bath: Clears lungs, hastens dehydration, smooths skin.
Sauna: Relaxes nerves and muscles.
Body massage: Serious muscle relaxation.
also Medical, Kinesiological, and Beauty and Health Services.

Daily hotel prices range from US$39 to US$77 for a bunk to US$52 to US$123 per person double occupancy. Suites and duplexes are also available. Prices include three meals and tax but not lift tickets. Neither ski week prices nor daily rates include use of the spa facilities which run from US$5 to US$22.

Other Lodging

There are several other lodges down the road from the Termas. The **Parador** and **Pirineos** are both comfortable and modern options. These also fill on weekends and reservations need to be made in season. Prices were unavailable.

Future Plans

Ownership considers the current resort 20% developed. A new base "villa" complete with a hotel, a condominium complex, and an apartment building is being constructed on privately owned land below the lodge. A total of five new lifts including a double chair to link the base areas and lifts to access the Tres Marias area west of the existing lifts are planned. Other plans call for paving the remaining unpaved section of the access road and building a nordic trail system.

Getting There

From Chillán

Via Private Auto:
Chillán-Recinto: via Pinto, 53km (33 miles), 45min, paved.
Recinto-Termas: 29km (18 miles), 30min, unpaved.
Via Bus:
From Termas office: weekends and holidays only, 7.00am, free with lift ticket purchase, 1½hr.
Local bus: to Recinto, then hitch.

Further Information and Reservations

In Santiago:
Termas de Chillán
Hotelera Somontur, 2237 Providencia, Loc P41. Tel: 251-5776
In Chillán:
1042 Libertad, Tel: 223-887
In Concepción:
734 O'Higgins, Tel: 234-981

CHILLÁN

The city of Chillán is one of Chile's most interesting places to visit. It is the capital of Ñuble Province and has a population of 120,000. Chillán is the birthplace of Bernardo O'Higgins, Chile's greatest revolutionary hero and has a tragic but inspiring history of destruction and reconstruction. It also hosts one of the country's most colorful markets.

The city was founded in 1565 as a defensive position to counter attacks coming over the mountain pass from the east. Due to its strategic location, Chillán was destroyed by foreign invaders and rebuilt by Chilean forces several times until 1751 when the city was relocated to the present site of Chillán Viejo. Then, earthquakes began to take their toll. The city was completely wiped out at least five times throughout its tragic history. The last major earthquake was in 1939, destroying 90% of the city while taking some 15,000 lives.

Since none of the buildings are over 50 years old, Chillán has a very modern look. The city center is 12 blocks wide and is surrounded by a quadrangle of tree-lined boulevards. The heart of the city is at the **Feria Municipal**, or central marketplace. It is one of the best places to buy Chilean handicrafts and art work, and the farmers' market is spectacular. Adjacent to the market is an area of *marisquerías* (food stalls) where anyone can enjoy a delicious, inexpensive meal.

On the southwest side of the city is Old Chillán with a monument and cultural museum dedicated to Bernardo O'Higgins. The highlight of the exhibit is the 60m (200ft) long stone mural which depicts the life of the great liberator. Another attraction is the murals of the Mexican School. The school was donated to the city by the Mexican government in a fraternal gesture after the 1939 earthquake. The paintings by Mexican artists David Alfaro Siqueiros and Xavier Guerrero are located in the library on the second floor. There are four murals which have historical themes and they can be seen anytime during school hours.

All of these locations are within an easy walk from the central Plaza de Armas. Plan a trip to Chillán in late September to avoid crowded slopes and to enjoy the city when its plum trees are in full spring bloom.

Transportation

From Santiago
Via Private Auto:
Santiago-Chillán: Hwy5, 407km (253 miles), 5hr, paved.
Via Bus:
Santiago-Chillán: LIT, TurBus, others, hourly, 5hr, US$5.
Via Train:
Santiago-Chillán: 2/day, 6hr, US$5 Salon Class.

From Los Angeles
Via Private Auto:
Los Angeles-Chillán: Hwy5, 110km (68 miles), 1¼hr, paved.

Termas de Chillán

Via Bus:
Los Angeles-Chillán: many companies, hourly, 1½hr, US$1.
Via Train:
Los Angeles-Chillán: 2/day, 2hr, US$2 Salon Class.

Hotels
First Class:
Isabel Riquelme: 600 Arauco, Sgl:US$30-40, Dbl:US$35-55, overpriced, unhelpful.
Moderate:
Cordillera: 619 Arauco, Sgl:US$21, Dbl:US$29, on Plaza, good.
Budget:
Quinchamali: 634 El Roble, Sgl:US$13, Dbl:US$18, friendly, clean, warm, central, recommended.
Ruiz de Gamboa: 497 O'Higgins, Sgl:US$11, Dbl:US$15, good.
Libertador: 305 Libertad, Sgl:US$11, Dbl:US$17, cheaper rooms too.

Restaurants
International:
La Estancia: in Parque O'Higgins in Old Chillán.
Typical:
Café Paris: 666 Arauco, best in town, dining room in back.
Budget:
Marisquerías: between 5 de Abril, Riquelme, Maipon, and Roble.

Important Addresses
Foreign Exchange: Difficult, try Banco Concepción.
Post Office: 501 Libertad.
Telephone: 625 Arauco; 455 Libertad.
Tourist Office: by O'Higgins Park in Old Chillán.
Car Rental: First, 380 18 de Septiembre.
Bus Terminal: Brasil at Constitución, opposite train station.
Train Station: end of Libertador at Brasil. Tickets at 656 18 de Septiembre.
Cinema: Central, 690 Constitución; O'Higgins, 210 Libertador.
Ski Shop: Sparta, 635 5 de Abril; Ski Center, 261 Barros Arana.
Ski Area Office: 1042 Libertad.
Parque Monumental O'Higgins: Calle O'Higgins in Old Chillán.
Escuela México: 250 O'Higgins.
Feria Municipal: 700 block of Maipón (at 5 de Abril).

Antuco ski trails

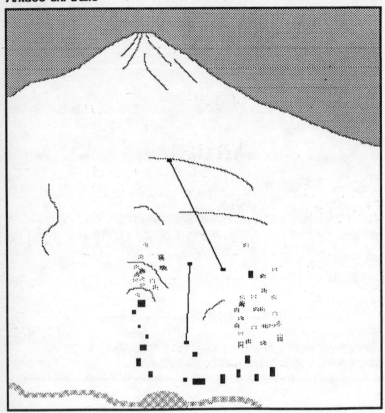

Chapter 14

Antuco

Ski Area Facts and Figures

Elevation: Top: 1,850m; 6,100ft.
Bottom: 1,400m; 4,600ft.
Vertical Drop: 450m; 1,500ft.
Season: Early July to Late September
Lifts: 2 Poma Lifts
Runs: 2:
                    20% Beginner, 50% Intermediate, 30% Advanced
Ticket Prices, 1990:
   Weekends: US$11 Adults Full Day, US$8 Youths under 17.
   Weekdays: US$ 7 Adults Half Day, US$7 Youths.

Introduction

Antuco is the second and highest (3,585m; 11,762ft) of Chile's southern volcanoes. The ski area is typical of the small, club-run resorts of South America. Antuco's two surface lifts climb about a third of the volcano and offer open-slope skiing for all levels. It is known by the locals as a less expensive alternative to Chillán. The volcano is positioned in a climatic transition zone where the frequent wet storms from the south meet the cold air of the north. For many skiers, this would conjure up images of frequent storms leaving thigh deep powder, but Antuco's slopes face north and any fresh snow soon thickens under the hot Chilean sun.

The ski runs and the surrounding area all lie within the Laguna de La Laja National Park. The Laguna de La Laja is a huge reservoir near the base of the ski area. It is the first of the sprawling, deep, trout-filled lakes of Southern Chile. Important hydroelectric projects at and below the lake make road maintenance a priority to the local government for which local skiers are thankful. The approach to the ski area is one of the most spectacular on the continent; stark black lava beds are interspersed by grassy meadows crossed by overflowing brooks which are fed by waterfalls pouring down dark postpile cliffs.

History

Antuco is run by the Club Esquí de Los Angeles which owns about 500 hectares around the north side of the volcano. The Club was founded in 1938, and members skied various sites in the area before deciding to set their foundations on Antuco. The poma lifts were built in the late 70s, and 1980 was the first full season of lift operation. The Club had a *refugio*, but it burned down several years ago.

Geography

Antuco is located at the eastern end of the Cordillera Pelada which is the range to the right as the ski area is approached. While the south side of Antuco has more desirable snow conditions, that area is extremely remote with impossible access. Although it was one of the few places that had consistent snow in 1990, the season is relatively short due to the poor slope orientation. The project at Caviahue in Argentina is just 50km (30 miles) by air to the southeast.

Skiing Tips

The main run here is called La Lola. It is the intermediate run just to the left (east) of the lower half of the upper poma. The run is frequently blanketed with moguls but can be groomed as well. The right (west) side of the lift is skied less frequently because it is usually rockier. Since the ski area lies well above treeline, all the other runs are formed by natural canyons and ridges and are nameless.

The best skiing is found with traverses of varying lengths east from the top of the upper poma. Antuco's signature run is the thin, elevated gully that begins about 300m east of the upper lift and makes a "Z" shape as it descends toward the bottom. The northern orientation of the runs make it imperative to start skiing early in the morning and conclude at lunchtime.

Adventure Skiing

Adventure skiers have three options. All involve serious hikes of several hours. The obvious indication is to climb the volcano and ski back to the lifts, but the reality is that the top of the cone is littered

Antuco

with rocky, exposed ridges and there is usually no clean fall-line. A better alternative is to hike and ski the conspicuous southeast-facing bowl on the opposite side of the parking lot. A final option is to traverse west to the east-facing chutes from the Los Cóndores poma. There is no avalanche danger in the ski area, but use prudent judgement in these last two out-of-bounds areas.

Nordic Skiing

Cross-country enthusiasts will really enjoy the Antuco area. The best place to ski is on the south side of the lake on the road which skirts the lakeshore. There is a great deal of rolling terrain to explore here so bring a lunch and plan a full-day excursion. The lake surface rarely freezes but provides many kilometers of flat terrain when frozen. Expert telemarkers may be able to reach a high plateau north of the ski area. Ride the lifts first to view the shelf (it is not visible from the road) and plan the approach.

Skier Services

Both the Ski Club and DIGEDER have small ski schools which could provide basic instruction. Enquire at DIGEDER's *refugio* or at the ticket office. There are volunteer ski patrollers from the Patrullas de Chile and they claim to have a doctor at the site at all times. The nearest hospital is in Los Angeles.

Base Facilities

Tickets are sold from the hut at the base of the lower poma. There is no locker or changing area so use your vehicle. Equipment can be rented from the Club or DIGEDER both of whom have large if tired selections.

Dining

The Club has two restaurants that are leased to different operators. The first is located in the round structure to the left of Condorito and offers a full service, home-style lunch with tablecloths and wine. It is highly recommended for a late lunch. Adjacent to this is a smaller cafeteria with quick sandwiches and pizza.

Lodging

Only the **DIGEDER** lodge has overnight accommodations for the public. It is dormitory style with bunks and a common bath and fills

A DAY IN ANTUCO

Antuco is the site of one of those rare travel experiences that you imagine but don't really believe will happen when you plan a trip to the distant land of a foreign culture.

It was late September in 1987 when I was just beginning my first tour of Chile's southern volcanoes. After a relaxing "day off" at the port city of Concepción, I approached Antuco in an evening slush storm. My compact rental car could not quite make it in the blizzard, so I parked the car, reclined the seat, and turned up the volume on the stereo. The next morning dawned with a spectacular blue sky and without a cloud in sight.

With some difficulty, the Toyota made it to the ski area but it seemed deserted. I found Jorge by tracking the source of his music to his sturdy cabin. He had just arisen and invited me inside to share his breakfast. As we munched on bread with butter and sipped *maté*, I explained that Mammoth and Antuco were completely alike in that they both served skiers from Los Angeles. This weak attempt at human bonding fell apart a bit when I showed him my trail map with 30 lifts and 150 runs. It must have worked, however, because after a few radio transmissions he told me to boot-up and meet him at the base of the poma. In no time we were at the top of the second poma, about a third of the distance to the volcano's summit. He came up to check the towers and told me to ski to my heart's content, and then he would close. Really? Okay.

The slopes were covered with a clean slate of a micro-thin rain crust over five centimeters of dense windpack. The surface was the purest virgin white, and I experienced a euphoric vertigo during my descent in the featureless terrain in spite of the sunny weather. I snaked my signature on all the obvious fall-lines, in each tiny canyon, on every elevated ridge, and left proud.

I was amazed to find a few hundred skiers when I returned in 1990. I didn't think anyone ever skied here. I imagined that it was a simple public service for ignorant foreigners who naively presume Chileans partake in the winter sport. It was actually enjoyable though, watching the youthful crowd wiggling through the soft moguls, but my smile of contentment was from those vivid memories when, for a day, Antuco was mine.

on the weekends. Reservations can be made at the DIGEDER office in Concepción.

A pristine resort called **Lagunillas** is set creekside amongst pine trees and lava beds 4km below the ski resort. Although closed in the

Antuco

winter, individual cabins can be leased for extended stays. Try Turismo Magallanes in Santiago at 231-5973 or other tourist agencies in Concepción.

The only acceptable lodging found between Los Angeles and the ski area is at the **Hostería El Bosque**. It is 16km (10 miles) east of the town of Antuco and 15km west of the ski area on the south side of the road. Prices are US$5 each in a private room and US$9 with excellent meals. Skiers are encouraged to try the Hostería for tea if nothing else.

Getting There

From Los Angeles
Via Private Auto:
Los Angeles-Antuco(town): Hwy180, 62km (39 miles), 45min, paved.
Antuco-Antuco(ski area): Hwy180, 31km (19 miles), 45min, unpaved.
Via Bus:
None from Los Angeles.
Try Turismo Ritz in Concepción: 721 Barros Arana, weekends only.

Further Information
Club Esquí de Los Angeles
520 Valdivia, Los Angeles, CHILE. Tel: 322-651

LOS ANGELES

Los Angeles, Chile, is a typical central valley agricultural community of 70,500 people. It sits in the middle of the Isla de La Laja, a large and fertile chunk of land between the Laja River and the Biobío, Chile's longest river. Los Angeles was Chile's fastest growing city in the '80s with fruit and timber the leading industries.

The town is typical Chile with the main street **Colón** passing the central Plaza de Armas. The bus terminal is located a convenient half block from the Plaza which makes the usual taxi to a hotel unnecessary. There are many good restaurants in the city, but there is a very poor and overpriced selection of hotels, none of which are strongly recommended.

Transportation

From Temuco
Via Private Auto:
Temuco-Victoria: Hwy5, 63km (39 miles), 40min, paved.
Victoria-Los Angeles: Hwy5, 102km (63 miles), 1hr, paved.
Via Bus:
Many companies: hourly, US$2, 2hr.
Via Train:
Temuco-Los Angeles: 2/day, US$3, 3hr.

From Chillán
Via Private Auto:
Chillán-Los Angeles: Hwy5, 110km (68 miles), 1¼hr, paved.
Via Bus:
Many companies: hourly, US$1.50, 1½hr.
Via Train:
Chillan-Los Angeles: 2/day, US$2, 2hr.

Hotels
Moderate:
Gran Hotel Müso: 222 Valdivia, Sgl:US$40, Dbl:US$50, Suite:US$95, on Plaza, around corner from terminal, overpriced, new.
Mariscal Alcazar: 385 Lautaro, Sgl:US$40, Dbl:US$50, cheaper with shared bath, central, remodeled, overpriced.
Mazzola: 579 Lautaro, Sgl:US$30, Dbl:US$40.
Budget:
Santa Maria: 504 Caupolicán, US$8 each, next to bus terminal, friendly.

Restaurants
First Class:
Centro Español: on Plaza.
Prymos: 410 Colón, downstairs for ice cream, upstairs for fine dining, best in LA.
Moderate:
Julio's Pizza: 452 Colón, good pizza, dine upstairs.
El Arriero: 235 Colo Colo.
El Rancho de Julio: 720 Colón, popular *parrilla*.
Budget:
Chi Wei: 324 Paseo Quilque (between Colón and Almagro), good Chinese food, creekside.

Important Addresses

Foreign Exchange: Exchange in Santiago or Temuco.
Post Office: on Caupolicán at Plaza.
Telephone: Galleria at Rengo and Colón, Loc 36; also 583 Caupolicán.
Tourist Office: on Caupolicán at Plaza.
Bus Terminal: 540 Caupolicán.
Train Station: 21 de Mayo and Ercilla.
Car Rental: First, 471 Valdivia; Auto Club, Villagrán and Caupolicán.
Books: El Rincón del Libro, 638 Almagro, Loc 24, follow the signs, excellent used English selection.
Cinema: Imperial, 330 Rengo.
Ski Shop: Sparta, 350 Colón; Taller, 270 Villagrán.
Ski Area: Club Esquí de Los Angeles, 520 Valdivia.

Explore the Lake District with

ANDEAN LEISURE

A British-run company in the heart of the Chilean Lake District. We can advise and organise all types of adventure travel in this beautiful region. We are fully aware of the fragility of the environment and are careful to avoid the negative effects of tourism.

- Hotel bookings
- Car hire
- Map sales
- Guides

— tell us your needs and we'll organise it.

Come and see us at Egaña 82, Puerto Montt (near the railway station), or phone/fax (065) 258555.

Chile

Lonquimay ski trails

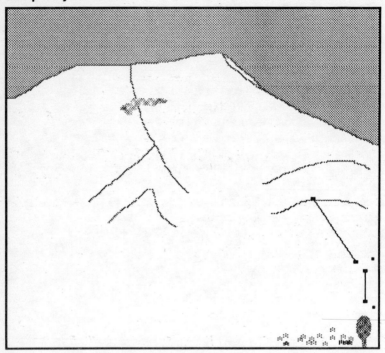

Chapter 15

Lonquimay

Ski Area Facts and Figures

Elevation: Top: 1,850m; 6,070.
 Bottom: 1,650m; 5,413ft.
Vertical Drop: 200m; 655ft.
Season: Early July to Late September.
Lifts: 1 Poma Lift, 1 Portable Tow
Runs: 2: 100% Beginner
Ticket Prices, 1990:
 US$8 Adults Full Day, US$7 Children under 12.

Introduction

Chile's third skiable volcano is the majestic white cone of Lonquimay. South America's northernmost grove of araucaria (monkey puzzle) trees surround the slopes. The forested area on the approach to the ski hill frames the stark white volcano and gives the scene an extremely serene but alien aura. The ski area is one of the continent's newest and most unknown. A secluded hotel with its own hot spring baths provides first class accommodations nearby.

There are two small surface lifts at Lonquimay that access a tiny hill at the southeast base of the *volcán*. Lonquimay's summit is, however, the most inviting of all of Chile's volcanoes. The south face supports two wide bowls both bisected in the middle by a 15-30m high cliff band. Access to the top of the volcano is not particularly difficult or technical. The entire volcano is above the araucaria treeline where the new and friendly *refugio* of the ski resort is located.

The first lift was built in 1985 by the city government of Curacautín, a small town 46km (29 miles) west of the lift site. A group of skiers headed by a lawyer from Los Angeles obtained a 20-year concession to operate the lift on the property. A smaller, portable lift was added by the concessionaire.

Geography

Lonquimay is surrounded by several volcanoes with the summits of Antuco, Callaqui, Copahue, Tolhuaca, and Llaima visible from the top. The headwaters of Chile's longest river, the Biobío, are nearby, and South America's longest tunnel, Las Raíces, provides access to the town of Lonquimay just past the turnoff to the ski area. Lonquimay's summit is 2,890m (9,482ft) high.

The star of the regional flora is the araucaria tree. It is a distinctive member of the pine family that has long, twisting, spindly arms that bear broad, triangular, and sharp needles. Araucarias are found naturally in a limited region of Chile and Argentina. In Chile, the trees range from Lonquimay in the north to Villarrica in the south but are widely found in many public parks and squares outside of their natural range. The cones produce a large nut that the Mapuche tribes came from afar to collect each fall. Bags of the raw nuts (*piñones*) are available in the local markets.

Skiing Tips

Experienced skiers will want to climb to the summit of the volcano. The best route is on a southeast ridge to the right of the main south-facing bowl. No special climbing equipment is needed for the ascent, but avalanche danger can be extreme after a winter storm. Expect to spend about four hours on the hike (the lift saves fifteen minutes of climbing). Start in the morning and enjoy a full descent to the *refugio* to order their excellent hot lunch. This excursion covers about 1,400 vertical meters (4,600ft) and is recommended as one of the best in South America.

Nordic Skiing

Outstanding nordic touring terrain surrounds the base of the volcano. From the *refugio*, circle right (east) over gentle cones to the steaming site of the 1988 eruption. There is a wide expanse of both open and araucaria-filled wilderness that is a cross-country skiers dream.

Base Facilities

At the base of the lifts there are a couple of very small structures which serve as a storage shed and a ticket booth. Be sure to check

Lonquimay

at the ski area office in Los Angeles or at Sernatur in Temuco before coming up to make sure everything is open.

The *refugio*, located one kilometer below the lifts, is nestled in the araucarias just below treeline. They have ski instructors (US$10 for a private) and rental equipment (US$10/day). The modern wooden structure has warm rooms for 32 people. Rates run from US$8/night with lunch or dinner selling for US$4. They also have a van which may be able to pick up skiers in Malalcahuello (arrange in Los Angeles).

Other Lodging

The **Termas de Manzanar** is an outstanding hot springs resort 28km (17 miles) from the ski area. The hotel and bathhouse are located on well-maintained grounds alongside the rushing Río Cautín. The popular summer resort has 25 comfortable rooms some of which are plumbed with the spring water (be sure to ask). They serve outstanding home-style fare and the place is very quiet in the winter season. Transportation to the ski lift may be available. Rates run from US$20-30 each depending on meal plan and room type. It is highly recommended.

There are a few hotels in Curacautín which may be a more viable option for some although the town is not of much interest. Try the **Turismo** (140 Tárapaca) or the **Plaza** (157 Yungay). Otherwise, stay in Temuco.

Getting There

From Temuco
Via Private Auto:
Temuco-Lautaro: Hwy5, 30km (19 miles), 15min, paved.
Lautaro-Curacautín: 54km (34 miles), 1hr, 20km paved.
Curacautín-Manzanar: 18km (11 miles), 15min, paved.
Manzanar-Malalcahuello: 13km (8 miles), 15min, unpaved.
Malalcahuello-Volcán: 15km (9 miles), 30min, unpaved.
Via Bus:
Weekend trips: check at Sernatur office in Temuco.
Local buses to Victoria, then Lonquimay, disembarking at Manzanar or Malalcahuello.

From Los Angeles
Via Private Auto:
Los Angeles-Victoria: Hwy5, 102km (63 miles), 1hr, paved.

Victoria-Curacautín: 56km (35 miles), 45min, paved.
Curacautín-Manzanar: 18km (11 miles), 15min, paved.
Manzanar-Malalcahuello: 13km (8 miles), 15min, unpaved.
Malalcahuello-Volcán: 15km (9 miles), 30min, unpaved.
Via Bus:
Local buses to Victoria, then Lonquimay, disembarking at Manzanar or Malalcahuello.

Further Information and Reservations
Lonquimay
228 Tucupel, No 5, Los Angeles, Chile. Tel: 321-684
Termas de Manzanar
Km 18, Camino Internacional Paso Pino Hachado, Casilla 38 Curacautín, Chile. Tel: 1 x 3, Manzanar

---

LONQUIMAY ERUPTS!

It was a lazy Sunday in Santiago and the local ski areas had decided to cancel all efforts at trying to stay open with three centimeters of snow. It was a perfect opportunity to wander around the market area by the Mapocho River on the west side of the city. I stumbled upon the old gutted railroad station and entered to see what today's exhibit was about. High school students representing each of Chile's 13 political divisions were discussing the physical attributes and economic opportunities of their home towns.

The display of dynamic earth physics in Chile's Region of the Araucarias perked my senses. I noticed a picture of Lonquimay, but it was spewing molten lava. "My God, man," I pulled an intelligent looking kid aside, "when did this happen?" He calmly explained that the eruptions began on Christmas Day in 1988. "I've skied this volcano. Is the mountain still there, is the lift still standing?," I prodded, unconcerned that thousands of native people may have perished in the cataclysm.

The kid was from a small farming community northwest of the volcano and knew nothing of skiing. I was able to learn that the eruption occurred at a small cone on the northeast side of the volcano about as far away from the ski lift as possible. Apparently none of the locals were killed, but the town of Lonquimay was evacuated due to the choking ash clouds that the new Cono Navidad emitted for a period of about twenty days. It's not that I was really concerned about the modest lift facilities, it was just that I had never before skied on anything that had erupted *after* I had skied it.

Chapter 16

Llaima

Ski Area Facts and Figures

Elevations: Top: "Old" Llaima: 1,600m; 5,250ft.
"New" Llaima: 1,800m; 5,900ft.
Bottom: 1,400m, 4,600ft; and 1,500m, 4,900ft.
Vertical Drop: 200m, 650ft; and 300m, 1,000ft.
Season: July to October.
Lifts: "Old" Llaima: 5: 2 T-Bars, 3 Cable Tows.
"New" Llaima: 2 Poma Tows.
Runs: "Old" Llaima: 5: 70% Beginner, 30% Intermediate.
"New" Llaima: 2: 100% Intermediate.
Ticket Prices, 1991:
"Old" Llaima: Negotiable.
"New" Llaima: US$10 Adults Full Day.

Introduction

There are two small ski areas on the southwest flank of the still active Llaima volcano. Both claim the name "Llaima" for their slopes, and both rightfully claim to be the legitimate heirs to the ski pioneers of the Club Andino Cautín of Temuco (as does Villarrica-Pucón).

While Villarrica-Pucón attracts an international crowd, the more modest areas at Llaima attract less experienced local skiers and students. "Old" Llaima is at the site which was all but abandoned after the club's magnificent *refugio* burned to the ground in a 1984 fire. A dedicated Spanish ski instructor named José Luis Sanz is desperately trying to keep the fabled slopes active.

Meanwhile, at "New" Llaima, a few kilometers north of the older site, a group of investors has purchased a small parcel and has built a more modern and challenging lift network. They seek a middle-ground to serve the unsatisfied market between the entry-level "Old"

Llaima and the internationally-oriented Villarrica-Pucón. While the downhill ski facilities at Llaima may seem almost trivial to some travellers, the natural splendor of the region, remote ski touring terrain, and the desire of the hosts to carry on a vital ski tradition makes a visit to Llaima imperative.

History

Llaima's intriguing story begins in 1918 when Sr Casimiro Escribano bought much of the land on the western flank of the volcano. Although he was a conservationist, the exploitation of the rare araucarias by other settlers motivated the government to create the Parque Nacional Las Paraguas. The name refers to the umbrella-like appearance of the unusual, top-heavy araucarias. Complete expropriation of his prized lands was avoided by cooperation with a new ski club from Temuco that had eyes on a parcel of his property.

The Club Andino Cautín was founded in 1938. The club was originally a northern branch of the Club Andino Osorno which was instrumental in constructing access roads and the *refugio*. Important figures in this early period include the French ski instructor, Andres Bossoney, who helped to build the lodge and lift, Jimmy Tinkler, the first Club President, and Carlos Della Maggiora, who led the Club to national prominence and whose grandson, Carlos Urzua, is the developer of the Villarrica-Pucón ski resort.

The first ski lift (a 12 minute T-Bar) was completed in the Spring of 1948 on the run called La Cancha de Valparaíso at the site of "New" Llaima. But, the 4km distance between the lift and the lodge proved to be an obstacle that excessively limited ski time. The T-Bar was thus moved in the late 1950s to the run in front of the lodge called La Cruz.

What really made Llaima special in those days was not so much the runs, which were famous for holding snow until late in the season, but the five-story, 170-bed *refugio* of the Club Andino. The structure was first inhabitable in 1938 and was continually upgraded and enlarged, most significantly by the architect-daughter of Sr Della Maggiora, Elsa. It attracted all the important people of the era including the President of Chile, Gabriel Gonzalez, who, when asked if he would like to try a bit of skiing, replied, "My friend, with the responsibility that I have, I cannot risk injuring myself in this foolhardy and dangerous sport."

When the *refugio* burnt completely to the ground in 1984, skiing at Llaima all but died. Although the lodge was fully insured, the fond memories and rich traditions could never be replaced. While the slopes of Llaima are unlikely to see such grandeur again, there is still a unique ski experience awaiting visitors.

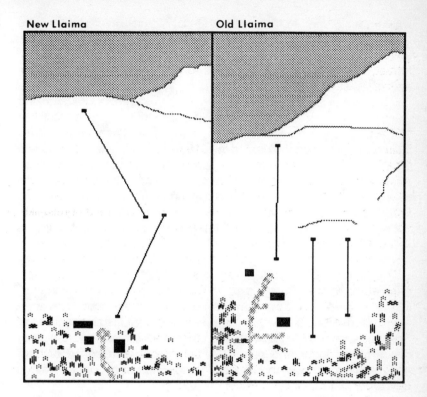

Geography

Llaima is one of the more active volcanoes in Chile with about 10 eruptions this century. As the ancient araucarias in the area attest, no eruptions have disturbed the western flanks of the mountain. There are actually two summits; the highest is 1km west of the other at 3,125m (10,253ft). "New" Llaima climbs a steep cone called the Montón de Trigo, or Wheat Mound, some 6km southwest of the volcano's summit. "Old" Llaima is located about 4km south of the new development just below treeline. Both are located inside the Las Paraguas National Park.

Skiing Tips

"New" Llaima has installed two refurbished Doppelmayr retracting poma tows one of which is from Gunstock, Vermont. All of the runs here are rated intermediate and provide the best access for a summit expedition. Snowcat tours may be available as well.

"Old" Llaima boasts five lifts of regional manufacture but only one cable tow normally operates. It opens in July to school groups and later in the season to the general public. All runs at "Old" Llaima are rated beginner, and most of the trails are at the araucaria treeline.

Adventure Skiing

Most extreme skiers will want to ski the volcano, but its smoking summit is distant and hostile. An ascent would take at least five hours and complete mountaineering equipment is needed. An easier alternative with better skiing is the west slope of the large hill called El Colorado just east of "Old" Llaima whose summit could be reached in an hour. At "New" Llaima, good off-piste skiing is found by traversing along the ridge north or south from the summit of the upper lift. On a good day, many descents could be made on the face of this broad expanse by utilizing the lift system. Avalanche hazard at Llaima is minimal.

Nordic Skiing

There is a variety of rolling terrain all around the south and west sides of the Volcán Llaima. Nordic skiers will enjoy easier access to these areas from "Old" Llaima and could easily pass several days in the area exploring the region. As snow is commonly found well below the ski lodges, there is also a significant amount of terrain in the araucaria groves.

Base Facilities

Expect to find inexpensive homemade fare at "Old" Llaima where they serve an outstanding US$0.40 hot lunch to famished visitors. Meals of a higher standard and price can be found in the modern restaurant at "New" Llaima.

Lodging

At "Old" Llaima there are several lodges, but apparently only the lodge of José Luis rents beds to the public. The dorm style rooms would be comfortable only if there were no student groups there at the time. Lodging with meals is provided for US$17 each per day and half-price for kids under 10. Most international tourists will prefer the more modern amenities and better slopes offered at "New" Llaima. An apartment building and a hotel with a total of about 150 beds is available. The Club Andino Cautín also has a new *refugio* at the site. Because it is new for 1991, prices are unavailable.

Llaima

LEGENDARY LLAIMA

It was with high expectations that I first approached the araucaria-lined ski slopes of the Llaima volcano. After all, my brochure touted Llaima as the "favorite of Chilean skiers, particularly in late winter." My first doubts began to surface when I had to abandon my vehicle several kilometers short of my destination due to the deep and heavy snow that remained on the road from a storm that had passed weeks ago. I arrived at a dilapidated lodge an hour later with soaked feet and dampened spirits. An old man emerged to relate a proud story of past greatness, of how Llaima once ranked with Portillo as the top ski area in Chile. Viewing the antiquated and exhausted T-Bar in front of the lodge on the grey, gloomy day, I imagined that I had somehow entered some bizarre ski horror flick. Actually, I was just 20 years too late.

Getting There

Drivers can rarely reach "Old" Llaima. The normal procedure is to park as high as possible and walk up the snow covered road (3-5km). Passengers and gear are often loaded in a rickety sled pulled by an ancient tractor for the ascent to the lodge (as they have for 50 years). This system is slow and noisy but functional. Nordic skiers will enjoy skiing in. As the "New" Llaima has better equipment to maintain their road, access should become easier in future seasons.

From Temuco

Via Private Auto:
Temuco-Cajón: Hwy5, 9km (6 miles), 5min, paved
Hwy5-Vilcún: 29km (18 miles), 30min, 11km paved.
Vilcún-Cherquenco: 19km (12 miles), 30min, unpaved (road improves after San Patricio).
Cherquenco-Llaima: 23km (14 miles), 30min, unpaved, snow covered.
Via Bus:
Check at Sernatur or JAC offices in Temuco for weekend buses.

Further Information and Reservations

"New" Llaima: **Sociedad de Ski Frontero, SA**, Casilla 49-D, Temuco, Chile or check with Sernatur.
"Old" Llaima: José Luis Sanz, Casilla 624, Temuco, Chile. Tel: No 1, Volcán Llaima or check at Hotel Nicolás for José Luis.

TEMUCO

Temuco is the fourth largest city in Chile and capital of the IXth Region of the Araucanía. The city was incorporated into Chile with the signing of the 1881 peace treaty with the Mapuches. Although Temuco is often called the Mapuche capital, the Indians of the region were actually nomadic in lifestyle and lived in small clan groups. While visitors can expect to encounter costumed Mapuches in Temuco, it is not an Indian town as some sources indicate. With a population of about 20,000, they are greatly outnumbered in this city of 158,000. Temuco's population is distinctly young and the pace in the city is one of the fastest in South America.

Temuco is situated next to the River Cautín in the heart of an area known as the breadbasket of Chile. Wheat, barley and oats are grown extensively as are a variety of fruits especially apples, cherries, and berries. For a good view of the city, go to the top of the Cerro Ñielol where there is a restaurant and public swimming pools.

The market areas of the city feature a wide variety of Mapuche handicrafts and should not be missed. Best buys include the traditional silver jewelry of the Mapuches and wood carvings and wool products. The Mapuches will haggle, but remember that the authentic pieces have involved weeks of tedious labor. There are two markets: one by the train station and the other indoors at Portales and Aldunate.

The center of the city has a modern Plaza de Armas and the main commercial street is **Bulnes**. The Panamerican Highway passes through the city west of the center and is called **Caupolicán**. It is a safe and clean city where walking is an appropriate means of transportation to visit all the interesting sites.

Transportation

From Osorno
Via Private Auto:
Osorno-Temuco: Hwy5, 242km (150 miles), 2½hr, paved.
Via Bus:
Many companies: US$4, 5hr.
Via Air:
LANChile: US$24.

Llaima

From Los Angeles
Via Private Auto:
Los Angeles-Victoria: Hwy5, 102km (63 miles), 1hr, paved.
Victoria-Temuco: Hwy5, 63km (39 miles), 40min, paved.
Via Bus:
Many companies: hourly, US$2, 2hr.

From Pucón
Via Private Auto:
Pucón-Villarrica: Hwy119, 25km (16 miles), 30min, paved.
Villarrica-Freire: Hwy119, 60km (37 miles), 45min, paved.
Freire-Temuco: Hwy5, 27km (17 miles), 15min, paved.
Via Bus:
JAC: every ½hr, US$2, 1¼hr.

Other Air
Ladeco: from Santiago, daily, US$102, 1hr; from Puerto Montt, daily, US$41, 40min; from Coyhaique (Balmaceda), 3/wk, US$103, 1hr.
LANChile: from Santiago, 5/wk, US$102, 1¾hr: from Punta Arenas, weekly, US$180, 2½hr.

Hotels
First Class:
Nuevo Hotel de La Frontera: 726 Bulnes, Sgl:US$66, Dbl:US$82, outstanding, indoor pool, sauna, TV, in-room bar, best restaurant south of Santiago, Villarrica-Pucón ski area info.
Moderate:
Hotel de La Frontera: 733 Bulnes, Sgl:US$33, Dbl:US$42, good value.
Nicolás: 420 MacKenna, Sgl:US$29, Dbl:US$39, TV, central, clean.
Budget:
Continental: 708 Varas, Sgl:US$15-18, Dbl:US$24-27, good restaurant, popular with businessmen.
Turismo: 636 Solar, Sgl:US$8-17, Dbl:US$15-25, friendly.

Restaurants
International:
Nuevo Hotel de La Frontera: 726 Bulnes, best international cuisine.
Club Alemán: 772 Estebanez, formal.
La Nueva Estancia: 2351 Ortega (Panam Hwy), good steaks, disco.

Typical:
Julio's Pizza: 778 Bulnes, excellent food and service, big menu.
Dino's: 360 Bulnes, another in the chain, good sandwiches.
Locals' Favorite:
Dell Maggio: 536 Bulnes, good sandwiches, pastries, and coffees, very popular, named for Carlos Della Maggiora.

Important Addresses

Foreign Exchange: Turismo Money Exchange, 655 Bulnes, Loc 1.
Post Office: Portales and Prat.
Telephone: 565 Prat; 368 Bulnes.
Tourist Office: Sernatur, Bulnes and Solar (at Plaza).
Airlines: LANChile, 635 Bulnes; Ladeco, 370 Bulnes.
Car Rental: Auto Club, 763 Bulnes; First, 1036 Varas; Avis, 800 Prat; Budget, 498 Montt.
Bus Terminal: No central terminal, several around Solar and Lagos; JAC, MacKenna and Bello.
Train Station: end of Lautaro, tickets at 582 Bulnes also.
Newsstand: Nuevo Hotel de La Frontera, front desk.
Laundry: 1185 Portales.
Cinema: Central, 840 Varas.
Ski Shop: Sparta, 822 Montt.
Ski Area Information:
Villarrica-Pucón: Nuevo Hotel de La Frontera.
Llaima and Lonquimay: Sernatur office.

For a map of the Temuco area see page 125.

Chapter 17

Villarrica-Pucón

Ski Area Facts and Figures

Elevation: Top: 2,440m; 8,005ft.
               Bottom: 1,550m; 5,085ft.
Vertical Drop: 960m; 3,150ft.
Season: Early July through November.
Lifts: 9:
           3 Double Chairs, 5 T-Bars, 1 *Va et Vient*
Runs: 22:
           20% Beginner, 30% Intermediate, 30% Advanced, 20% Expert
Ticket Prices, 1990:
  Weekends: US$12 Adults Full Day, US$11 Youths 12-21, US$7 Children under 12, Seniors over 65.
  Weekdays: US$9 Adults Full Day, US$8 Youths, US$5 Children and Seniors.

Introduction

Villarrica-Pucón is the newest ski resort in South America. The ski resort is called Villarrica-Pucón to stress the completeness of the resort. Rather than stay up at the cool climes of the ski area, skiers return to the lakefront hotel where a wide variety of other activities take place. The ski area is the highest in the southern Lakes Region and can legitimately boast skiing in November. It is possible to ski the spring corn snow in the morning and come back to the lake in the afternoon to fish, sail, water ski, golf, bike, hike, or just lounge in a natural hot spring.

The three-year project has seen massive development in the area. Nine lifts were built on the north side of the Villarrica Volcano. A new road was carved on the volcano to access the modern base lodge. A 27-room condominium complex was recently installed alongside the hotel; a new sports facility with an indoor pool and racquetball courts sits on the beach. A casino has been opened in the west wing of the hotel which has undergone complete renovation.

History

The first skiers to descend the slopes of the Volcán Villarrica were Germans from Osorno and Valdivia. The first ski area was located on the north face due to the ease of access, and the Club Andino Cautín soon erected their first *refugio* there. But on October 18 1948, Villarrica erupted, and their lodge "*despareció totalmente*" (disappeared completely). After this setback, all the Club's activities were moved to Llaima which was thought to be a less volatile site.

It wasn't until 1966 that a second attempt was made at putting a ski resort on Villarrica. Max Kaiser built a modest lodge and three lifts, one an 1,800m (5,900ft) long Doppelmayr with single chairs alternating with T-Bar fixtures. He struggled almost 20 years before succumbing to recurring maintenance problems caused by excessive icing on the lift parts.

The new ski resort was built by Carlos Urzúa, grandson of Carlos Della Maggiora, one of Temuco's ski pioneers, at a site west of the old ski area where the volcano is less likely to cause problems. The new resorts's first season was 1988 when just one lift operated. In 1989 three more were added, and by the end of 1990, eight lifts had been installed on the volcano. The last lift was constructed in 1991. Now the challenge is to find skiers to fill the lonely slopes.

Geography

Like Antuco and Osorno, the Villarrica Volcano stands alone in its Fuji-like splendor. Its large crater is filled with bubbling magma that casts an orange glow onto its own steam cloud on clear evenings. Geologists have discovered that this is actually the third Villarrica earth has seen (a fact to which any local ski historian can also attest), and that this volcano is the most active in Chile. The ski area is located in the Villarrica National Park which extends southeast to the Lanín Volcano.

Villarrica's summit currently reaches an elevation of 2,840m (9,318ft). The resort's relatively high elevation ensures one of the latest seasons in South America in spite of the fact that all the runs face north. Normal snow depth is three meters at the base and up to 12 meters higher up the mountain!

Storms arrive saturated but warm from the Pacific Ocean. A problem unique to Villarrica is caused by the huge lake of the same name at its base. This large body of water increases the humidity when the windy storms approach inducing a buildup of rime ice that

Villarrica-Pucón

Chile: Victoria to Villarrica

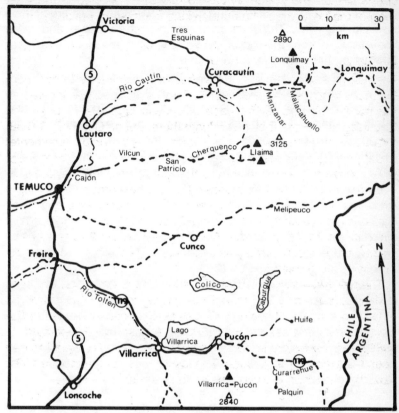

is known to reach one meter in thickness. The weight of the ice was responsible for tearing down lift towers at the old ski area and poses a formidable challenge to the new management.

To counter nature's fury, the ski area has adopted a strategy in which some surface lift cables are lowered to the ground and tied to the lift towers if a prolonged storm front appears to be approaching. Chairs are left rigged in the hope that their swinging will be adequate in breaking loose the larger rime formations. To skiers, this means the lifts may open a bit late after storms. It also ensures a deep, dense, velvety wind-pack base for ego-feeding snow conditions.

Skiing Tips

Few of the runs are identified by name, but the ski area can be classified into three sectors. The first is a mostly intermediate area which fans out from the top of T-Bar 4 and incorporates the Pyramide slope on the west side of the ski area around lifts 1, 2, 3, and 4. This area is separated from the other four lifts by a wide expert canyon that is the second main sector. Both these areas have north-facing runs. The third major area is the steeper and more varied terrain from the top of the *Va et Vient* to the bottom of T-Bar 6. Most of these runs face northeast.

Beginner skiers will enjoy the security of the Coñaripe run in front of the lodge. Intermediates will find gently sloped and wide open terrain in the upper Piramide area around T-Bar 4. The long T-Bar 6 has a good variety of challenging runs on both sides of the lift for advanced skiers. Experts should try traversing into the upper reaches of the main canyon from either lift 7 or 8. The resort owns three Pisten Bully snowcats, but nature often does a far better job at maintaining the slopes at Villarrica than any machine.

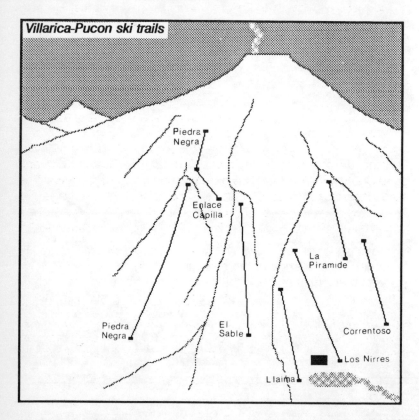

Adventure Skiing

Professional skiers will want to reach the top of the volcano for a full descent of the mountain. The route is not difficult and may take 2-4 hours depending on what lifts are operating. Crampons are needed for the ascent and are available in Pucón. At the summit, climbers are treated to a spectacular lesson in the earth's dynamic origins when viewing the domed mass of glowing molten lava rising and subsiding as if the mountain was breathing. Confirm plans with Ski School Director and mountaineer, Claudio Diaz, before ascending to the volcano's summit.

Avalanche danger is minimal on the north face although the main canyon could be a major path under the right conditions. Large avalanches have been reported on the west face. The south face is glaciated and large crevasses pose a grave threat to skiing there.

Nordic Skiing

There is very little flat, snow-covered terrain at Villarrica which could provide good ski touring. Talk to Claudio Diaz for ideas. He may suggest trying an area near the Termas de Palguín and the Quetrupillán Volcano southeast of Villarrica.

Skier Services

The ski school at Villarrica-Pucón is headed by Claudio Diaz who has skied and taught extensively in Chile. He is also a graduate of the Chamonix Mountain School and is thus a qualified mountain guide. There is a capable staff of instructors who can teach all levels of skiing. Ski school rates begin at US$16 for a one-hour private and go to US$85 for a full day (7hr) group lesson for up to six skiers. The ski school desk is located on the ground floor of the ski lodge.

There is a close group of professional ski patrollers who have a good first aid facility in the base lodge. The nearest modern hospital is in Temuco although Pucón's is adequate.

Base Facilities

Tickets can be purchased on a daily basis at the window on the east side of the lodge. Ski week packages at the Gran Hotel Pucón include lift tickets. Half-day lift tickets are available in all categories. Wednesdays were designated Ladies Day in 1990, and all women skied for half price.

The rental shop at Villarrica-Pucón is located on the first floor in the west end of the lodge next to the ski school desk. Full equipment rental was US$12 in 1990 and US$10 for a half day. All rental equipment is in new condition. There is also a good sport shop in the lodge.

Dining

The lodge's top level houses the cafeteria, bar, and a comfortable fireplace lounge. Large windows provide sweeping views of the volcano. A wide menu is served and anything from sandwiches to hot lunch specials can be ordered from the cafeteria line. Prices are average for Chile with a complete lunch costing about US$4.

The Hotel

The ski area's hotel is the **Gran Hotel Pucón** which sits at the front of a small cove on the east end of the giant Lake Villarrica. The hotel is bordered on its south side by a two block wide park and is located at the north end of the small town of Pucón. A broad, black-sand beach separates the hotel from the lake. The hotel was built in 1934 by the national railroad company and has undergone complete restoration by the ski area developer who purchased it in 1987. The building was designed by Martín Lira who also designed the ski lodge at Portillo. It is a hugely popular summer resort with a pink patio in front that beckons guests on warm afternoons.

The main hotel includes an ample lobby, video theater, sport shop, travel agency, bank, a large cocktail lounge with a fireplace and live music, and two large dining rooms with picture windows providing views of the lake. There are at least seven different room options. The most expensive rooms are located on the fourth floor and have wet bars and lake views. The less expensive rooms face a courtyard and have huge bathrooms with giant bath tubs and antique brass fixtures. Nightly rates run from US$50-93 for a single, US$61-120 for a double, and US$141-150 for a suite. Rates include breakfast, dinner, and transportation to the ski area. When inclement weather prohibits skiing, trips to the hot springs resorts at Huife and Palguín are arranged for guests.

The lakefront condominium building just west of the hotel opened in January 1989. The rooms have comfortable furniture, TV and stereo, terraces, a fireplace, and a fully equipped kitchen. Three and five bedroom plans are available on a daily or weekly rate and come without meals or with breakfast and dinner included. The condominium option is the most economical for large groups.

A sports and recreation complex opened on the lakeshore in August 1989, located at the east side of the hotel. It has an indoor swimming pool, two racquetball/squash courts, gymnasium, private sauna rooms, jacuzzi tubs, and tennis courts. The hotel owns a large fleet of sailing craft including Lasers, dinghies, catamarans, and windsurfers which all come out by the end of October for the summer season, and also has water ski boats and equipment. New for the 1991 season is a gambling casino in the hotel's west wing.

Getting There

From Pucón

The new road to the ski area is unpaved but kept in good repair by the ski area's heavy equipment. The road has yet to close in its short existence but could with heavy snow. Chains are nearly always needed, so be sure you have them in your vehicle before starting.
Via Private Auto:
Pucón-Access Road: Hwy119, 2km (1 mile), paved.
Hwy119-Ski Lodge: 13km (8 miles), 30min, unpaved.
Via Bus:
From Gran Hotel Pucón: 9.00am, US$5rt, free for hotel guests.
JAC: 9.00am weekends only, US$2, 45min. Also from Temuco.

Further Information and Reservations

In Santiago:
Centro de Ski Villarrica-Pucón
3144 Napoleon, Santiago, Chile. Tel: 232-1787, FAX: (562)246-6935
In Temuco:
Nueva Hotel de La Frontera, 733 Bulnes. Tel: 212-638
In Pucón:
Gran Hotel Pucón, 190 Holzapfel. Tel: 441-001

PUCÓN

Pucón is a small tourist community on the eastern shore of the rectangular Lake Villarrica. It is bordered on the north and west by small bays formed by a peninsula which supports a nine hole golf course. Before the completion of the road to Pucón in the 1940s, everyone arrived by ferry from Villarrica. On the hill south of the town is a pretty monastery of Capuchin monks. There are about 5,000 year-round residents in the community and the main economic activity is tourism.

    The 24km (15 mile) stretch of lakeshore between the towns of Villarrica and Pucón is the second most important region in Chile for tourism behind Viña del Mar/Valparaíso. Summer tourism centers on the lake. Popular water sports include sailing, windsurfing, fishing, and water skiing. Other activities in the area include mountain biking, hiking, camping, horseback riding, golf, tennis, and relaxing at one of the many natural hot springs which lie east of the lake.

    Many of the hotels and restaurants are closed in the winter season, especially those by the lakeshore. Expect these to open as summer approaches and as the ski area becomes busier. Many of the bus lines, like those to Junín de Los Andes across the Mamuil Malal pass to Argentina, do not operate in the winter.

Transportation

From Temuco
Via Private Auto:
Temuco-Freire: Hwy5, 27km (17 miles), 15min, paved.
Freire-Villarrica: Hwy119, 51km (32 miles), 40min, paved.
Villarrica-Pucón: Hwy119, 25km (16 miles), 30min, paved.
Via Bus:
JAC: every ½hr, US$2, 2hr.

From Osorno
Via Private Auto:
Osorno-Loncoche: Hwy5, 137km (85 miles), 1½hr, paved.
Loncoche-Villarrica: 41km (25 miles), 30min, paved.
Villarrica-Pucón: Hwy119, 25km (16 miles), 30min, paved.
Via Bus:
From Temuco only.

From Santiago
Via Bus:
JAC: nightly executive service, US$18, 12hr, recommended.

Hotels
First Class:
Gran Hotel Pucón: 190 Holzapfel, see above.
Antumalal: Hwy114 3km from Pucón, Sgl:US$60, Dbl:US$100, Suite:US$133, cabins also, nice grounds, small, snooty, overpriced.
Moderate:
La Posada: 191 Pedro de Valdivia, Sgl:US$15-24, Dbl:US$23-33, also cabins, very nice, friendly, recommended.
El Principito: 291 Urrutia, Sgl:US$18, Dbl:US$26, homey, nice.
Budget:
Milla Rahue: 460 O'Higgins, US$5 each, great restaurant, on main street next to bus station.
Hot Springs Resorts:
Termas de Huife: 33km northeast, US$30 each in cabins, US$1 for bathing, nice setting, modern, good restaurants.

Termas de Palguín: 30km southeast, US$18 each w/meals, US$2 for bathing, more rustic, closer to nordic skiing.

Restaurants

Typical:
El Fogón: 480 O'Higgins, popular with locals.
Bakery:
Holzapfel Bäckerei: 524 Holzapfel, fantastic German bakery, serves meals also, make reservations.

Important Addresses

Foreign Exchange: Exchange in Temuco.
Post Office: 183 Fresia.
Telephone: 560 O'Higgins.
Tourist Office: Brasil and Caupolicán.
Travel Agent: Sol y Nieve, O'Higgins and Lincoyán.
Bus Terminal: JAC, 500 O'Higgins; others on Palguín.
Ski Shop: Sol y Nieve, O'Higgins and Lincoyán; Shop at 361 Palguín; both have mountaineering equipment to rent.
Mountain Bike Rental: 550 Palguín.

Centro de Ski
Villarrica ~ Pucón

Antillanca ski trails

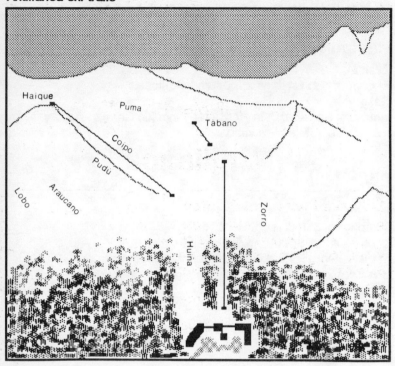

Chapter 18

Antillanca

Ski Area Facts and Figures

Elevation: Top: 1,534m; 5,033ft.
             Bottom: 1,070m; 3,510ft.
Vertical Drop: 464m; 1,523ft.
Season: Early July to Mid September.
Lifts: 3:
             2 T-Bars, 1 Surface Tow
Runs: 7:
             40% Beginner, 30% Intermediate, 30% Advanced
Ticket Prices, 1990:
   US$13 Adults Full Day.

Introduction

In the heart of the dense and steamy temperate rainforest of Chile's Lakes District rises a small volcano which the local Mapuches call "Birthplace of the Sun." At the base of this multi-coned mountain, a small group of dedicated skiers has built two comfortable lodges exclusively with materials found in the local surroundings. They built the stairs and support beams with robust *lenga* trunks, manufactured walls and roof shingles from dense *alerce* wood, and ornamented the ceilings and wicker furniture with cane-like *colihue*. Best of all, the 108 members really enjoy sharing their "clubhouse" with any visitor looking for good skiing and warm friendship. Their manager explained "the fundamental difference between Antillanca and the other ski areas is that this is an open club; members mix with the guests, and even the staff doesn't know who is a member and who is a tourist."

Like Portillo, Antillanca is accessed from a major pass between Chile and Argentina. The border is just 51km (32 miles) east of the turn-off at Puyehue, and Bariloche is just 178km (111 miles) distant. Antillanca has two T-Bars, but only one offers a variety of open trails to advanced skiers. This lift is named Haique, short for the expression "*Hay que ver que lindo!*" (Look how pretty!), which is exclaimed by people as they admire the view. From the top, Osorno, Puerto Montt and its bay, three major lakes, and six important summits are seen.

History

Like their neighbors in Bariloche, Antillanca has a long and rich skiing tradition. The Club Andino Osorno, or CAO, was founded on June 5 1935 by the brothers, Federico and Alfredo Matthei, who learned how to ski in Europe. When they came to Osorno, they found that many other German colonists in the city were interested in this new, exotic sport. Their first skiing activities took place by the *refugio* at La Picada which the club built on the north side of the Osorno volcano. The CAO also constructed 15km of new road to their lodge which could sleep 50 members.

The decision to move all skiing activities to the Antillanca site was made in 1944. Several factors led to this bold and challenging transfer. First, although Antillanca is a bit farther from Osorno, it promised to have easier access (the Puyehue Pass was to become the major southern artery between Chile and Argentina). In addition, the site at Osorno did not have a long season because the slope faces north. The final impetus was given by Alberto and Octaviano Bertín who donated some 1,200 hectares of land around the Antillanca volcano to the CAO for the purpose of building a lodge and ski area.

The new project required more road construction and a new *refugio* to house the skiers. In 1950 the CAO introduced the first ski lift, and the road and hotel were inaugurated the following year. With the addition of a second lift and a snowcat from Europe in 1951, the modern ski era began at Antillanca. The *refugio* was financed by a plan whereby each interested member purchased a room at a price equal to the construction costs of two. Thus, a member would build two rooms but give the Club a gift of one room for public use. In this same manner, a second hotel was constructed in 1983, and Antillanca now boasts over 600 beds in 145 rooms.

Geography

Antillanca sits in the middle of the Puyehue National Park 99km (62 miles) from the city of Osorno. The volcano is called either Casa Blanca or Antillanca, its Mapuche name, and the summit reaches a modest altitude of 1,990m (6,530ft). While there are many hot springs in the park, no volcanic activity has been recorded in the

Antillanca

area in modern times.

The most interesting aspect of Antillanca's geography is the surrounding forest. As the ski area is approached, travellers suddenly find themselves amidst what resembles a tropical rainforest. It is difficult to believe there can be snow nearby. Misty clouds cling to the vertical green slopes of the surrounding hills. It rains here frequently, and water runs everywhere. Everything is always wet. At times the colder temperatures at the higher elevation of Antillanca turns this rain to heavy snow. At other times, it doesn't. A sunny day is a real, and rare, treat.

Skiing Tips

Four runs are generally groomed from the top of Haique, and all have a consistent pitch with little terrain variation. The two runs on either side of the T-Bar are the steepest and are often used for race training.

Adventure Skiing

Antillanca's greatest asset is the terrain offered outside the lift-serviced areas around the many cones and craters of the volcano. There are at least seven different cones in the immediate vicinity, and all offer easy access and tame slopes for complete skiing freedom. From Haique, the closest opportunity lies west at the Taza Chica. This is a small crater reached by a 15 minute hike. Ski this crater a few times (5min hike out) before returning to the lodge on a long, south-facing slope.

The summit of Casa Blanca lies east of Haique. The best access route follows a corniced ridge past two smaller cones before ascending the volcano's west flank. It is an easy traverse route and can be completed in two hours. Avalanche danger is minimal, and only the south face of Casa Blanca appears to slide with frequency.

Nordic Skiing

Antillanca is the only ski area in Chile that rents nordic equipment. A trail is maintained through the trees at the base of the hotel when there's enough snow. As this is rare, don't count on skiing below treeline. Instead, head for the rolling craters east of the ski area discussed above. All around the south side of Casa Blanca, gentle plateaus are covered with consistent snow for great ski touring.

Skier Services

Antillanca has a small ski school with young, local instructors who specialize in teaching introductory skiing techniques. A full day private sells for US$15. Six group lessons are included in the price of a ski week. There is a strong youth racing program here, and many of Chile's best ski racers have come out of the CAO system. There are no FIS homologated runs at Antillanca, but they have applied to have a GS and downhill course certified.

The ski patrol is made up of volunteer members of the Patrullas de Chile from Osorno and Valdivia. There is an excellent infirmary at the hotel which is staffed by a doctor from Osorno and a full-time nurse. On weekends and holidays there is usually an ambulance standing by as well. The best hospital in the region is the Clinica Alemana in Osorno.

Base Facilities

Tickets can be purchased by the rental shop and ski check in the gallery between the two hotels. A rental package with nice Kneissel skis sells for US$13. There are three separate ski rooms; one in both hotels for guests and one in the gallery for visitors. Lifts run from 9.00am to 5.00pm seven days a week.

Dining

Antillanca's restaurant is generally a self-service cafeteria but, when it's not too crowded, the waiters will serve guests. The food is excellent and typical Chilean fare is served. The dining room is tiered on the upper levels of the central gallery and many tables have views of the slopes. All meals are included in the room price.

The Hotels

Antillanca has two connected hotel structures. The first (as you enter the complex) is the older of the two and is referred to as the *Refugio*. It has a large lobby area surrounded by club memorabilia. The video viewing room is actually what remains of the very first *refugio*. Visitors stay in the rooms on the first level as all rooms on the second floor are owned by club members. Rooms here are generally larger but sleep only three and have wooden floors. There is a ski room with a heated boot rack in front of the exit.

The new **Hotel** is on the east end of the complex. Each room has four beds and is carpeted. The rooms are more comfortable but cramped. Remnants of the first ski lift dangle majestically on a wall in the lounge area.

The central gallery is connected to each hotel with a covered walkway. It is the social center for *aprés* ski activities in Antillanca. In the lower level is a disco, a game room with ping pong tables, the parquet-floored gym, a wood-heated sauna with massage rooms, and inside access to the outdoor swimming pool. The upper level has a cozy bar and the restaurant.

The club generates its own electricity with a small hydroelectric generator that is located a few kilometers from the hotel. It is not quite sufficient to supply all the power they would like however. The lifts are thus gas powered and the hotels are heated by wood-fired boilers. The dim lights in the rooms are due to a lack of spare power rather than an attempt to create a false ambience which the homey lodge does not need.

Future Plans

The biggest problem at Antillanca occurs when warm temperatures or rain wash away the snow at the bottom of the mountain. When this happens, there is still good skiing up on Haique, but there is no access. The first priority is to replace the Flecha T-Bar with a chairlift to carry skiers from the base to the top of the 1,650m (5,415ft) Cornisa ridge. This would not only provide a longer season but would also greatly increase the amount of skiable terrain. Since the ski area is run not-for-profit, this plan has a good chance of becoming reality, but probably not for several years.

Other Lodging

Termas de Puyehue

A less expensive option is found at the beautiful **Hotel Termas de Puyehue** 22km (14 miles) from Antillanca and 77km (48 miles) from Osorno. It is easier to get to than Antillanca, and they offer a free daily bus service to the ski hill. The hotel is first class and is packed in the summer with fishermen and other outdoor enthusiasts. In the winter months it is deserted.

The hotel was constructed in 1947 and covers 26,500 square meters. Built with natural rock, it sits on a hill overlooking their grassy grounds, golf course and Lake Puyehue ("Place of Fresh Water Fish"). The hotel has its own springs, and water is bottled in a plant behind the hotel. The hot springs are used to fill the indoor swimming pool which is probably the most beautiful in all of South America. Indoor tennis courts are located in the hotel for those rainy days in Antillanca.

Prices range from US$57/night for a basic room to US$297/night for a suite with a balcony for two people. A variety of meal plans can be included. Ski week packages including six lift tickets, transportation to the ski hill, breakfast and dinner are available for US$328 each.

Aguas Calientes

2km toward Antillanca from Puyehue is **Aguas Calientes** which rents cabins and offers baths to day visitors. An indoor pool and several open-air hot pools alongside a pristine river are the attractions here. It is fairly popular with bathers, even in winter, and if a day off from skiing is desired, arrange a trip here to bathe. There is also a campground and an office of the Puyehue National Park nearby.

Getting There

From Osorno

Via Private Auto:
Osorno-Puyehue: Hwy 215, 77km (48 miles), 1hr, paved.
Puyehue-Antillanca: 22km (14 miles), 30min, unpaved.
Via Bus:
There is no public bus service from Osorno to Antillanca. One option is to take local buses to Puyehue via Entre Lagos (inquire at tourist office in Osorno bus terminal). Another is to pay for the ride to Bariloche but unload at Puyehue. From Puyehue, someone from Antillanca will meet guests with hotel reservations.
Osorno-Antillanca, the club's service: available anytime, 1½hr, US$56, private car.
Puerto Montt/Osorno-Bariloche (ask to get off at Puyehue): every morning, several companies, 2hr, US$20.
Osorno-Entre Lagos-Puyehue: local bus, 4/day, 3hr, US$2.

From Bariloche

Via Private Auto:
The Puyehue Pass is open 8.00am to 8.00pm only as the customs stations close at night.
Bariloche-Chacabuco: Hwy 237, 20km (12 miles), 15min, paved.
Cacabuco-Villa La Angostura: Hwy 215, 75km (47 miles), 1hr, paved.
Villa La Angostura-Puyehue: Hwy 215, 83km (52 miles), 2hr + customs time, mostly unpaved.
Puyehue-Antillanca: 22km (14 miles), 30min, unpaved.
Via Bus:
Bariloche-Osorno/Puerto Montt (ask to get off at Puyehue): every morning, several companies, 5hr, US$20.

Further Information and Reservations
Centro Turistico y Deportivo Antillanca
Mackenna 716 — 3er Piso, Casilla 765, Osorno, Chile. Tel: (064)232-297, Telex: 271513.
Antillanca Office: Tel: 5114
Termas de Puyehue
Vitacura 2902, Of 1404, Santiago, Chile. Tel: 231-3417, FAX: 231-3582. Telex: 240572 TRANS CL
Osorno Office: (064)232-157. Telex: 273146 TERMA CL
Complejo Turistico Aguas Calientes
Tel: (064) 236-988

OSORNO

Osorno is a town of 95,000 located in the center of Chile's Lake District. The region is very similar to the Lakes Region of Argentina although activities are not as concentrated as in Bariloche. The city lies between the rivers Rahue and Damas. The main street, **Ramirez**, leads from the main cathedral to the rivers' confluence. The city's Farmers' Market is open every morning and is the largest in Chile. Osorno is also famous for its German hospitality.

The principal economic activity in the area is agriculture with grains, potatoes, asparagus, and a variety of berries the most common products. Dairy farming is also important in the region. Tourism is a the most vital summer industry with camping, fishing and other water sports the main activities.

Transportation
Osorno is something of a transportation hub because it sits on the Chilean end of the Puyehue Pass, the second most important road between Chile and Argentina. Thus, overland trips to Bariloche, Coyhaique, and Punta Arenas originate here. Osorno sits just west of the Pan American Highway and has excellent travel connections in all directions.

From Puerto Montt
Via Private Auto:
Puerto Montt-Osorno: Hwy5, 107km (66 miles), 1½hr, paved.
Via Bus:
Puerto Montt-Osorno: Varmontt every ½hr, others, US$2, 2hr.
Via Air:
Ladeco: 4/wk, 25min, US$14. LANChile: US$14.

From Temuco
Via Private Auto:
Temuco-Osorno: Hwy5, 242km (150 miles), 2½hr, paved.
Via Bus:
Temuco-Osorno via Valdivia: many companies, US$4, 5hr.
Via Air:
LANChile: US$24

From Santiago
Via Private Auto:
Santiago-Osorno: Hwy5, 946km (588 miles), 10hr, paved.
Via Bus:
Santiago-Osorno: many companies, many classes including sleeper, US$16.
Via Air:
Ladeco: via Valdivia, 4/wk, 2¾hr, US$116.
LANChile: 2 stops, 5/wk, 3hr, US$121.

To Coyhaique
Via Bus:
Osorno-Coyhaique: Turismo Lanin, 1/wk, 22hr, US$23.
Via Air:
Ladeco: via Puerto Montt, 4/wk, 2¼hr, US$69.

To Punta Arenas
Via Bus:
Osorno-Punta Arenas: Turismo Lanin, 1/wk, 34hr, US$50.

From Bariloche, Argentina
Via Private Auto:
Bariloche-Chacabuco: Hwy 237, 20km (12 miles), 15min, paved.
Cacabuco-Villa La Angostura: Hwy 215, 75km (47 miles), 1hr, paved.
Villa La Angostura-Puyehue: Hwy 215, 83km (52 miles), 2hr + customs time, mostly unpaved.
Puyehue-Osorno: Hwy 215, 77km (48 miles), 1 hr, paved.
Via Bus:
See *Chapter 6*.

Antillanca

Hotels

First Class:
Hotel Del Prado: 1162 Cochrane, Sgl:US$47, Dbl:US$63, Suite:US$85, in residential neighborhood 7 blocks from center, pool, fireplace, cozy, like staying in a very nice home. German owners.
Hotel Garcia Hurtado de Mendoza: 1040 Mackenna, Sgl:US$46, Dbl:US$64, Suite:US$77, central location, new.

Moderate:
Hotel Waeger: 816 Cochrane, Sgl:US$27, Dbl:US$53, Suite:US$85, long tradition in Osorno, newly remodeled, German run.
Hotel Inter Lagos: 515 Cochrane, Sgl:US$26, Dbl:US$41, Suite:US$56.
Gran Hotel: O'Higgins at the Plaza, Sgl:US$22, Dbl:US$35, Suite:US$45, old hotel, overlooks plaza.

Budget:
Residencial Riga: 1058 Amthauer, US$11 each, popular.

Restaurants

International:
Peter's Kneipe: 1039 Rodriguez, outstanding German food
Hotel Waeger: 816 Cochrane, German and Chilean fare.

Typical:
Lucas Pizza: 551 Cochrane, good pizza and pasta.
Dino's: 898 Ramirez, cafeteria style sandwiches.

Important Addresses

Foreign Exchange: Change in Puerto Montt or Temuco.
Post Office: 645 O'Higgins.
Telephone: 1004 Mackenna.
Tourist Office: 665 O'Higgins; also at Bus Terminal.
Airlines: LANChile, 862 Matta; Ladeco, 976 Mackenna.
Bus Terminal: Errazuriz and Colon.
Car Rental: Auto Club Chile, 463 Bulnes; Hertz, 857 Bilbao; First, 959 Mackenna.
Cinema: Cine Lido, Ramirez 650.
Hospital: Clininca Alemana, 1530 Zentero.
Antillanca Office: 716 Mackenna.

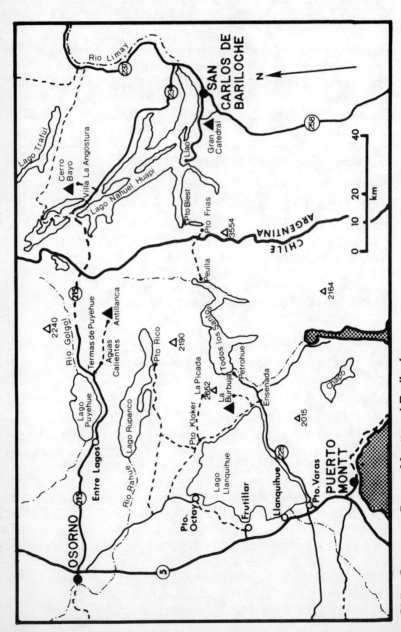

Chile: Osorno to Puerto Montt and Bariloche

Chapter 19

La Burbuja

Ski Area Facts and Figures

Elevation: Top: 1,620m; 5,315ft.
                Bottom: 1,300m; 4,265ft.
Vertical Drop: 320m; 1,050ft.
Season: Mid July to Early October.
Lifts: 1 T-Bar, 1 Tow Lift
Runs: 3:
                20% Beginner, 30% Intermediate, 40% Advanced, 10% Expert
Ticket Prices: Unavailable.

Introduction

La Burbuja is the southernmost ski area of Chile's Lakes Region. The modern lift climbs a small part of the south face of the glaciated Osorno Volcano (2,652m; 8,701ft), the most rugged and alpine of all of Chile's southern volcanoes. The renowned beauty of Osorno is the main attraction of La Burbuja. Political analyst, James Whelan, urges armchair travellers to "imagine a conical shape of sculpted perfection, a crown of eternal snow, green forested flanks, all mirrored in the deep blue of Lake Todos Los Santos, and you have an impoverished word picture of glorious Osorno."

La Burbuja serves as the ski area for the local population from the summer resort towns of Puerto Varas, Llanquihue, Frutillar, and the port city of Puerto Montt. While most skiers may need only a day to fully explore the terrain of La Burbuja, the area in and around Puerto Montt deserves several days of sightseeing. From the fish markets of Angelmo and the bucolic island of Chiloé, to the ferry ride across All Saints Lake and the isolated hotel at Peulla, Puerto Montt offers the foreign visitor a glimpse at several cultures and lifestyles.

History

The Osorno volcano was first skied by enthusiasts from the Club Andino Osorno at La Picada on the north slope of the peak. In 1940 they were joined by skiers of the Teski Club (tennis + ski) of Puerto Varas who built a *refugio* in the area called Portezuelo de Contrabando. A lift was never built in this region, but the huts are still maintained and see heavy use by climbers in the summer.

When the Osorno Club decided to move to Antillanca in 1944, the Teski Club also chose to desert La Picada. Teski went to La Burbuja whose south-facing slopes offered better snow and a longer season. La Burbuja is also much closer to Puerto Varas. The Teski Club eventually erected a *refugio* and a surface lift at the site, but skiing on a commercial scale did not begin until 1985 when the municipality of Puerto Varas built a T-Bar adjacent to Teski's poma lift.

The local government's professed interest in skiing was to offer an off-season attraction to balance the busy summers. Others claim the city was trying to divert attention from their gross mismanagement of the once-thriving grand hotel and casino on the hill above the town. The ski area proved to be another management nightmare for the *Municipalidad* who finally offered an administrative concession to private interests. In 1990, the parent company of the Hotel Vicente Perez Rosales in Puerto Montt secured a contract to operate the lift and lodge at La Burbuja.

Geography

The Osorno volcano rises from the center of a large glacier-carved valley. The ski resort sits above Lake Llanquihue on the southwest face of the monolith. When viewing Osorno from Puerto Varas, the lift lies directly below — and aligned with — the summit. The volcano is not dormant and last erupted in 1850. An 1835 eruption is described by Darwin in his *Voyage of the Beagle*. Heavy winds are common and make chairlift construction impractical. La Burbuja (The Bubble) is named after a small crater of the same name that one passes on the road to the ski run.

Skiing Tips

La Burbuja's runs are unnamed. Beginners should have no problems if they unload at Tower 5 and ski the gentle slope on either side of the lift. Intermediate slopes are located on the west (left) side of the T-Bar, and all advanced and expert skiing is in a hidden bowl behind the ridge east of the lift.

La Burbuja

La Burbuja ski trails

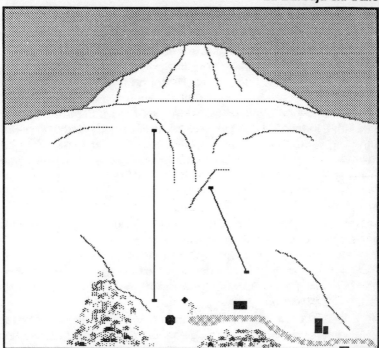

Adventure Skiing

There is little safe off-piste skiing at La Burbuja. The summit of Osorno can be reached only with full mountaineering equipment. Crevasses, ice-falls, avalanches, and high winds are just a few of the hazards that have claimed many experienced climbers. Better adventure skiing opportunities lie with longer descents from the ski area to a variety of points along the access road. There is some avalanche hazard in the advanced bowl described above and on the entire south face of the volcano to the right of the T-Bar.

Nordic Skiing

Although there are no trails, there are several adequate areas for nordic skiing at La Burbuja. Many benches and plateaus are found below the south face right (west) of the poma lift. Snow is common below the base lodge and treeline, and the Los Pumas *refugio* might be a good spot for basing cross-country ski adventures at lower elevations.

Base Facilities

When arriving at the ski area, the first structures are a ranger station on the left and the lodge of the Teski Club on the right. Teski's *refugio* has a small bar, restaurant, and overnight accommodation. Several hundred meters higher there is a private *refugio* which offers primitive ski rental equipment and good homestyle food.

The round stone building past the end of the parking lot is the main lodge for La Burbuja. It is built around a central fireplace and has three levels. The top level currently houses a bar and cafeteria. Rooms may become available for overnight stays in the future. The small kiosk in front of the lodge is the ticket booth. With the recent change in management, prices for the various services were not available.

Lodging

The *refugio* of the Teski Club at La Burbuja rents beds in a dormitory-style arrangement. The **Los Pumas** *refugio* is closed in the winter season although a caretaker resides there (skiers may be able to arrange something). Los Pumas is located 12km (7 miles) from Ensenada on the La Burbuja road, and there are plenty of signs indicating its location.

In Ensenada, the classic if dilapidated *Hotel Ensenada* is closed in the winter. **Las Brisas del Lago** rents several good cabins and seems to be the only available accommodation in the winter season in Ensenada. Stop here for information about the ski area if arriving from the north.

There are several first class lodging options in Puerto Varas 70km (43 miles) from La Burbuja. Puerto Montt (17km south of Puerto Varas) was chosen as the base for La Burbuja excursions because it is a more interesting town. Transportation to La Burbuja is also easier to arrange from Puerto Montt. For skiers with a car, the modern, clean, and quiet lakefront town of Puerto Varas may prove to be a more desirable option, and several hotels are listed.

Getting There

From Puerto Montt

Via Private Auto:
Puerto Montt-Puerto Varas: Hwy5, 17km (11 miles), 15min, paved.
Puerto Varas-Ensenada: Hwy225, 50km (31 miles), 30min, paved.
Ensenada-La Burbuja: 19km (12 miles), 30min, unpaved.
Via Bus:
Check at Hotel Vicente Perez Rosales.
Check at travel agencies in Puerto Montt and Puerto Varas.

Further Information
Hotel Vicente Perez Rosales
447 Antonio Varas, Casiila 607, Puerto Montt, Chile. Tel: 252-571.

PUERTO MONTT

Puerto Montt is the capital of Chile's Lakes District (Region X) and is located at the northern end of the Reloncaví Sound. Geographically similar to Vancouver in Canada, it is the transport and economic center for the entire archipelagic region of Chile and its timber and marine products. The city boasts 120,000 inhabitants and faces south on a long strip of flat land between the bay and the coastal highlands. West of the city is the humble port and fishing town of Angelmó, and Pelluco is a small but wealthy community 5km east of the city.

The main commercial zone parallels a grassy park on the waterfront. The park has several kilometers of well-maintained oceanside paths that promote lingering strolls from Angelmó to Pelluco. The main street, **Antonio Varas**, is one block off the coast and stretches about 2km from the train station on the east end of town to the bus terminal on the west side.

The pastoral island of Chiloé attracts tourists from around the world in spite of frequent fog and heavy rain. This unique part of Chile is renowned for its distinctive architecture. Stilted wooden houses are perched along the coast, and a variety of shingled churches are scattered about the island. Quality wool products from Chiloé are best purchased on the island or in the streets of Puerto Montt.

The port of Angelmó is reached by an interesting 30 minute walk. In case of rain, taxis and *colectivos* are easily hailed along the route. At the far west end of the coastal road, visitors will discover the fish market and many amazing types of seafood. The locals enjoy slurping the delicate orange meat of sea urchins (*erizos*) while negotiating the price of *congrio* (conger eel) or *almejas* (clams). The fishermen's wives compete vociferously to entice passers-by into their identical *marisquerías* where locals and visitors dine on a variety of fresh catches.

The seafood is cooked in a common kitchen and is completely safe in spite of the primitive appearance of the market. While the plates are not inexpensive, the freshness of the seafood will bring epicureans back time and again. Lunch is the most popular meal, and the market closes before 8.00pm. Highly recommended dishes include *locos* (mini-abalones), and the giant barnacle called *picoroco* which has a sweet, crab-like meat.

Transportation

Puerto Montt is the transportation hub for excursions to Chile's archipelagic and Patagonian regions. The Carretera Austral begins here and now extends over 1,000km (620 miles) south to Cochrane and beyond. Three southern ferry lines are based at the port, and the bus terminal is always active. In addition, the Cruz de Lagos ferry trip to Bariloche operates from this city.

The bus terminal is on the waterfront towards Angelmó. Ride with Varmontt and use their secondary terminal on Copiapó to avoid the hectic central terminal. There is a good airport 10km north of town, taxi US$10. Many summer ferries don't run in the winter months.

South
Via Private Auto:
Puerto Montt-Chaitén via Chonchi: Hwy5, 187km (116 miles), 4hr, paved, plus 6hr ferry.
Puerto Montt-Chaitén via Río Negro: Hwy7, 205km (127 miles), gravel, plus 4½ hours on 3 ferries, full day.
Chaitén-Coyhaique: Hwy7, 420km (260 miles), 2 days, gravel.
Via Bus:
All connections except to Chiloé are from Osorno.
Via Ferry:
Navimag has service twice weekly to Chacabuco for Coyhaique on the ship *Evangelistas* and three times/month to Puerto Natales on the *Tierra del Fuego*. Both carry cars and passengers as well as freight, and the passenger salons are comfortable with airplane style seats, video movies and news programs. *Evangelistas* has a simple cafeteria which serves microwave food. Cabin and bunk guests have real meals in a separate dining room and can use the shower facilities (bring towels). On the *Tierra del Fuego*, all prices include meals. There is plenty of space for walking about, but the weather is almost always gloomy, preventing full enjoyment of the magnificent fjords through which the ships navigate. Bulky luggage goes into an inaccessible container, so carry whatever may be needed. Make reservations in Santiago early for cabins or beds.
Puerto Montt-Chacabuco: two/week each direction, 26hr.
Cabin 1:US$130 each; Cabin 2:US$110 each; Bunk (*Litera*):US$40; Seat (*Butaca*):US$25; Auto:US$63.
Puerto Montt-Puerto Natales: three/month each direction, 72hr.
Cabin 1:US$390 each; Cabin 2:US$325 each; Cabin 3:US$250 each; Bunk:US$117; Seat:US$85; Auto:US$145.

La Burbuja

Via Air:
To Coyhaique:
LANChile: Daily except Sunday, US$62, 1hr.
Ladeco: Daily except Saturday, US$57, 1½hr.
To Punta Arenas:
LANChile: Daily, US$136, 2hr.
Ladeco: Daily, US$136, 2hr.

North

Via Private Auto:
Puerto Montt-Osorno: Hwy5, 109km (68 miles), 1¼hr, paved.
Via Bus:
Puerto Montt-Osorno: Varmontt, others, US$2, 2hr.
Via Air:
LANChile: to Santiago, 2/day, US$121, 1½hr.
Ladeco: to Santiago, 2/day, US$117, 1½hr.
Also connections to Osorno, Valdivia, Temuco and Concepción.

To Bariloche
See *Chapter 6*.

Hotels

First Class:
Vicente Perez Rosales: 447 Varas, Sgl:US$61, Dbl:US$70, best in town, snooty, ocean views, good restaurant, ski area info.
Moderate:
Montt: 301 Varas, Sgl:US$26, Dbl:US$34, popular, good location, friendly, outstanding inexpensive restaurant.
Millahue: 64 Copiapó, Sgl:US$21, Dbl:US$24.
Colina: 81 Talca, Dbl:US$32.
Budget:
El Candil: 177 Varas, Dbl:US$17.

In Puerto Varas

First Class:
Licarayan: 114 San Jose, Sgl:US$30-39, Dbl:US$35-47, waterfront, central, jacuzzi baths, fireplaces, outstanding.
Cabañas del Lago: 195 Klenner, Sgl:US$38, Dbl:US$43, Cabin:US$40, grassy grounds, great views.
Gran Hotel Puerto Varas: 351 Klenner, Sgl:US$28, Dbl:US$38, old classic, run down, nice grounds and view.

Moderate:
Asturias: 233 O'Higgins, Sgl:US$30, Dbl:US$36, city center.

Restaurants
International:
La Terraza de Pelluco: 3km to Pelluco, best food, atmosphere, and service.
Club de Yates: over bay past train station, good seafood.
Moderate:
Rail car on south side of train station.
Dino's: 550 Varas, upstairs for dining, downstairs for snacks.
Locals:
Marisquerías: in Angelmó, eliminate the middleman.

Important Addresses
Foreign Exchange: 595 Varas, Loc 3; others around Hotel Rosales.
Post Office: 126 Rancagua.
Telephone: 160 Pedro Montt; 98 Chillán.
Tourist Office: Kiosk in park between Rosales and train station.
Travel Agent: Andina del Sur, 437 Varas, for Bariloche ferry.
Newsstand: Best at Bus Terminal.
Books: 232 Quillota, small used selection in English.
Navimag: 2187 Angelmó.
Car Rental: Auto Club, 75 Cauquenes; Avis, 878 Benavente; Hertz, 1036 Urmeneta; First, 437 Varas; Budget, 200 San Martín.
Airlines: LANChile, 305 Benavente; Ladeco, 350 Benavente.
Train Station: 50 San Felipe.
Bus Terminal: Portales w/Lota.
Cinema: Rex, 621 Varas.

Chapter 20

El Fraile

Ski Area Facts and Figures

Elevation: Top: 1,825m; 5,990ft.
Bottom: 1,025m, 3,390ft.
Vertical Drop: 800m; 2,600ft.
Season: Mid July to Early October.
Lifts: 1 T-Bar, 1 Poma Lift
Runs: 4:
30% Beginner, 20% Intermediate, 40% Advanced, 10% Expert
Ticket Prices, 1990:
US$6.50 Adults Full Day, US$3.50 Children.

Introduction

In the heart of archipelagic Chile, in a region only recently accessible to international tourists, lies a small ski area called El Fraile. It is without a doubt the most remote and unknown ski area in South America. El Fraile was built by the federal government to provide recreation for the hearty pioneers they hope to attract to the region. The theory is that a modest but modern ski hill will help entice young, free spirited people considering a new life in the pristine area.

El Fraile is located 29km (18 miles) from the modern and inviting town of Coyhaique, capital of the Chile's XIth Region. The area was recently integrated with the rest of Chile with the completion of the northern section of the Carretera Austral Presidente Pinochet. The "Longitudinal Highway" promises to open Chile's last frontier. For now, this unsullied land of frozen glaciers, misty fjords, giant trout, and an unpretentious ski hill remains a secret even to Chileans.

The ski area was completed in 1978 with the construction of the short poma lift at the base. In 1982, the long T-Bar was added. The government gave an administrative concession to a group of Argentine and Chilean entrepreneurs in 1987. But high ticket prices asked by the concessionaire made the cost of skiing prohibitive to locals and the concession was revoked. The ski area is now administered by DIGEDER, Chile's national sports body.

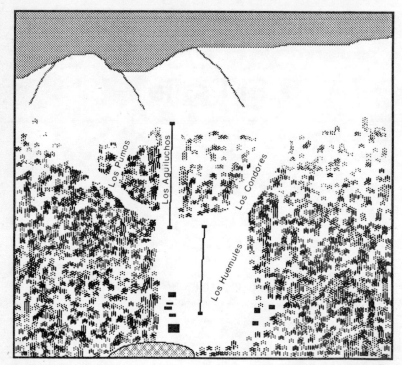

El Fraile ski trails

Geography

Cerro El Fraile, or "Friar Mountain," is so named because from Coyhaique the summit resembles the classic round head of a bald, cherubic monk. The hill anchors the western end of the MacKay Range, and while rocky and foreboding on the northwest side, the southeast side is forested and better protected from the prevailing winds.

Storms normally come in cold and dry from the northeast, but a far wetter and warmer system will approach occasionally from the southwest. These storms can deposit a deep blanket of "Coyhaique curd," or completely wash out the area. The snow is usually deeper below the treeline, as the higher exposed ridges are often swept clean by the wind.

The trees in the area include firs as well as the hardwood ñires and lengas found throughout southern Chile. Unlike the Lakes

Region, the forest here is not choked with *caña*, and many glades are skiable.

Skiing Tips

There is a very wide area around the lower poma lift for the beginner skiers who form the majority of the skiing public here. This is the only area on the mountain that can be groomed. The only truly intermediate area is around the first four towers of the higher T-Bar. Above this, it's all advanced. The Kamikaze run is tree-lined with a consistent steep pitch. Los Pumas is preferred by the ski instructors who call it Embudo for the large bowl in the middle. It is a natural run of tiny canyons, small bowls, and sheer faces filled with copious amounts of snow. The varied and open terrain gives skiers a sense of big mountain skiing.

Adventure Skiing

Like many of the smaller ski areas in South America, El Fraile has great adventure skiing reached with a nominal effort. A 20 minute hike up the obvious ridge above the top of the T-Bar leads to expansive views and a dozen skiing options. Advanced skiers will have no trouble descending the tolerant bowl just right (east) of the access ridge. Expert skiers can head farther east to the heavily corniced and lengthy headwall that looms over Kamikaze. To the west, two major bowls can feed back to the traverse road at the bottom of Embudo.

These areas have run-out zones inside the ski area which pose a potentially significant avalanche hazard. While the new snow is usually heavy enough that it bonds well, slides could run down Embudo past the cutoff road. The traverse to Kamikaze is also at risk. Under such conditions, the lifts are sure to be closed and the greatest concern will be returning to Coyhaique. The ski patrollers also ski cut the areas if there is a threat, but be aware.

Nordic Skiing

Organized nordic skiing is accessed from El Fraile's lifts. From the top of the T-Bar, ski northeast between the above mentioned headwall and Kamikaze, bearing left to ascend to the top of the ridge. One kilometer north is a large oval crater used by the military for winter training exercises. Although the entire ridge is appropriate for cross-country skiing, it is often stripped clean by the wind. The crater catches and holds the snow better, although skiers may get a bit dizzy skiing around and around and around....

Skier Services

While El Fraile does not have its own ski school, there are several private ski schools with certified instructors in Coyhaique. Inquire at the DIGEDER office for details or ask for Gonzalo Nogués at Turismo Pollux.

El Fraile has four full-time patrollers who are certified with the Patrullas de Chile. Be sure to inform them of off-piste ski plans, especially if going alone. There is an excellent, modern hospital in Coyhaique which serves as the main medical facility in the region.

Base Facilities

The lifts run six days/week with the day off varying each week. Weekend hours are from 10.00am to 5.30pm. Some weekdays the lifts don't open until 2.00pm. Be sure to check with the DIGEDER office in Coyhaique before going up.

There is no storage facility, but belongings can be safely left in a corner of the lodge. Adequate if short skis rent for a dollar, and a full rental package including ski pants will set skiers back US$4.

The public lodge is the large orange and black structure above the parking lot flying the festive banners of El Fraile. The entry has a wood stove and ample space to change into ski attire. The rental desk and ticket window are also here. The comfortable cafeteria seats about 60 people and is dominated by a large fireplace in the middle of the room. A basic selection of hot and cold sandwiches is served (US$2-3), and a well-stocked bar is found in the corner.

There are about 15 other structures around the base of El Fraile. These all belong to a variety of groups including ski clubs, the local hospital staff, *carabineros*, the military, and local families.

Getting There

From Coyhaique follow the Longitudinal Highway south towards Balmaceda. The road is unpaved but is in great shape as it is the major highway in the area. After 16km (10 miles), make a left turn at the signs indicating El Fraile and Lago Frio. Before turning though, continue a few meters south to see the waterfall of the Pollux River and the Simpson Valley on the right side of the road.

About 2km after the turn at the waterfall, take another left on the ski area road. Grandiose signs mark the government project. From here, the road is less travelled and becomes muddy, icy, and narrow. Do not attempt to approach the ski area without chains or a four-wheel drive vehicle.

Just before reaching the ski area, the road descends steeply to

El Fraile 155

the main parking lot. Many skiers park at the top of this hill and walk in because slick conditions prevent vehicles from escaping this depression.

With extra time and nice weather, skiers should return to Coyhaique by the longer (25km, 16 miles) but more interesting road to Lakes Frio, Pollux, and Castro, all outstanding fisheries in season.

There are no public buses to the ski area. Many of the local travel agencies will carry passengers in their jeeps, but this is a costly service. A better alternative is to rent a four-wheel drive vehicle for a few days to explore the area and ski.

From Coyhaique
Via Private Auto:
Coyhaique-Pollux Waterfall: Hwy7, 16km (10 miles), 25min, unpaved.
Pollux Waterfall-El Fraile: 13km (8 miles), 35min, unpaved.

Further Information
DIGEDER
376 Dussen
Coyhaique, Chile
Tel: 221-690

COYHAIQUE

Coyhaique is an Indian term that means "The Camp between Two Rivers." The River Coyhaique comes from the east and meets the larger River Simpson from the south and then continues west to the ocean at Puerto Aisén. Coyhaique is situated in a transition zone between the dry Argentine *pampa* and the drenched fjords of coastal Chile. While the coastal islands are inundated with over 3500mm (138in) of rain annually, Coyhaique receives a more reasonable 1095mm (43in) per year. South of Coyhaique are expansive and remote glaciers and glacier lakes, and thick forests make most of the area to the north inhospitable.

The modern town was founded in 1929. The area was originally inhabited by Scottish sheepherders, and Chileans did not really settle in the area until a 1937 program enticed a new colonist class to the region. Early pioneers left a tragic environmental legacy in the area. In order to quickly clear the land for grazing and agriculture, they set fire to the ancient forests. The fires were so intense that, 20 years later, underground root systems were still smoldering. The zone around Coyhaique was gravely scarred, and an ecological disaster of great scale is evidenced by the fallen tree trunks scattered about on the sterile, desertified land.

Timber harvesting and livestock grazing remain the main economic activities of the region with tourism gaining importance. Coyhaique has become something of a mecca for summer tourists who come mainly to fish for the monstrous trout and salmon crowding the multitude of lakes and rivers. Aquaculture in the deep fjords is also increasing with the salmon headed for Japanese and North American tables.

The city is dominated by a five-sided Plaza de Armas which creates a schizophrenic mess of the normal street grid found everywhere else in South America. **Arturo Prat** is the main commercial street, and most of the hotels are found on the northwest side of the town. The community claims 38,000 residents. Perhaps because of its remoteness, Coyhaique is one of the safest and friendliest towns in all of South America, and if you don't come for the skiing, come for the travel adventure (but bring skis).

Transportation

Coyhaique's main travel connections are by air by and sea via an excellent paved road to the port of Chacabuco. I recommend flying in and sailing out on the ferry back to Puerto Montt. Travel connections are easier this way, and visitors won't arrive tired from a long bus or ferry ride. Although the ferry is very comfortable and modern, the weather can be depressing. The bus from Osorno journeys via Bariloche and Esquel and is the cheapest way to get to Coyhaique. The drive from Puerto Montt is difficult but far easier and faster if the vehicle is put on the ferry from Chonchi on Chiloé to Chaitén. The ferry from Puerto Montt to Chacabuco carries vehicles as well.

Via Air

The Coyhaique airport has an excellent gravel runway and cozy new terminal similar to the one at Chapelco. The bus to town (6km) is US$2 while a taxi costs US$10. Some flights land on the longer paved runway at Balmaceda 55km (34 miles) south and then bus their passengers to Coyhaique.

LANChile: daily except Sunday, from Santiago:US$165, 3hr; from Puerto Montt:US$62, 1hr.

Ladeco from Santiago via 3 other cities: daily except Saturday:US$150, 5½hr; from Puerto Montt:US$57, 1½hr.

Ladeco to Balmaceda: 3/wk, from Santiago, 3½hr; from Temuco:US$104, 2hr; from Puerto Montt:1hr.

El Fraile

Via Bus
The minimal terminal is at Magallanes w/Lautaro. The terminal at Puerto Aisén is also poor but has an excellent restaurant upstairs. The last stop in Chacabuco is the ferry terminal.
Coyhaique-Puerto Aisén/Chacabuco: Expresso La Cascada, 4 buses daily, to Puerto Aisén:US$1.75, 2½ hours. Sit on south side of bus, will pick up passengers at Coyhaique hotels, change buses at Aisén for Chacabuco:US$.50, 20 min.
Osorno-Coyhaique: Turismo Lanin, new service, one each way per week, US$23, 22 hours.
Puerto Montt-Coyhaique: NO direct buses. Try local bus from Puerto Montt to Chonchi, ferry to Chaitén, local bus to Coyhaique.

Via Private Auto

From Puerto Montt:
Puerto Montt-Chaitén via Chonchi: Hwy5, 187km (116 miles), 4hr, paved, plus 6hr ferry.
Chaitén-Coyhaique: Hwy7, 420km (260 miles), 2 days, gravel.

From Chacabuco:
Chacabuco-Coyhaique: 72km (45 miles), 1½hr, paved.

From Esquel:
Esquel(Arg)-Coyhaique via Río Mayo: Hwy40, 642km (400 miles), unpaved.

Via Ferry
See *Chapter 19* for details.
Puerto Montt-Chacabuco: twice/week each direction, 26hr.
Cabin 1:US$130 each; Cabin 2:US$110 each; Bunk (*Litera*):US$40; Seat (*Butaca*):US$25, (Best seats: 15A, B, T, and U); Auto:US$63.

Hotels
First Class:
Hostería Coyhaique: 131 Magallanes, Sgl:US$50, Dbl:US$67, very comfortable and popular.
Moderate:
Hotelera San Sebastian: 496 Baquedano, Dbl:US$45, excellent view, quiet.
Hotel Los Ñires: 315 Baquedano, Sgl:US$23, Dbl:US$35, loud, fair

restaurant, poor service.
Donhotel: Moraleda 448, Sgl:US$30, Dbl:US$47, newly remodeled, good restaurant.

Budget:
Residencial Serrano: 91 Serrano, Sgl:US$10, Dbl:US$25, clean, cold.
Residencial Puerto Varas: 168 Serrano, US$7 each, homey.
Also, many homes offer *hospedaje*, check with Turismo Pollux.

Cabins:
Río Simpson: km 3, Aisén Road, US$20 each, gorgeous setting.
Most other cabin rentals are closed in the winter.

Restaurants

International:
Hostería Coyhaique: 131 Magallanes.

Typical:
Q'iubo: 712 Baquedano, beautiful dining room, very enjoyable.

Locals' Hangout:
Café Oriente: Condell w/21 de Mayo, good coffee and pastries.

Important Addresses

Foreign Exchange: Better in Puerto Montt; El Libertador, 340 Prat; Banco del Estado, Condell w/Moraleda.
Post Office: 230 Cochrane.
Telephone: 626 Barroso.
Tourist Office: Sernatur, 320 Cochrane.
Travel Agents: Turismo Pollux, 357 Dussen.
Newsstand: Millaray, Prat w/Bilbao.
Ski Shop: Tiempo Libre, 140 Condell, Loc 3, small but good.
Cinema: 321 Cochrane.
Ferries: Navimag, 340 Dussen.
Airlines: Ladeco, 190 Prat; LANChile, 215 Parra.
Bus Terminal: Magallanes w/Lautaro.
Car Rental: Auto Club Chile, 583 Bilbao; Hertz, 420 Moraleda.
DIGEDER (ski area office): 376 Dussen (at Plaza).

Chapter 21

Cerro Mirador

Ski Area Facts and Figures
Elevation: Top: 450m, 1,475ft.
             Bottom: 100m, 325ft.
Vertical Drop: 350m, 1,150ft.
Season: Early July to Late September.
Lifts: 1 Double Chair
Runs: 20:
             10% Beginner, 50% Intermediate, 30% Advanced, 10% Expert
Ticket Prices, 1990:
  Weekends: US$10 Adults Full Day, US$5 Children.
  Weekdays: US$7 Adults Full Day, US$3 Children.

Introduction

Cerro Mirador is easily the best ski area in Patagonia. It is reminiscent of some of the smaller ski resorts in Vermont and is one of the few ski hills on the continent with all tree-lined runs. Although there is just one chairlift, some 20 trails of varying difficulty fan out in every direction from the top. The panorama from the summit includes the strategically located city of Punta Arenas, the legendary Strait of Magellan, and the fabled island of Tierra del Fuego. The late sunrise, though welcome, doesn't alter the constant chill in the air, and the snow is typically thin and wind-packed. Cerro Mirador is located just a few kilometers west of the port city of Punta Arenas.

History

Cerro Mirador is owned and operated by the Club Andino of Punta Arenas. The club was founded on November 18 1938, a few months

Cerro Mirador ski trails

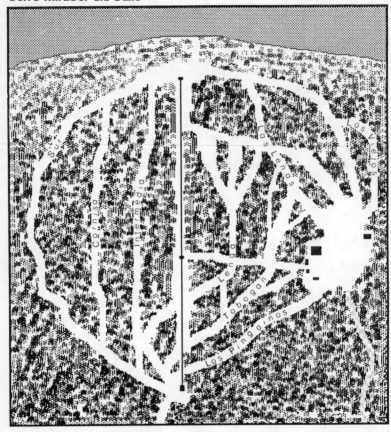

after a heroic rescue by two local skiers of the region. A major winter storm had stranded a bus 150 kilometers north of the city at the Morro Chico hotel. Marooned on this bus with the passengers was a famous and anxiously awaited film of the era called *El Rancho Grande*. After waiting a week, the cinema owner offered a valuable reward for whoever could rescue the film and bring it to the entertainment-starved population of Punta Arenas. Two young nordic skiers succeeded in the highly publicized mission, and skiing captured the hearts and minds of sports enthusiasts throughout the region.

A comfortable *refugio* was constructed for the 1939 season on a hill chosen for its convenience of access from the city. Momentous changes came in the year 1947 when the first primitive ski tow was constructed and the public land at the ski area was given to the club. The following year, a road to the *refugio* was completed. The chairlift was constructed in the late 1970s.

Geography

Cerro Mirador is located on an east-facing slope 7km (4 miles) southeast of the city and 8km from the edge of the Strait of Magellan which twists around the island of Tierra del Fuego to link the Pacific and Atlantic Oceans. While the latitude is extreme for the southern hemisphere, the ski area is as far from the pole as the heli-ski resorts of the Canadian Rockies or the European cities of Berlin and Liverpool.

The climate in the area is notorious for extreme winds and high humidity. The gale force winds arrive in the spring, and winters are characterized by cold and cloudy conditions with rain or snow a constant threat. Big storms are rare, and typical weather is sun in the city and light snow in the surrounding hills.

Skiing Tips

Cerro Mirador's runs are usually well-groomed by the club's new snowcat. The trees and bushes that line the trails grow densely making the woods impenetrable and unsafe for even expert skiers. Because of the rounded hills and thick forest, there is no good off-piste or adventure skiing terrain in the area.

True beginner skiers may have a difficult time at Cerro Mirador. The easiest descent is to follow the trails which circle around the north side of the ski area and pass in front of the *refugio*. Intermediate skiers will enjoy three long and consistent runs on the south side of the chairlift. Sur has a challenging drop at its midpoint for advanced skiers. Expert skiers will find three short but demanding chutes just below the top of the lift.

Nordic Skiing

Like Ushuaia, Punta Arenas is optimal for cross-country skiing because of its low elevation, consistent snow, and abundance of flat terrain. Races are held at the bottom of the chairlift along the flat base south of Cerro Mirador. There is a good parking area by a corral in this area. Normally there is sufficient snow to ski along the coast on either side of the city. Another idea is to head south towards the restored Fort Bulnes where skiers can enjoy a more remote and forested environment. Use your imagination as the region is completely covered with snow throughout the year.

Skier Services

The Club Andino has one of the most economical programs in South America to introduce the local population to skiing. At least 10 different programs are offered to residents. For visitors, beginner lessons run from US$16 for a one-hour private. Arrange classes with Señora Cofré in the tourist kiosk.

Base Facilities

The lodge is located at the midpoint of the hill. Most skiers arrive at the base of the chairlift, purchase their tickets there, and ride to the unloading ramp at the lift's halfway point. It is then a short walk along a contoured road to the lodge complex where skiers boot-up. That scenario is marginally easier than walking up the steep access road directly to the lodge. Only the strongest four-wheel drive vehicles can access the *refugio* on this road.

Tickets can be purchased at either the bottom of the chairlift or in the *refugio*. Half-day tickets are available on weekdays and single rides cost US$3 for adults and US$2 for children. Lift hours are 9.00am to 4.30pm seven days/week.

Change into ski attire before leaving Punta Arenas. Shoes and other equipment can be safely deposited in a corner of the lodge. Tired equipment can be rented in an annex adjacent to the *refugio* for US$5/day.

Dining

An excellent hot, home-cooked lunch can be purchased in the *refugio* for about US$3. Sandwiches and soft drinks are also available. Be sure to dine before or after the rush hour as the cafeteria is hectic when crowded.

Getting There

From Punta Arenas

The road to Cerro Mirador from Punta Arenas can be very icy. If driving, plan on using chains. Follow signs to the "*aerosilla*" for the parking lot below the bottom of the chair and the "*refugio*" for the steep access to the lodge. Otherwise, use the club's bus service. Taxis cannot succeed on the icy road and are not recommended (US$5 each way).
Via Private Auto:
Punta Arenas-Cerro Mirador via Ave Independencia: 7km (4 miles), 10min, unpaved.
Via Bus:
From Tourist Kiosk, 700 Colón: 8.30, 9.00, and 10.00am, return 4.00-5.00pm, US$2rt, 10min, Suburban-type vehicle.

Further Information
Club Andino de Punta Arenas
Oficina de Turismo, 700 Colón, Casilla 6, Punta Arenas, Chile.
Tel: 220-016

PUNTA ARENAS

Punta Arenas is unlike any other city in Chile. The town is clean, modern and upbeat and has a geography and climate that are unique in the world. Punta Arenas claims to be the southernmost city in the world, but both Río Grande and Ushuaia are farther south. The entire area is very interesting and there are many things to do which lie outside the scope of this guide. One clear day is sufficient to know Cerro Mirador; many more are needed to explore the region from Fort Bulnes to Puerto Natales.

The area has many fascinating histories which begin with glacial carving that left a flat, barren landscape, and continue with the migration of four physically and culturally diverse native tribes through the region. Western exploration began in 1520 when the Portugese navigator, Ferdinand Magellan, sailed in the region. Sir Francis Drake also explored the area in 1578. Charles Darwin studied local natural history with Captain Robert FitzRoy on the Beagle in 1833. Many of the significant geographic features bear the names of these early explorers.

Chile first established sovereignty in 1843 at Fuerte Bulnes. . In 1848, the population was moved 58km (36 miles) south to Punta Arenas ("Sandy Point") which was better situated to support an enduring community. The main economic activities in those days included sealing, whaling, and servicing the steam ship traffic with water and coal. Border disputes with Argentina were settled with an 1881 treaty that cleared the way for the development of huge *estancias*. Sheep were brought from Chiloé and the Malvinas, and wool soon became the most important regional product.

The most important industries today include the exploitation and processing of fossil fuels, commercial fishing, and international tourism. Natural gas and coal are only now beginning to be extracted on a significant scale, and the area supplies Chile's only domestic oil. These opportunities led to a 48% population growth in the region from 1972 to 1980. Punta Arenas currently boasts a young population of about 100,000. As the city has a well-developed summer tourism industry, it is very comfortable and inexpensive in the winter.

Punta Arenas stretches out along a flat plain between the ocean and the mountains. The small port facility is at the end of **Avenida Independencia** which also leads to the ski area. The main street is **Bories**. The commercial center is contained in about seven square blocks. The center of the Plaza de Armas has a huge bronze statue of Ferdinand Magellan standing tall in full regalia with naked Ono Indians cowering at his feet. The legend claims that if you kiss the polished big toe of a certain Indian, you will return someday to Punta Arenas.

Transportation

Punta Arenas has a diversity of travel connections that are slightly scaled down in the winter season. The modern airport is 17km (11 miles) north of the city. The only air connections are to Puerto Montt, but charters are also available. LANChile has an excellent bus service (US$2) that will pick-up or drop-off passengers at their hotels. A taxi can be haggled down to US$6.

There is no central bus terminal and each company has their own office from which their buses leave. Most will stop at the major hotels when leaving if arranged in advance. The ferry terminal (for Porvenir) is 1km past the *Zona Franca*. The buses and *colectivos* use it as a turnaround point (US$0.50), or take a taxi (US$3). There is no indoor facility and tickets are sold no sooner than ½hr before sailing time. The ferry ride can be cold and crowded. See *Chapter 6* for more travel details. See *Chapter 37* for a regional map.

From Puerto Montt\Osorno
Via Bus:
Osorno-Punta Arenas: Ghisoni, two/wk, US$38, 36hr.
Via Air:
LANChile: 8/wk, US$136, 2hr.
Ladeco: 6/wk, US$136, 2hr.
Via Ferry:
See *Chapter 19* for details.

From Río Gallegos
Via Private Auto:
Río Gallegos-Chile customs: Hwy3, 61km (38 miles), 1hr, unpaved.
Customs-Hwy9: Hwy 255, 146km (91 miles), 4hr, unpaved.
Hwy255-Punta Arenas: Hwy9, 55km (34 miles), 45min, paved.
Via Bus:
Río Gallegos-Punta Arenas: El Pinguino and Ghisoni, daily, US$10, 6hr.

From Ushuaia
See *Chapter 6*.

From Puerto Natales
Via Private Auto:
Puerto Natales-Punta Arenas: Hwy9, 254km (158 miles), 5hr, mostly paved but potholed.
Via Bus:
Puerto Natales-Punta Arenas: Bus Sur, 2/day, US$3, 6hr.

Hotels
First Class:
Cabo de Hornos: 1039 Gamero (east side of Plaza), Sgl:US$70, Dbl:US$83, very good, professional, ocean view, classiest restaurant.
Los Navegantes: 647 Menendez, Sgl:US$57, Dbl:US$67, nice bar, rude.
Moderate:
Colonizadores: 1690 21 de Mayo, Sgl:US$35, Dbl:US$40, Suite:US$50, closest to ocean, several blocks from center.
Mercurio: 595 Fagnano, Sgl:US$31, Dbl:US$35, older but nice, good restaurant.
Plaza: 1116 Nogueira, Sgl:US$29, Dbl:US$36, very helpful, central.
Savoy: 1073 Menendez, Sgl:US$18, Dbl:US$24, super nice, best value, businessmen's favorite.
Budget:
Montecarlo: 605 Colón, Sgl:US$8-13, Dbl:US$13-17, run down closest to tourist kiosk and ski bus.
Paris: 1116 Nogueira, 4th floor, US$8 each, central, good.
Central: 545 Balmaceda, US$6 each, common bath, well-kept.

Restaurants
Many sources tempt with talk about the king crab (*centolla*) which is unavailable in the winter months. Salmon, shellfish, and lamb are other local specialties.
International:
Union Club: on Plaza, in the Palace of Sara Braun, formal.
Centro Español: on Plaza above theater.
Typical:
Garage: 988 Montt, classic '50s decor, not to be missed.
El Infante: 875 Magallenes, tourist rip-off, avoid.
Iberia: 974 O'Higgins.

Budget:
Café Monaco: Menendez and Bories, good burgers and beer.

Important Addresses

Foreign Exchange: many, especially on Navarro between Montt and Fagnano.
Post Office: 955 Bories.
Telephone: 1116 Nogueira, 729 O'Higgins.
Tourist Office: Sernatur, 680 Seguel; Kiosk on center divider at 700 Colón.
Travel Agent: Many everywhere.
Airlines: LANChile, Navarro w/Montt; Ladeco, 924 Roca; Varig, Bosco w/Yugoslavia; Iberia, 839 Pinto; KLM, 1066 Navarro.
Car Rental: Avis, 1099 Navarro; Auto Club, 931 O'Higgins; Budget, 964 O'Higgins; Hertz, 1064 Navarro.
Bus Terminal: Bus Sur, 556 Menendez; El Pinguino, 915 Roca; Ghisoni, 975 Navarro; others by Chiloé and Menendez.
Ferry Terminal: For Porvenir: Tres Puentes, 5km N of city, 1km north of *Zona Franca*. For Puerto Montt: Navimag, 840 Independencia.
Cinema: Gran Palace, 932 Bories, classic.
Laundromat: Lavasol, 969 O'Higgins.
Ski Area Office: In tourist kiosk at 700 Colón, see Jaunita Cofré.

Part III

ARGENTINA

Geography

Argentina is South America's second largest country (2,776,900km^2, 1,072,162 miles^2). It is shaped like an elongated wedge aimed at Antarctica and is divided politically into 24 provinces. The nation's territory extends from the Atlantic seaboard in the east to Chile in the west. The crest of the Andes forms the western border (if the water flows east, it's Argentina). The *Cordillera* is highest in the north, from Malargüe to Bolivia, and becomes more rounded in the south.

The country stretches south through Patagonia, the desolate, windswept, and forsaken land south of the Río Colorado, to the 52nd parallel. The eastern half of the legendary Tierra del Fuego also belongs to Argentina. In the northeast are the Chaco and Mesopotamia, fertile areas where sheep are raised and a variety of crops are grown. These northern frontiers are shared with Uruguay, Brazil, Paraguay, and Bolivia, with most of the borders demarcated by the many rivers of the Chaco.

The center of Argentina is dominated by the vast heartland of the Pampa, a huge, featureless expanse of open prairie which supports various grasses and shrubs. The region is divided into huge *estancias* where Argentina's famous beef is produced for domestic and international markets. Argentina also claims the Islas Malvinas, or Falkland Islands.

History

Development in Argentina came late by South American standards. No large ore deposits attracted the oppressive *conquistadores*, and the local Indians were particularly hostile to early settlers. Juan Diaz de Solís "discovered" the uncharted region in 1516, and Pedro de

Mendoza proclaimed a city at Buenos Aires in 1536. The city was finally made secure around 1600 by Juan de Garay who is credited with having founded Buenos Aires on June 11 1580.

Even after independence was declared at the Congress of Tucumán on July 9 1816, the residents were not too keen on the federalist concept. Local *cabildos*, authoritative offices dominated by the upper class, actually ran the provinces until 1853 when a new constitution instituted a federalist system. Buenos Aires achieved supremacy in this period after La Plata and Paraná had served as the young nation's capital. Unlike Chile, Argentina's history is rife with episodes of military takeover. In the last 50 years alone there have been five major military *coups d'etat*.

Economics

The Argentine economy is the daily topic of conversation throughout the nation. Theories abound as to why one of the world's richest countries at the beginning of the century has since become one of the world's greatest debtors with little hope for recovery. Beginning in the 1940s, Argentina became engaged in a "reversal of development" which some scholars blame on a government preoccupied with a paranoia of leftist revolution instead of promoting economic development. Others blame the disaster on the Argentines' poor work ethic and their tendency to spend more than they earn. Massive public and private sector overspending in the 1940s and '50s was justified by an optimism that the country's vast resources would rescue it from serious debt problems.

Recent programs to control the rampant inflation, which averaged about 200% annually through the 1980s, have proved largely ineffective. From October 1989 to February 1990, the newly created Austral currency sank from 660 to 5,700 to the US Dollar! Even this aberration was taken in stride by the cynical Argentines who play a complex financial game to maintain some value in their earnings.

The main commodities produced in Argentina include beef, leather, wool, and grains. The Argentines are notorious beef eaters consuming about 80kg (175lb) each annually. Some 70% of the country's exports are agricultural, but the country maintains a large current accounts deficit in spite of huge import tariffs and other trade barriers. The nation is self-sufficient in energy due to the oil fields of Tierra de Fuego, natural gas production around Neuquén, and hydroelectric projects in the north. Argentina is the world's fifth largest wine producer, and the best vineyards are in the Mendoza and San Juan Provinces. Economic growth was nonexistent in the stagnant decade of the '80s.

Argentina

Demographics

Argentina's 32 million habitants (1990) are the continent's most sophisticated people. They are far more European than any other group on the continent, and the native population has been all but wiped out. From 1857 to 1930, six million Europeans relocated to Argentina with Italians and Spaniards predominating. Many Germans also immigrated at the end of World War I, and there is a significant British community.

Argentina's population is 85% urban with 40%, or about 13.5 million, living in the greater Buenos Aires metropolitan area. South America's highest standard of living is evidenced by a 95% literacy rate and a per capita income of around US$2,750. The residents of Buenos Aires, called *Porteños*, are proud that their city was once considered the "Paris of South America."

What really sets the Argentines apart, however, is not their sophistication but rather their pride and gregariousness. This tradition is passed down from the *gauchos*, Argentina's men of the plains. The people of the Pampas were proud and independent and lived with a certain code of honor, bravery, faith in their country's future, and complete disregard for the law. The richly costumed, *maté* drinking *gauchos* wandered the Pampas in search of wild cattle and horses whose skins they tanned and backs they broke. Living a lifestyle of exploiting the seemingly limitless resources of the endless Pampas, the *gauchos* were free-wheeling subsistence hunters. Their glory years lasted from 1775 to 1875 when the Pampas came to be controlled by large *estancieros*. As the lands were fenced to control the wandering herds, the *gauchos* were reduced to the indentured service of the ranches as lowly cowhands. The romantacized lifestyle of the *gaucho* survives today in every Argentine.

Modern Politics

Argentina's most famous modern politician is Juan Domingo Perón who with his wives, Eva, and later Isabelita, ruled Argentina from 1946 to 1955 and again in 1973 and 1974. Perón was a colonel in the army when he entered politics and built his strength around several huge labor unions which he basically organized and controlled for his own political gain. Although Perón was extremely powerful and popular, he is largely credited with destroying the Argentine economy.

After Perón's death in 1974, the government was run for a short time by his wife and vice-president, Isabelita. She was overthrown by the military in 1976 due to the virtual anarchy that controlled the streets. General Jorge Videla was installed as the Junta's appointed

President in 1978 and began the "Dirty War" to control the mayhem that had mocked the political and economic life of Argentina. His policies were continued by Generals Roberto Viola, and Leopoldo Galtieri. An estimated 20,000 citizens simply disappeared in this brutal period. General Reynaldo Bignone finally led the nation to war with Great Britain over the long-festering dispute over the possession of the small chain of South Atlantic islands they call Malvinas.

Due to the quick and humiliating defeat at the hands of the British Navy, the generals were forced to return the country to civilian rule. On October 30 1983, Raúl Alfonsín, the standard bearer for the UCR (Radical) party, was elected President with great hopes for economic recovery and justice to the generals. The highlight of Alfonsín's administration was the Austral Plan which introduced a new currency and actually controlled inflation for nearly 18 months. By the time his term was over though, Argentina's lack of confidence had plunged the economy back to where it was at the heady times of Alfonsín's inauguration. The generals were in jail however, after receiving short sentences.

Carlos Menem's election in 1989 represented a turn away from the pragmatic approach of Alfonsín. Without a concrete plan, but with an Argentine flair for the dramatic, Menem's victory represents a return to power of the Peronists, formally called the *Partido Justicialista*. A former provincial governor of Syrian descent, Menem presents a flamboyant personality with long, wavy hair and silver, lamb chop sideburns that reach his chin. His term began ominously with the sudden death of his finance minister the day after his inauguration. In spite of this initial setback, Argentina seems to be recovering slowly.

Chapter 22

Los Penitentes

Ski Area Facts and Figures	
Elevation:	Top: 3,194m; 10,479ft.
	Bottom: 2,580m; 8,465ft.
Vertical Drop:	614m; 2,014ft.
Season:	Early July to Late September.
Lifts:	7:
	2 Double Chairs, 1 T-Bar, 4 Poma Lifts
Runs:	25:
	20% Beginner, 30% Intermediate, 30% Advanced, 20% Expert
Ticket Prices, 1990: US$20 Adults Full Day.	

Introduction

Los Penitentes is a mid-sized ski resort on the international highway between Santiago and Mendoza. Penitentes began operations in 1979 and fills the huge gap between Mendoza's local resort, Vallecitos, and the international-level development of Portillo, 30km (19 miles) west. It serves a national market of weekenders from Mendoza and ski weekers from the cities of Santa Fe, Córdoba, Tucumán, and Buenos Aires.

Penitentes is characterized by a few simple lifts which ascend the base of some magnificent mountains. With the summit of Aconcagua, the highest peak in the Western Hemisphere, about 25km (15 miles) distant, it is easy to imagine the ruggedness of the terrain. But unlike Portillo which has a higher elevation, the snow at Los Penitentes is often thin even when Las Leñas and Portillo have good coverage. When it does snow, the avalanche problems at Penitentes are more severe than at any other ski resort in South America, and many local *Mendocinos* refuse to risk skiing these slopes.

History

The Penitentes region, being located in the Uspallata Valley and on the route of the Trans-Andean Railroad, shares much of its early ski history with Portillo. The British and Scandinavian engineers who worked on the railway undoubtably skied in this area, too. Once the railway was completed, Argentine skiers also used the train for access to the ski runs, although the skiing activities were not as organized as they were at Portillo.

In the days before the highway was completed, Los Penitentes, which is actually the name of a nearby peak on the opposite side of the valley, was known as Kilometer 151. This was a railroad stop between Punta de Vacas and Puente del Inca where trains detoured from the main track to allow others to pass and refill water tanks. The ski hill was 1km east of and below this depot. The army group stationed here inaugurated a portable ski lift on July 9 1957 and invited the public to join in the novel sport. In addition, skiers could usually stay overnight in the *casino* of the Compañia de Esquiadores de Montaña, also owned by the army.

In the early 1970s, a group of Mendozan skiers organized the Club de Esquí Cruz de Caña to further develop skiing in the area. This title comes from the name of a river and peak in the Penitentes ski area. In support of their goals, the provincial government of Mendoza gave the club a 99-year concession to some 300 hectares (750 acres) of land in 1973. This land was administered by an organization formed by the club for this purpose called the Associación Mendocina Actividad de Montaña, or AMAM. With a donated *refugio* and surface lifts locally built by Pedro Lauryssens of Matriceria Cuyo, skiing finally took root in the Uspallata Valley in 1975.

This arrangement worked well for club members, but skiing was still not commercially viable. So, in the interest of the sport, the ski club cooperated when it was approached by a private concern to develop a ski resort at the site. The contractual arrangement called for the club to renounce its concessionary rights in order that the investment group could then purchase the land to build their base. After the land was purchased, a parcel would be donated to the club for its own purposes. This scenario progressed until it was time to return a parcel to the club, and the group has yet to comply with the agreement.

The Modern Era

By 1979, the new Penitentes group had the Las Pircas double chairlift and a few short poma lifts operating. In the early '80s, two more lifts and a hotel were added, and in 1986, four other modern

Los Penitentes

hotels were built at the base of the young ski area.

With about 25% of the potential ski area now utilized, there is ample space for more runs. The future lies in an area which they call Tres Mil, a large area around the summit of the Cruz de Caña mountain east of the existing lifts. They hope to reach it with either a long gondola or two triple chairs, but it is doubtful that these plans will be realized soon.

Geography

Los Penitentes is located in the Valley of the Cruz de Caña which branches north from the Uspallata Valley. The ski area is surrounded by the high peaks of Santa María to the west, Cerro Leñas to the north, and Cerro Cruz de Caña to the east. On the south side are the Río de las Cuevas and the opposing slopes of Cerro Penitentes, so named because of the multitude of rocky spires which cover its north face.

Skiing Tips

More than one day will not be required for most skiers to fully explore the slopes, and the ski area is best visited as a brief stop between Portillo and Las Leñas. The first chairlift, called Las Pircas, reaches the top of the Lomo, a flat bench which splits the ski area into two vertical parts.

All the beginner terrain is spread out east from the base complex on four popular rope tows with a run on either side of each. Intermediate skiers will find a challenge at the top of San Antonio. Advanced and expert skiers will traverse left from the top of the Guanaco chairlift to ski the Morro Godoy and Tobogan runs. On the right side, try the Valle Azúl bowl which drops into the Cruz de Caña Valley. Or, try traversing high across this canyon to ski the west and south-facing slopes of the Cruz de Caña Mountain.

Adventure Skiing

There are many off-piste skiing possibilities in the Penitentes area. The most obvious areas are on the slopes of Cruz de Caña and Cerro Leñas, but more serious overnight tours can originate from the ski area as well. The main chute at the ski area is reached with a high traverse, past Tobogan, to the wide and looming east-facing chute on Cerro Santa María. Skiing the main bowl itself is not an extremely technical challenge, but some of the entrances are demanding. Another popular excursion is to ski to Punta de Vacas from the top of Cruz de Caña.

Los Penitentes ski trails

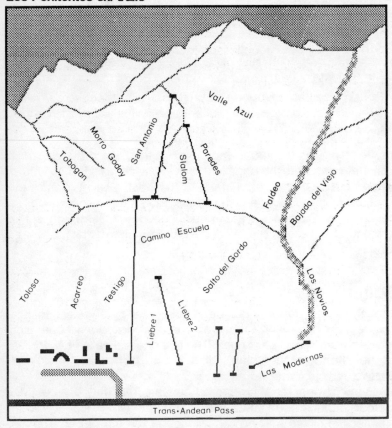

Extreme avalanche danger exists at the ski area. The bottom of the Guanacos chair has been wiped out several times by avalanches. Most avalanches are directed away from the base area by the ridge at the top of Las Pircas. Slides from the Valle Azúl and other starting zones often run down the Cruz de Caña canyon to the beginner areas. Skiers should use extreme caution when skiing at Los Penitentes, and should probably avoid the area after storms.

Nordic Skiing

Good ski tours could also be based at the ski area, but the extreme avalanche danger again demands serious attention. If the snow coverage is sufficient, the Uspallata Valley is wide and flat enough for great touring between the small villages.

Skier Services

The ski school at Penitentes is headed by Arturo Delgado who oversees a group of about 45 local instructors. Rates range from US$10 for a half-day group lesson to US$20 for a 55 minute private. Day-care rates run from US$10 for a half-day to US$100 for a week's worth of all-day supervision.

The ski area has a group of 12 professional ski patrollers who are qualified in first aid procedure but engage in little avalanche control. A fully equipped medical clinic with X-ray facilities is located at the base, and the nearest hospital is in Mendoza.

Base Facilities

Tickets can be purchased in the slopeside building with the orange-colored roof. Lift hours are from 9.00am to 6.00pm. There is a check facility in the cafeteria for visitors. Otherwise, ski and boot storage rooms are located in each of the hotels.

The Le Trac ski rental facility is located next to the ticket window. Rentals in 1990 cost US$12 for an adult and US$9 for minors. The equipment consists of Head skis, Tyrolia bindings, and Dolomite boots, with some competition-level equipment available at a higher price. Nordic gear may also be available.

Dining

The **Barraca del Lomo** is a snack bar located on the ridge by the top of the Pircas chair lift. Basic sandwiches and drinks are available. At the base, most of the hotels and the *refugio* of the Cruz de Caña Club have restaurants. Breakfast and dinner are included with some hotel packages. **La Herradura** is the busiest lunch spot at the base with cafeteria-style service and prices.

The Hotels

The ski area operates seven different lodging options. The most economical is at the **Hostería Puente del Inca** located 7km east of the ski area (daily transportation is included to and from the ski area). The most economical at the ski area is the **Hostería Penitentes**. The **Apart-Hotel Lomas Blancas** is the most expensive with condominium-type rooms for up to five guests. The **Edificio Portezuelo, Horcones, Juncal,** and **Tolosa** hotels complete the list of options.

Prices are difficult to compare because each hotel has distinctive meal, transportation, lift ticket, and insurance programs. The resort prefers to sell packaged ski-weeks. Individual nights are accepted only when the rooms cannot be filled with week-long guests.

Other Lodging
Ayelen is a modern lodge located across the highway from the ski slopes. This complex features both a hotel with suites and jacuzzi tubs and a less expensive *hostería*. Prices range from US$50 to US$140 for double occupancy with breakfast in the hotel, to US$20 to US$56 for a single in the hostel. Three and seven-night plans are also available and more complete meal packages can be arranged. The most economical option at the ski area is in the *refugio* of the Cruz de Caña Club. Space is limited, so check in Mendoza before leaving.

The only other good option for staying in the region is at Uspallata's new and recommended **Valle Andino** hotel. The hotel at Portillo is a close but impractical option due to customs formalities at the borders. Otherwise, Mendoza has plenty of inexpensive lodging and good daily transportation to the ski area.

Getting There

From Mendoza
Via Private Auto:
Mendoza-Uspallata: Hwy7, 99km (62 miles), 1¼hr, paved.
Uspallata-Los Penitentes: Hwy7, 67km (42 miles), 1hr, paved.
Via Bus:
Penitentes car: US$200 for 4 people, private auto.
Expresso Uspallata: local bus, daily 6.00 and 10.00am, also 7.00am weekends and holidays, 4½hr, US$5.
Turismo Jocoli: daily, 3½hr, included with lift ticket purchase.
Try other travel agents on Las Heras in Mendoza.

From Portillo
Via Private Auto:
Portillo-Los Penitentes: Hwy7, 30km (19 miles), 2hr w/customs, paved.
Via Bus:
Arrange Santiago to Mendoza car service: 2hr, US$16 each.
Ask for rides from Los Libertadores customs house near Portillo.

Further Information and Reservations
Operadores Penitentes
420 Las Heras, Loc 3, (5500) Mendoza. Tel: (061) 234-049, FAX:

Los Penitentes

(061) 233-239, Telex: 55154
In Santiago:
Agustinas 1022, Of.702, Santiago, Chile. Tel: 717-559
Los Penitentes Centro de Esquí, SA
62 Rivadavia, Piso3, (5500) Mendoza. Tel: 241-979, Telex: 55374 SKIAR
Ayelen
1248 España, Of 55, or Martínez de Rosas 489, (5500) Mendoza.
Tel: (061) 250-609, FAX: (061) 250-729, Telex: 55240 UNION AR.

Los Penitentes Centro de Esquí S.A.

Argentina: Mendoza to Malargüe and Portillo

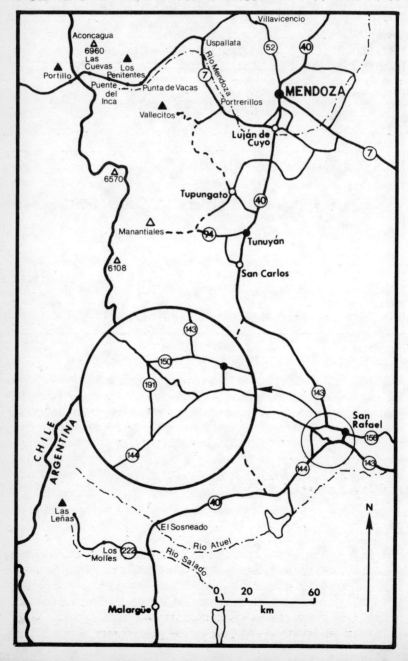

Chapter 23

Vallecitos

Ski Area Facts and Figures

Elevation: Top: 3,300m; 10,825ft.
Bottom: 2,900m; 9,510ft.
Vertical Drop: 400m; 1,315ft.
Season: Late June to Late September.
Lifts: 5:
1 Double Chair, 2 Single Chairs, 1 T-Bar, 1 Surface Tow
Runs: 8:
20% Beginner, 60% Intermediate, 20% Advanced
Ticket Prices, 1990:
  US$10 Adults Full Day, US$6 Children Full Day.

Introduction

Vallecitos is a small ski area owned and operated by the Ski Club Mendoza. Skiing at Vallecitos is characterized by open, treeless, rolling slopes covered with abundant snow. It is popular with the local *Mendocinos* when they just want to get on the snow for a day or when they can't afford the pricier skiing at Los Penitentes or Las Leñas. There is plenty of advanced terrain both in the ski area and out-of-bounds and most skiers will need only one full day to fully explore the lift-serviced slopes.

History

Vallecitos is the oldest ski area in the Mendoza area and ranks a distant second to Bariloche in Argentine ski history. The first skiers to test the snow in the wide moraine-valley came in 1947 when the provincial government first promoted skiing to develop the tourism industry in the mountainous and inaccessible region.

The first lift, financed and built by the government, was a 170m-long (560ft) funicular that carried skiers alongside a short run named San Bernardo in an area below the present-day ski area. Later, the road to Vallecitos was constructed and several *refugios* were erected at what was to be the base of an ambitious new ski area.

Unable to attract commercial interest, the land around the slopes of Vallecitos was given to the Ski Club Mendoza (founded 1952) which had recently split from the more climbing oriented Club Andino. In 1954, the first surface lift began operation and, in 1964, Mendoza's first chairlift was erected.

Fortunately for local skiers, Francisco Guiñazú was a dedicated skier and devoted member of the ski club. As an engineer who owned a large metal-working yard in Mendoza, Sr Guiñazú embraced ski lift construction as his new hobby and sideline. In 1964, he not only built the La Canaleta double chair at Vallecitos, but also installed Bariloche's first chairlift.

Vallecitos ski trails

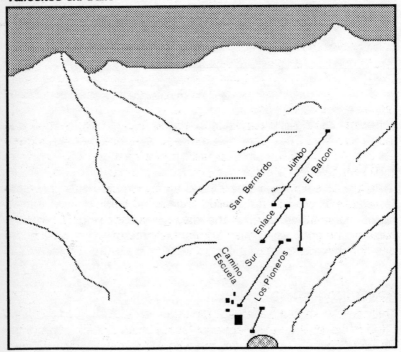

Geography

Vallecitos sits in one of the glacier-carved Valles del Plata. It is located on the north side of the wide, moraine valley of the Cordón de La Jaula, with most of the runs facing south-southeast. The ski area base is positioned just above the normal snow line, but good skiing can often be had below the ski area as well. Storms of various sizes approach from the southeast and the Atlantic Ocean.

Skiing Tips

All the lifts were built locally by Francisco Guiñazú and his crew. The prestige and economics of local manufacture is unmatched anywhere else on the continent, but it should be noted that the lifts do not really meet international standards. For example, the double chair can be very difficult to load due to poor loading ramp conditions and the sloped approach of the empty chairs. It is suggested that even experienced skiers attempt to load the narrow chair alone the first time.

In addition, both chairlifts sag low between towers. Skis ride along the snow pack for much of the ascent bringing new confusion to the term *aerosilla*. The Escuela single chair, also called Enlace, features an armrest-less seat with easy side exiting between towers. Derailments are not uncommon but are repaired expediently.

These problems are not listed to warn skiers of dangerous conditions. None represent a serious safety hazard due to the slow speed and low height of the lifts. It is noted, however, that all skiers need to pay attention to these situations and should expect some inconveniences. Please have patience when trouble occurs, and recall the low ticket price.

Beginner skiers are usually sent to the Escuela single chair and the Enlace run. They can then return to the base by following the School Road. Intermediate skiers should head up the valley to explore the variety of runs and pitches of the Las Morenas T-Bar.

Advanced skiers should ski the south-facing sidewalls above the Canaleta trail. This area is called the Filo de Loma Blanca. Take a high traverse from the top of the chair to access the long ridge that parallels the chair, to choose from a multitude of short, small bowls and thin, twisting chutes.

Adventure Skiing

Thrillseekers should traverse a bit farther around the Loma Blanca ridge to discover an excellent east-facing chute system north of the ski area. These can be accessed with the Canaleta chair if skiers remember to traverse out high enough to return to the base. Another idea is to ski the large bowl below the ski area that looms above one of the access road's switchbacks. A rocky traverse leads to this bowl but it is the easiest accessed off-piste skiing in the area.

Vallecitos has the best off-piste skiing in Argentina, and observant skiers will easily find a great deal of out-of-bounds skiing. Ideas include the large bowls northeast of the ski area. These are reached with an hour-long, ridgeline hike, and the long run-out canyon below empties to a convenient location on the Vallecitos road. More strenuous efforts can be made in the Rincón Valley south of the ski area. As with other locations in the *Alto Cordillera*, avalanche danger can be extreme.

Nordic Skiing

Good nordic skiing can be enjoyed in the Vallecitos area in spite of the high elevation. The two relatively flat glacier valleys in the area provide vast expanses of skiable terrain in a zone of otherwise rugged and inaccessible mountains. Follow either the main Vallecitos valley to its origin, or try the geographically similar Rincón Valley farther south.

Skier Services

A small group of local instructors is based in the La Canaleta lodge to assist new skiers with their developing techniques. In addition, the Ski Club has a body of nine professional ski patrollers to maintain the slopes and provide safety services. A new medical clinic with a local doctor has been assembled at the base, with the nearest hospital in Mendoza.

Base Facilities

Tickets can be purchased on the deck outside the main base lodge. Lift hours are from 10.00am to 5.00pm, but the lifts generally open about one-half hour after the bus arrives.

Equipment can be safely stashed in a corner of the main lodge. Fairly modern Atomic ski equipment is available for rent at the ski area. This service is in concession to a new Mendoza shop, and prices were unavailable.

Dining

A small snack bar operates at the top of the double chairlift. Basic sandwiches and beverages are also available in the **La Canaleta** base lodge. Prices are inexpensive and service adequate. More formal meals can be found at the other *refugios* in the area. Ask around for current offerings.

Vallecitos

Lodging

There are some 30 structures around the base of Vallecitos. Several are private homes, but a few offer public lodging. Check with the **Plaza Hotel** in Mendoza for the best lodging, including the **Gran Hotel Potrerillos**, located 20km (12 miles) below the ski area. They also have management concessions for the **San Antonio** (6km below Vallecitos) and the **Cerro Nevado** lodges. Other options include the **Refugio Ski Club**, the **San Bernardo**, and the older **Club Andes Talleres**. There is also a good new hotel called **Valle Andino** 53km (33 miles) north of Potrerillos in Uspallata. Most skiers will be more comfortable in Mendoza.

Getting There

From Mendoza

Via Private Auto:
Mendoza-Potrerillos: Hwy7, 44km (27 miles), 40min, paved.
Potrerillos-Vallecitos: Hwy86, 21km (12 miles), 30min, ½ paved.
Via Bus:
Turismo Jocoli: Leave 8.00am, Return 8.00pm, 2hr, included with lift ticket purchase.
Try also Turismo Mendoza, Turismo Vitar, Maguitur, or Alventur in Mendoza.

Further Information

Valles del Plata
España 1340, P 10, Of 10, (5500) Mendoza, Argentina. Tel: 250-972.
Plaza Hotel
1142 Chile, (5500) Mendoza. Tel: 23-3248, FAX: 23.3000 INT 178, Telex: 55243 PLA HO

MENDOZA

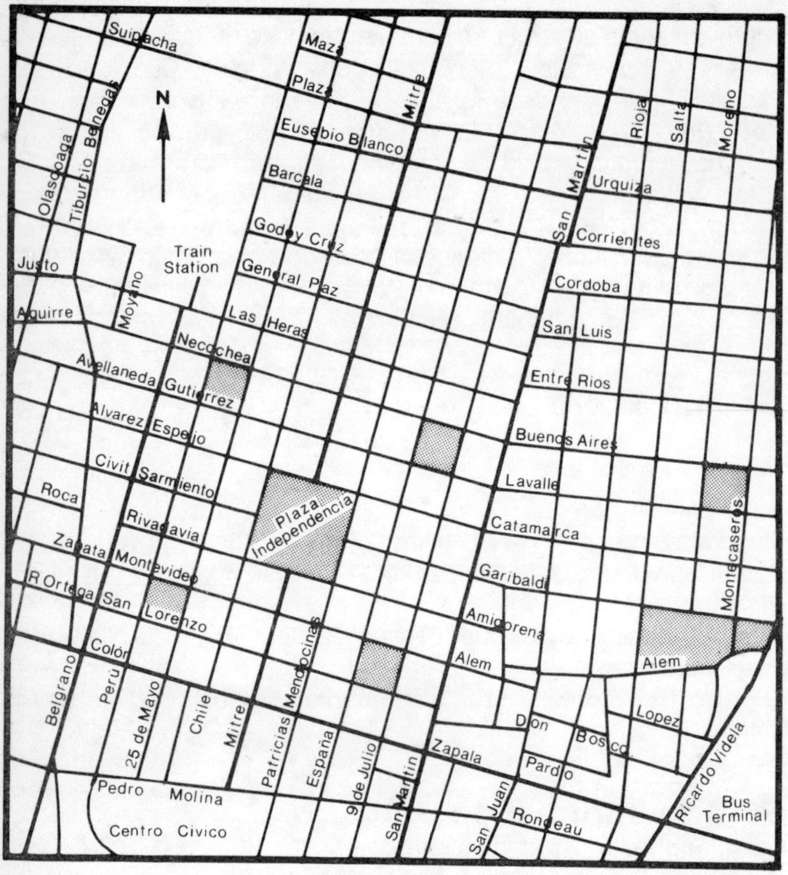
Suipacha
Maza
Plaza
Eusebio Blanco
Barcala
Godoy Cruz
General Paz
Las Heras
Necochea
Avellaneda
Gutierrez
Alvarez
Espejo
Civit
Sarmiento
Roca
Rivadavia
Zapata
Montevideo
R Ortega
San Lorenzo
Colón
Belgrano
Perú
25 de Mayo
Chile
Mitre
Patricias Mendocinas
España
9 de Julio
San Martin
Pedro Molina
Centro Civico
Olascoaga
Tiburcio Benegas
Justo
Aguirre
Moyano
Train Station
N
Mitre
Plaza Independencia
San Martin
Rioja
Salta
Moreno
Urquiza
Corrientes
Cordoba
San Luis
Entre Rios
Buenos Aires
Lavalle
Catamarca
Garibaldi
Amigorena
Alem
Montecaseros
Alem
Lopez
Don Bosco
Zapala
Pardo
San Juan
Rondeau
Ricardo Videla
Bus Terminal

Chapter 24

Mendoza

Introduction

Mendoza is a refreshing change from Santiago, its neighbor on the opposite side of the Andes. It is a much smaller city that doesn't suffer from the omnipresent smog which chokes the Chilean capital and is also more modern. The verdant streets and clear air complement the new, low structures mandated by the regions frequent earthquakes. Tiled sidewalks and a young, active, and healthy-looking population augment the invigorating and refreshing spirit of Mendoza.

Standing in the middle of a downtown street, it is difficult to believe that this is one of Argentina's biggest cities. With large and leafy trees growing at specific intervals along the sidewalks, every street in Mendoza is covered with a lush arch that blocks all views of the surrounding concrete walls. These green tunnels are maintained by a system of *acequias*, meter-deep water channels that flow alongside or underneath every sidewalk in the city. The troughs are flooded each day, cleansing the city, and reinvigorating the trees and Mendoza itself. The city's motto is painted on just about every available surface, unnecessarily reminding residents that they live in "*una ciudad en flor*," a blossoming city.

History

Mendoza was founded on March 2 1561 by Pedro de Castillo. It served as the base for the Liberator General José de San Martín in his support of the Chilean independence movement.

Mendoza was actually a part of Chile for many years, and at times the city seems to have more in common with Chile than Argentina. Mendoza has been destroyed or damaged several times throughout its long history by the strong earthquakes which frequently rock the region. The worst destruction occurred on March 20 1861, and a 1985 quake left several thousand homeless.

Geography

Situated on the northern edge of Argentina's *pampas* and at the base of the east slope of the Andes, Mendoza is geographically similar to a smaller and drier Denver. It has a far more moderate climate than the Colorado city though, and its 755m (2,475ft) elevation means snow is a rare sight on the city's streets. The weather is characterized by dry, warm days and clear, cold evenings. Storms which blanket the nearby mountains often bring gusty, hot winds that raise fine dust and scatter dead leaves throughout the city.

Mendoza is Argentina's gateway to the *Cordillera*. In the summer, the city is the base for international climbing expeditions to Aconcagua, the Americas' highest peak. In the winter, Mendoza is the headquarters for Argentina's best alpine skiing, with four ski areas within a three hour drive.

Historically, all the skiing activity was centered up the dramatic Uspallata Valley at Puente del Inca and Portillo. In those days, die-hard skiers drove all day, bouncing along cross ties through dripping and frozen railroad tunnels, to reach the privileged slopes of Portillo.

The Andes in this area are distinguished not only by Aconcagua but also by the existence of two frontal ranges with high summits east of the main *Cordillera*. The Cordón del Plata features the small ski field of Vallecitos on its northern end. The Cordón de Portillo is the southern extension of the frontal range and planners hope to someday develop the Manantiales project on its east flank.

Demographics and Economics

Mendoza is a rapidly growing region of about 650,000 people who call themselves *Mendocinos*. Included in the greater metropolitan area are the cities of Godoy Cruz, Las Heras, Guaymallén, and Maipú. Mendoza is the capital of the province of the same name and the biggest city in the Cuyo region.

Important economic activities include manufacturing and agriculture. Most of the cultivated land is covered with vineyards, and Mendoza is Argentina's most important wine-producing region. Alfalfa and a variety of fruits are also grown in areas close to the mountains where irrigation is easier.

Oil is an important product of the region, and there is other mining activity in the Andean foothills.

The City

Mendoza is a well-planned city of one-way streets and wide sidewalks. The downtown area is bordered by the park-like Civic Center on the south and the huge Parque General San Martín with a golf course, lake, zoo, and university to the east. The west end of the city is bordered by the Cacique Guaymallén Canal, across which lies the central bus terminal.

The main street, **San Martín**, runs north-south and is one of the few bidirectional streets in the city. Everything in Mendoza can be described in relation to this main commercial boulevard which is lined with many sidewalk cafes. The downtown quadrangle can be described as lying east of San Martín with Colón, Belgrano (which parallels the railroad tracks), and Las Heras forming the other borders. Mendoza's center is at the four block wide Plaza Independencia. Four other block-sized plazas, named Chile, Italia, España, and San Martín, are symmetrically positioned in the downtown area.

Other noteworthy streets in the city include **Lavalle** for movies and entertainment, **San Juan** for books and culture, and **Las Heras** for travel agencies, ski shops, and handicrafts. **Sarmiento** is the new *paseo*, or walking street, which runs from San Martín to the Plaza Independencia and eventually reaches the municipal park. Mendoza is great for safe and wandering walks, but street hikers need to be alert for uneven tiles on the sidewalks and the deep, rock-lined water courses which are crossed with little cement bridges in varying degrees of repair.

Things to See and Do

Business hours in Mendoza are from 9.00am to 2.00pm in the mornings and from 4.30pm to 8:30 or 9.00pm in the evenings. Around 3.00pm, it is impossible to do any sort of business. Good purchases include leather and wine with prices moderately less than in Buenos Aires.

Be sure not to miss the Parque San Martín and its stadium and hill where romantic views of the city are enjoyed after dark. In front of the office of the city's news daily, *Los Andes*, on San Martín, current national and international headline stories are displayed on chalkboards in flawless handwritten script for passersby.

Transportation

Mendoza has a clean, modern, and well-organized bus station located 2km from the center of the city. If walking, follow Alem to the underpass which exits between the enclosed international wing and the outdoor regional section. Across the modern C-shaped terminal is the wing for local buses. Warren Miller's ski movies are often shown, in Spanish, on the terminal's 20 video monitors. A good *guardería* is located in the international wing. Excellent travel connections are made to all points of South America from Mendoza's bus terminal.

The train station, on the other hand, is decrepit and no services are available. It, too, is located just 2km from the city.

The El Plumerillo airport is about 6km from the city. A taxi costs around US$6 and there is no public bus service from the airport. Expect flights between Santiago and Mendoza to increase significantly as relations between the new democratic governments of Chile and Argentina improve.

From Buenos Aires
Via Private Auto:
Hwy7: 1037km (644 miles), 12hr, paved, rough.
Via Bus:
TAC, others: 14hr (overnight service), 1st:US$43, Regular:US$34.
Via Air:
Aerolíneas Argentinas: 22/wk, 1½hr, US$120.
Austral: 18/wk, 1½hr, US$115.
Via Train:
El Libertador: 2/wk, 13hr, bed:US$69, Pullman:US$48.
El Aconcagua: daily, 14½hr, bed:US$37, Pullman:US$26.

From Santiago
See *Chapter 6*.

From San Rafael
Via Private Auto:
San Rafael-Pareditas: Hwy143 to 156, 109km (68 miles), 1¼hr, paved.
Pareditas-Mendoza: Hwy40, 127km (79 miles), 1½hr, paved.
Via Bus:
TAC, Uspallata: 4/day, 3½hr, US$4.
Via Air:
Aerolíneas Argentinas: 5/wk, 40min.

From Bariloche
Via Bus:
TAC: 3/wk, 24hr, US$51.
Via Air:
TAN via Neuquen, or Aerolíneas Argentinas via Buenos Aires.

To Ski Areas
Las Leñas: TAC bus, daily 6.00am and 12.20pm in season, 7hr, US$8; Expresso Uspallata, weekends and holidays 7.00am, 7hr, US$9; others from Las Heras agencies leaving 1.00am.
Los Penitentes: Jocoli bus, daily, 3½hr, included with purchase of lift ticket; Expresso Uspallata, local bus, daily 6.00 and 10.00am, weekends and holidays 7.00am added, 4½hr, US$5.
Vallecitos: Jocoli bus, daily, daily 8.00am, 2½hr, included w/lift ticket purchase.

Hotels
Deluxe:
Plaza: 1142 Chile, Sgl:US$48, Dbl:US$64, on Plaza Independencia by Casino, classically formal, reserve here for Gran Hotel Potrerillos and Vallecitos hotels.
Aconcagua: 545 Aconcagua, Sgl:US$55, Dbl:US$70, modern, international tourists' favorite, 5 blocks from center.
Huentala: 1007 de la Reta (at end of Rivadavia), Sgl:US$43, Dbl:US$56, modern and central.
First Class:
International: 720 Sarmiento, Sgl:US$26, Dbl:US$37, in quiet neighborhood, many rooms w/balcony.
Balbi: 340 Las Heras, Sgl:US$32, Dbl:US$40, classic hotel on busy commercial street, good location for skiers.
Nutibara: 867 Mitre, Sgl:US$29, Dbl:US$38, quieter street, big sunny lobby, friendly.
Moderate:
Alcor: 86 Paz, Sgl:US$14, Dbl:US$18, best value, friendly.
Royal: 1550 9 de Julio, Sgl:US$16, Dbl:US$24, good location.
Rincón Vasco: 590 Las Heras, Sgl:US$16, Dbl:US$21, good restaurant.
Budget:
Casino: 688 Gutiérrez, Sgl:US$11, Dbl:US$14, all w/private bath.
Shorthorn: 1532 Mendocinas, Sgl:US$10, Dbl:US$15, good value but strange reception.
City: 95 Paz, Sgl:US$10, Dbl:US$14, dark, dismal.

Restaurants

A regional specialty in Mendoza is *paella*, the Spanish rice casserole that is served in its many forms at all the good Italian restaurants. Ask the waiter to make a good local wine selection.

International:
Trevi: 68 Las Heras, formal, mostly Italian, large menu.
Typical:
Vecchia Roma: 1615 España, best Italian food in Mendoza.
Montecatini: 370 Paz, excellent Italian food, popular.
Barbaro: 914 San Martín, good steaks.
Budget:
Il Tucco: 68 Sarmiento, good, inexpensive pizzas and pastas.
Locals' Favorites:
Auto Club: San Martín w/Amigorena, businessmen's coffee break.
Soppelsa: Civít w/Belgrano, popular ice cream spot, 50 flavors.
Juan Sebastián Bar: 757 Villanueva, sandwiches and beer, popular with young crowd.
Vegetarian:
Govinda's: 840 San Juan, Indian-type food, friendly.

Important Addresses

Foreign Exchange: Cambio Santiago, 1177 San Martín; Exprinter, 1198 San Martín; Maguitur, 1203 San Martín; Cash, 1173 and 1297 San Martín; others, shop around for best rates.
Post Office: San Martín w/Colón.
Telephones: 1574 Chile.
Consulates: Chile, Civít w/Rodriguez; Bolivia, 1357 9 de Julio.
Hospitals: Central, 376 Alem; Civít, San Martín Park; Lagomaggiore, Av Gordillo.
Tourist Office: 1143 San Martín.
Travel Agents: American Express, 80 Rivadavia; Jocoli, 601 Las Heras; Vitar, 494 Las Heras; many others on Las Heras.
Airlines: Aerolíneas, 82 Sarmiento; Austral, 921 San Martín; LANChile, 1126 9 de Julio, Loc 27; Ladeco, 144 Sarmiento; TAN, 126 Rivadavia.
Car Rentals: Avis, 228 Espejo; National, 127 Sarmiento, Loc 30; ACA, San Martín w/Amigorena.
Bus Terminal: end of Alem (through underpass) on Videla w/Zapata; TAC ticket office, 65 Sarmiento.
Train Station: end of Las Heras w/Belgrano.
Newsstands: along San Martín, especially by Sarmiento; Kiosk in center of *galería* at 43 Sarmiento.
Books: Centro Internacional del Libro, 1105 San Juan, English, French, and German, excellent selection.

Mendoza

Cinemas: 1-200 Lavalle, others.
Casino: 1123 25 de Mayo.
Laundromats: Laverap, 543 Colón; La Lavendería, 338 San Lorenzo.
Ski Shops: Andesport, 390 Rufino Ortega; Chamonix, 249 Barcala; several others on Las Heras.
Ski Area Offices:
Operadores Penitentes, 420 Las Heras.
Valles del Plata, 1340 España, 10th Floor, Of 7.
Valle de Las Leñas, 1233 San Martín, Galeria Caracol, Loc 70.
Other Ski Related Addresses:
Lahuen-Co (Los Molles), 12 San Lorenzo (at San Martín), 1st Floor, Of 8.
Ski Club Mendoza, 650 Acceso Este (by bus terminal).
Club de Esquí Cruz de Caña, 354 Clark.
Ayelen Hotel (in Penitentes), 1248 España, Of 55.
Valle Manantiales, 1169 Olascoaga.

Chapter 25

Valle Manantiales

The other Portillo pass, the one Darwin crossed in his journey to Mendoza, and the one General San Martín traversed in his return from a successful campaign to liberate Chile, is the site of the grand Manantiales ski area proposal. Located east of Tunuyán (half the distance between Mendoza and Las Leñas), the Manantiales Valley has abundant snow, an ideal climate, and huge mountains. Glaciers still carve the 6,000m mountains that lie within the developers' boundaries.

The plan calls for a staged construction of a resort with 5,000 beds in a variety of hotels, *refugios*, and cabins set in a compact, mountainside villa. A total of 10,000 skiers could eventually ride the seven chairlifts and nine surface lifts planned to serve the 60km (35 miles) of trails on 3,700 hectares (9,145 acres) of high Andean peaks.

The idea, however, is not to build another Las Leñas or Valle Nevado. Manantiales would be marketed as a sort of mountaineering park for higher-caliber athletes and adventurers. Although there will be luxury hotels and restaurants, an equal amount of bunk and dormitory space will be available for skiers with more restricted financial resources.

The driving force behind the project is Jorge Iñarra, an architect from Mendoza and an experienced mountaineer who has conquered several Himalayan and Andean peaks. He first visited Manantiales in 1966 and has since skied and climbed in the region extensively. The major obstacle to development is the difficulty and cost involved in completing a road to the site. As plans proceed to construct a second, southern highway between Santiago and Mendoza, a project hoped to be completed around the turn of the century, watch for new skiing in the Manantiales Valley.

Chapter 26

Valle de las Leñas

Ski Area Facts and Figures

Elevation: Top: 3,340m; 11,253ft.
Bottom: 2,240m; 7,349ft.
Vertical Drop: 1,100m; 3,904ft.
Season: Early June to Mid October.
Lifts: 12:
1 Quad Chair, 6 Double Chairs, 4 Poma Lifts, 1 Surface Tow
Runs: 40:
5% Beginner, 30% Intermediate, 25% Advanced, 40% Expert
Ticket Prices, 1990:
US$25 Adults Full Day.

Introduction

The gigantic ski area at Valle de las Leñas is aptly described in one simple statement — on a clear day, you can ski forever. What this means is that Las Leñas has more lift serviced ski terrain than any other ski area in the Western Hemisphere. More than Jackson Hole, more than Whistler/Blackcomb. Combine Vail and Snowbird, remove all the lifts that parallel each other, and you have a fair representation of Las Leñas.

The mountain's only flaw is that inclement weather and extreme avalanche danger often keep the majority of the mountain closed. In addition, only strong, experienced skiers are qualified to ski most of the upper slopes. But, this should not deter skiers of more modest abilities. Las Leñas also has plenty of groomed runs for intermediate and advanced skiers. And, the base facilities are of an international level. Some 13 separate hotel structures and over 10 diverse restaurants and bars cater to guests after skiing hours. The resort also offers a casino, a shopping center, and a complete infrastructure to serve its multi-national clientele.

The Valle de las Leñas Story

Valle de las Leñas has a short but interesting history full of political intrigue. It begins with the dry and barren land of the region, which has never really been of much use to anyone. It did appeal, however, to Joseph Connelly, a Californian industrialist who was so enamored with the land that he bought over seven million hectares of it in the 1950s! Nationalist sentiment soon threatened expropriation, so he eventually sold most of his land to local concerns.

One of these parcels, a 225,000 hectare (556,000 acre) plot in and around the Valle Hermoso, was sold in 1974 to one of Argentina's wealthiest business conglomerates, Bunge y Born. The huge food and manufacturing company made the purchase with the idea of building a destination ski resort and contracted with the Aspen Ski Corporation to complete a feasibility study. The final report gave the site a lukewarm possibility for success as a ski area. But, on September 19 1975, Jorge and Juan Born were kidnapped by Montoneros guerrillas who demanded a US$60 million ransom to be distributed to Argentina's suffering masses. After nine months and a partial payment including truckloads of consumer items to be left in rural districts (most of which were intercepted by the police), the brothers were released unharmed. At the conclusion of the ordeal, they sold the land to the current ownership group.

After searching in places like El Bolsón, Lake Argentina, and Mount Tronador, a group led by Ernesto "Tito" Lowenstein, a sixth-generation Argentine beef baron, purchased the Las Leñas site. Its main attraction was the ability to actually own — and thus control — all of the land within the ski area. Tito's partners included the French developers Grands Travaux de Marseilles who built the Superdevoluy resort in France and have a 25% stake in Las Leñas. Several doctors from Buenos Aires combined with Tito to complete the 75% Argentine share.

With his architect, Juan Schettini, his lawyer, Eduardo de Porto, and consulting help from the Les Arcs group, Tito opened Las Leñas in 1983. They started with six lifts, three hotels, and 400 beds that season and have since doubled the lifts and expanded the base facilities many times over. To help market the new resort, Tito invited the World Cup's "White Circus" and its accompanying press entourage for an early, South American-style event to show off his new snowy playground.

Valle de las Leñas

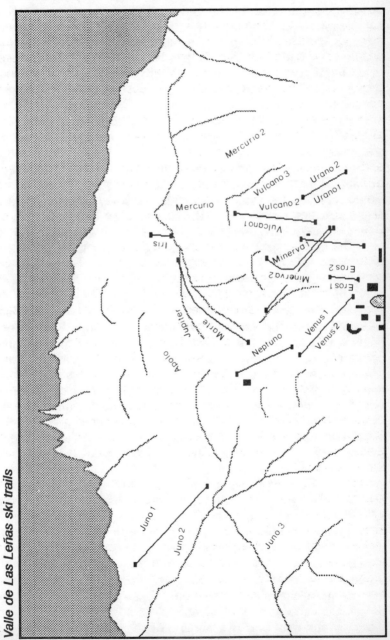

Valle de Las Leñas ski trails

Geography

The Valle de las Leñas is located at the southern end of the *Alto Cordillera* opposite the city of Curicó in Chile. The valley runs north-south before it turns west to the Valle Hermoso about 25km (16 miles) from the international border. Las Leñas is just south of the site of the plane crash of Uruguayan soccer players, described in the book *Alive*. Las Leñas means "the firewood," and is so named because of the profusion of a particularly woody bush in the treeless valley.

The high peak on the opposite side of the valley, often seen in ski area promotions, is called Cerro las Leñas. Other landmarks include Torrecillas, the highest mountain in the ski area (3,771m, 12,372ft), El Collar, the skiable mountain just east of Juno, and Entre Ríos which is adjacent to Torrecillas and has a huge bowl that is popular with off-piste skiers.

The mountain is known for the extreme winds and fierce blizzards that arrive most frequently in late July and August. The spring months are best for good snow and permissive weather. The early 1980s saw 65% sunny days in the ski season, with annual snowfall at the base averaging 3500mm (138in) but varying between extremes from 720mm (28in) in 1985 to 8450mm (333in) in 1982.

Skiing Tips

The ski area can be divided into three sectors. The first encompasses all the face runs and includes the short Eros access poma which has night skiing until 8.00pm, the C-shaped Minerva poma, and Urano, the northernmost lift in the ski area. The Vesta chair provides access to Vulcano which reaches farthest up the face and is a popular intermediate area. Finally, the new Caris quad chair accesses a snow-covered ridge above the ski area's central canyon.

The second sector includes the beginner Venus chairlift and the more advanced Neptuno which ascend a deep and broad avalanche canyon with steep walls and chutes on both sides. Marte carries skiers out of this canyon from the top of Neptuno and accesses the short but strategic Iris poma lift. Juno is the only lift in the third sector. It lies farther south than the other lifts and accesses the north-facing chutes of El Collar.

Trail ratings should not be construed as signifying that there is little beginner terrain, as 5% of a huge ski resort represents more area than 50% at smaller ski hills. Beginners should start with Venus 2, an easier and prettier run than the more popular Eros. Intermediate skiers should begin on Apolo and progress to Jupiter as confidence is gained. Advanced skiers flock to Jupiter 1, a run that dips and rolls over the moraine deposits in the glacial valley below Torrecillas.

Expert skiers are often frustrated in accessing some of the areas visible from below. For example, at the top of the main face is a large, featureless, wind-swept plateau that makes it very difficult to find selected bowls or chutes. Begin a traverse from the half-way point of the Iris poma and proceed carefully.

El Collar is reached with a very short hike to the top of a ridge left from the top of Juno. There is a remarkable variety of terrain here, and the snow is usually corned and unstable in the spring. Or, explore the terrain north of the top of Vulcano. Stay high for a long traverse to south-facing chutes and return via Urano, or hike behind the tiny patrol shack and discover the steep and untracked chutes which drop into a river gulch. Traverse left to avoid an unmarked and frozen 15m-high waterfall in the lower end of this gulch.

Rules need to be restated for Las Leñas. Never ski alone, beware of unmarked hazards off-piste, and know some avalanche basics before venturing too far. Bring and wear avalanche transceivers if you own them, even inside ski area boundaries. Be extra careful on cloudy or snowy days, as avalanche warnings and closures are minimal by US standards.

Here are a few special recommendations: Best (only) moguls: Vulcano 1; best powder: high traverse left (south) from the top of Vulcano; best high-speed cruising: Jupiter 2 (or 1, 3, or 4); best chute (highly subjective): the first on El Collar (go left from halfway down Juno 2); best bowl: Mercurio, from the top (not too steep but frightening in its sheer immensity).

Racing

Las Leñas has played a major role in globalizing international ski racing. Las Leñas was the first area in the Southern Hemisphere to host a World Cup event, and it has held a major race nearly every season since. It has thus become a mecca for national race teams who find the combination of consistent snow, open slopes, and the absence of European pressures ideal for their training needs. The first race was held in 1985, and World Cup events have been scheduled almost every season since. The events are usually downhills (there are four courses), but other events have been held as well. Las Leñas has more FIS homologated runs than any other ski area on the continent. In addition to the four downhills, three SuperG, two GS, and two slalom hills are laid out on the mountain.

Adventure Skiing

There's so much great lift-accessed skiing at Las Leñas that there is no need to venture outside of the ski area. But, some skiers still insist on exploring. A popular route with the ski instructors is the broad east face on south side of the Neptuno canyon. This is reached from Juno with a long traverse along the El Collar ridge. The return to the ski area is then completed with a pickup on the Las Leñas road a few kilometers south of the ski area.

Nordic Skiing

New trail maps have eliminated the cross-country track at the base of Las Leñas. This simply means that skiers should not expect to find groomed tracks at the resort. Good touring remains up the valley (north, then west) to the Laguna del Valle. Nordic skiers will find plenty of terrain here and also in the valley which continues west from the sharp right turn to Las Leñas about 4km before the ski area. Avalanche danger can be extreme, so keep an eye on the slopes above the valleys.

Skier Services

A multinational and multilingual group of about 90 certified instructors is on call at Las Leñas. The ski school is led by former Argentine skiing champion, Roberto Thorstrup. Instructors come from Europe, North America, and other South American countries.

Las Leñas has a group of about 16 professional ski patrollers who are trained at the beginning of each ski season by one of France's top mountaineering experts. They are led by Jorge "Coco" Torres, who was an explosives technician before arriving in Las Leñas. Patrollers maintain two high mountain huts, both called Bora Bora, at the tops of Marte and Juno, where they stay overnight during storms in order to continually control avalanches. While the first aid skills are top rate, avalanche control and safety are undertaken at a minimal level by US standards.

An excellent medical clinic staffed by two doctors functions at the base near the ticket booth. In life-threatening emergencies, the helicopter will be commandeered for evacuation to good hospitals in Malargüe, San Rafael, or Mendoza.

Base Facilities

The base of the ski area is dotted with about 25 north-facing, pyramid-inspired structures. Several roads and paths weave between the buildings, and a muddy parking lot is located near the bottom of the Vesta chair. If driving, stop at the information booth at the entrance to the resort for assistance in finding specific destinations. There is also a parking area for motor homes (*casas rodantes*) near the employee housing complex (1km northeast of the hotels), and a regular bus connects all the communities.

The **Pyramide** is the centrally located social area with several high-priced shops, a hair salon, a post office, a newsstand, the photo service, a post office, a bank, two restaurants, a nice bar, and corporate offices. In addition, exhibits rotate through the lobby. Downstairs is the **Cleopatra Discotheque** which opens at 1.00am for those real skiers and costs US$7 just to enter. A well-stocked supermarket with a deli, a bakery, and a good wine selection is located between the Dormy-Houses, and Esparta.

Tickets, Storage, and Ski Rental

Lift tickets are included with all hotel packages. They can be purchased at the ticket booth by the ski school desk behind the Acuario Hotel. Lift hours are 9.00am to 5.00pm, but the upper lifts close earlier.

Each hotel has its own ski and boot rooms with valets to take care of equipment. The boots are stored on a heated boot rack. There are no public storage facilities, so non-guests should be prepared to change in their vehicles.

Las Leñas has two rental shops. The first is at the top of the main parking lot and has a larger inventory of entry-level equipment. The other rental and repair shop is up by the ticket booth and has more modern equipment for more experienced skiers and a good repair technician.

Dining

There are several good restaurants at Las Leñas. On the hill is **Bacus**, a popular lunch stop, especially on sunny days. One evening each week Bacus hosts a special fondue dinner with a torchlight descent in the dark. It is located at the top of Neptuno and provides a warm shelter on windy and snowy days. Also slopeside is the tiny snack bar called **Torta Loca** (Crazy Cake). This is located just above the bottom of Vulcano and has a small sandwich menu. All seating is outdoors.

Most skiers opt to take their lunch in **El Brasero**, the cafeteria-style restaurant in the Acuario Hotel. El Brasero features a large selection of excellent but expensive food with seating for several hundred guests.

In La Pyramide is the exclusive French restaurant, **La Salamandra**.

Food here is expensive, but it is the most romantic dining room at Las Leñas. **Bankett**, across the hall, is the most reasonably priced dining facility at the ski resort. The menu is Italian with homemade pastas and pizzas. Downstairs is **Angelo's Piano Bar**, a popular spot for a cold beer after a long day of exploring Las Leñas' vertical terrain.

The Pisces hotel also houses two restaurants. **El Balcón** is a comfortable bar and lounge overlooking the pool and lobby areas. Good sandwiches and snacks make up the menu here. The hotel's other restaurant, **Las Cuatro Estaciones**, is the most fashionable at Las Leñas.

All other hotels have their own restaurants, but Apart-Hotel and Dormy-House guests dine in El Brasero if the half-pension option is chosen. Lunch is not included in any packages, and packaged guests are limited to dining in their own hotel.

The Hotels

The star of Las Leñas is the large **Pisces** hotel at the top end of the complex. The ground floor houses the casino while the lobby area has two restaurants, a large, mellow bar, and a conference room for 250 people. Pisces is the best and most expensive of the hotels. The eight junior suites feature bathtub jacuzzis, fireplaces, and the best views. **Aries** is the newest hotel and also has several suites. It is located north of the main complex (a bus provides frequent transport). Most foreign guests will be lodged in the comfortable **Escorpio** or **Acuario** hotels. These four lodges are the only ones which feature ski-in and ski-out convenience. **Géminis** is the least expensive and smallest hotel at the resort.

There are six large **Apart-Hotels** at Las Leñas. These are condominium-type accommodations with basic kitchens and gas fireplaces. The rooms are quite comfortable and reasonably priced. Five floor plans for two to six guests are available. The **Dormy-House** is the most economical lodging option at Las Leñas for large groups. There are two styles available for five to eight skiers. Meals add US$200 to the weekly rate in the Apart-Hotels and US$160 in the Dormy-Houses.

Other Lodging

Trying to beat the high cost of skiing at Las Leñas can be an exciting and financially rewarding game. For skiers who want to visit Las Leñas as a part of a longer South American ski vacation, here are a few tips no one is supposed to know.

The price structure for Las Leñas is different in each branch office,

Valle de las Leñas

and rates are lowest in Argentina. Arrange your visit in the Mendoza or Buenos Aires offices to save about a third of the US price. Save US$120 by arranging independent transportation to Malargüe. Stays of less than a week are possible only if purchased in Argentina. For one to three nights, divide the weekly rate by six and multiply by the actual number of days. For stays of four to six nights, divide by seven.

The hotels of **Lahuen-co** in Los Molles offer an excellent option. A hot-springs resort 19km (12 miles) from the ski area, Los Molles is popular with the local *Mendocinos* who prefer the outstanding home-style food and friendly ambience at the traditional resort. With two newly built hotels, Los Molles now offers an improved variety of accommodations. Weekly prices run from US$319-500 in **Lahuen-co II**, US$290-458 in **Hualum**, and US$258-328 in the older **Hostería** including two meals and hot springs use based on double occupancy. Nightly rates under US$50 are also available. The TAC and Uspallata buses will stop at the resort on the way to Las Leñas, and the hotel has a daily transportation service to the ski area. Make reservations in San Rafael or Mendoza.

Other options include staying in a hotel in Malargüe or San Rafael. Malargüe is a small and relatively uninteresting town with just a couple of hotels. The airport was rebuilt in 1981 to receive the jet-loads of skiers who fly in and bus out immediately. San Rafael is a much larger and more exciting town about 80km (50 miles) farther from Las Leñas.

Getting There

From Malargüe
Via Private Auto:
Malargüe-Hwy222: Hwy40, 30km (19 miles), 20min, paved.
Hwy222-Las Leñas: 49km (30 miles), 45min, paved.
Via Bus:
No public service.

From San Rafael
Via Private Auto:
San Rafael-Hwy222: Hwy143 to Hwy40, 159km (99 miles), 1½hr, paved.
Hwy222-Las Leñas: 49km (30 miles), 45min, paved.
Via Bus:
TAC: 10.00am daily, 2½hr, US$5.
Expresso Uspallata: 10.30am Fri, Sat, Sun, holidays, 3½hr, US$5.

Further Information and Reservations
Valle de Las Leñas
Arenales 707, Nivel Jardín, (1061) Capital Federal, Argentina. Tel or FAX: 313-2121, Telex: 28119 SKL AR.
In Mendoza:
Avda. San Martín 1233, Galería Caracol, (5500) Mendoza, Argentina. Tel: (061)231-628
In Brazil:
Avda. Brigadeiro Faria Lima 1570-5.A, 01452 — São Paulo. Tel: (011)815-1655, FAX: (011)212-2007, Telex: (011)83159 SKIL BR.
Rua México 98 — Grupo 302, 20031 Río de Janeiro. Tel: (021)220-1857
In Florida:
9592 Harding Avenue, 2nd Floor, Surfside, Miami, FL 33154. Tel: (800)862-7545, (305)864-7545, FAX: (305)861-2895, Telex: (23) 529476 SKIL MIA UD.
Los Molles
San Lorenzo 12, Piso 1, Of 8, (5500) Mendoza. Tel: 257-348.

MARTE

Marte. The chairlift of every skier's dreams. It's a silly place for a chairlift, really. Ascending over the throat of a 1,500m-long (5,000ft) double chute, it was destroyed by a midnight avalanche in 1987. New control and defense systems should prevent a similar occurrence in the future, but they won't. Who cares anyway, as long as they keep rebuilding it?

What's the big deal? Well, the "Mars" chair accesses more expert skiing terrain than any other lift on this planet. Glory seekers can jump into the wide bowl at the top and ski the chairline. Or, follow the east or west ridges around for a more challenging and spectacular approach to the twin gullies below. To escape the limelight, continue along the west ridge to the 20m-wide, never-tracked, south-facing chute system left of the chairline. Or, go the other direction, to ski the face of Las Leñas, which can be described, without exaggerating, as possessing 40 distinct and daunting chutes.

Marte. Forget the rest of Las Leñas. No skier could ever find — let alone ski — all the possibilities presented by this chairlift. Marte. Even the fittest World Cup racers could never complete a non-stop run from the top. Marte. With exposures on all sides, airy powder, velvety windpack, and granular corn are always available somewhere. Marte. So vertical, so narrow, it defines extreme. Marte. Thanks, Tito.

SAN RAFAEL

San Rafael sits in a large, flat plain near the base of the Andes 208km (129 miles) from Las Leñas. Even in winter, it is a warm and dry respite from the chilly snows at Las Leñas. Most of the ski area's work force comes from this city, and there is a reliable, daily bus service to the resort.

San Rafael was founded on October 4 1922. The streets and sidewalks are excessively wide in typical Argentine style. The preferred means of locomotion for the city's 80,000 residents is the bicycle, entirely appropriate considering the absolutely flat topography and distinctly dry climate. There are few taxis but the city is easily explored with an afternoon walking tour.

The primary economic activities of the region include agriculture, with walnuts, apples, and grapes grown in irrigated valleys. Mining of uranium, marble, coal, and other minerals in the nearby foothills is also important. Hydroelectricity is the region's newest resource and is generated at several artificial lakes near the city. The population is very outdoor-oriented with rafting, kayaking, and other water sports attracting summer tourists. Each summer, San Rafael hosts Argentina's biggest pentathlon, and the few locals who can afford it have embraced skiing.

Transportation

A busy outdoor bus terminal and quaint train station are located near the center of the city. As most travel connections arrive late in the day, independent travelers are likely to have an overnight stop here before catching a morning bus to Las Leñas.

From Mendoza
Via Private Auto:
Mendoza-Pareditas: Hwy40, 127km (79 miles), 1½hr, paved.
Pareditas-San Rafael: Hwy143 to 156, 109km (68 miles), 1¼hr, paved.
Via Bus:
TAC, Uspallata: 4/day, 3½hr, US$4.
Via Air:
Aerolíneas Argentinas: 5/wk, 40min.

From Buenos Aires
Via Private Auto:
Buenos Aires-Junín: Hwy7, 261km (162 miles), 3hr, paved.

Junín-San Rafael: Hwy188 and 143, 726km (451 miles), 8hr, paved.
Via Bus:
TAC: others, 14hr (overnight), US$35.
Via Air:
Aerolíneas Argentinas: 5/wk, 2hr.
Via Train:
El San Rafaelino: weekly (weekend schedule), 14hr, US$25-50.

From Bariloche
Via Private Auto:
Bariloche-Collón Curá: Hwy237, 67km (42 miles), 1hr, paved.
Collón Curá-San Rafael: Hwy40, 1000km (621 miles), 14hr, mostly paved.
Via Bus:
TAC: 3/wk, 20hr, US$45.

Hotels
First Class:
San Rafael: 30 Day, Sgl:US$20, Dbl:US$36, helpful, best in town.
España: 270 San Martín, Sgl:US$18, Dbl:US$28.
Los Alamos: 21 Salas, Sgl:US$18, Dbl:US$23.
Moderate:
Kalton: 128 Yrigoyen, Sgl:US$15, Dbl:US$27, closest to bus terminal, popular.
Tonin: 327 San Martín, Sgl:US$14, Dbl:US$26.
Viñas: 445 Mitre, Sgl:US$13, Dbl:US$22, nice but not central.
Budget:
Rex: 56 Yrigoyen, Sgl:US$9, Dbl:US$16, very central.
Bahía: 23 España, Sgl:US$6, Dbl:US$10, on side street but close to center and train, nice garden patio, recommended.
Cerro Nevado: 376 Yrigoyen, Sgl:US$9, Dbl:US$16.

Restaurants
International:
Club Español: Salas w/Day, most formal in city.
Typical:
La Vieja Posada: 17 Pellegrini, very good *parrilla*, best in town.
Las Rejas: 46 Day, basic but good.
Estancia Chica: 366 Yrigoyen, *parrilla*, popular with families.
Budget:
San Martín: 201 San Martín, basic sandwiches and coffee, popular evening spot with young crowd.

Valle de las Leñas

Important Addresses

Foreign Exchange: La Mundial, 24 Yrigoyen; Montenar, 13 Yrigoyen.
Post Office: 61 San Lorenzo.
Telephone: 127 San Lorenzo.
Hospital: Schestakow, Tel: 24-290, 24-291.
Tourist Office: Yrigoyen w/Ballofet, very helpful.
Travel Agencies: Lahuen-Co (for Los Molles), 19 Ballofet.
Airlines: Aerolineas, Day w/Pellegrini; Austral, Mitre w/Las Heras; TAN, 50 Almafuerte.
Car Rental: Avis, 30 Day.
Bus Terminal: Almafuerte or Godoy Cruz 100.
Train Station: end of San Martín (at Rivadavia).
Books: Feria del Libro, 112 San Martín, Loc 3, some English.
Cinema: Andes, 139 San Martín; Gran Sur, 36 San Martín; Roma, 280 Yrigoyen.
Ski Shop: Aire Libre, 48 Gutierrez; La Cabaña del Esquiador, clothing at 198 Yrigoyen, skis at 50 Salas, also in Malargüe at 999 San Martín.
Ski Club: Club Andino Pehuenche, 9 Salas, No 11.

JOURNEY LATIN AMERICA

Our latest Bespoke Tours brochure features competitive rates at the finest ski resorts in Chile and Argentina. Perhaps you're planning to ski at Valle Nevado, Las Leñas or elswhere in Latin America. Or you may simply wish to build a week's skiing into a longer itinerary. Whatever your requirements, we can make all the arrangements from this end, drawing on the most extensive pool of Latin American travel expertise in the UK. And to back this up, we offer a range of low cost flight options that is second to none.

Please ask for our tour brochures and Flights Bulletin.

Journey Latin America
14-16 Devonshire Road Chiswick London W4 2HD
Tours 081 747 8315   Flights 081 747 3108   24hrs 081 742 2320
Fully Bonded ABTA 86321

Chapter 27

Parque Caviahue

About half-way between Las Leñas and Bariloche, against the border of Chile between Antuco and Lonquimay, is the 2,980m (9,775ft) summit of the Volcán Copahue. On the east side of this broad mountain, near the west shore of the U-shaped Lake Caviahue, an international-level ski resort is being built. What's impressive about this plan is not the five-star hotels, the French restaurants, or the flashy discos, but the mountain itself. A study undertaken by Montistudio Sherpa of Bolzano, Italy determined that the ski area has a potential for 120km (75 miles) of runs. It is shaped like a smaller Mammoth Mountain, with steep bowls on top and gentle hills near the base. Some 1,330 vertical meters (4,365ft) lie between the base and the summit. That would make Caviahue America's biggest ski area.

The other attraction of this project is the pristine beauty of one of the most remote areas in Argentina. The volcano's crater is filled with the same hot sulfur water that surfaces at the nearby hot springs resort of Copahue. Between the mountain and the lake, araucaria groves fill the small valleys and cover the round hills. Hexagonal columns of basaltic rock form the surrounding cliffs, and the wide Río Agrio plunges over several edges. The protected paradise of Caviahue is being cautiously developed in cooperation with the watchful park management.

The development plan is spearheaded by a private company in Buenos Aires. It calls for an investment of US$16 million over seven years beginning in 1989. Three major hotels will eventually be built, but an Apart-Hotel, a double chairlift, and several surface lifts are scheduled for completion for the 1991 ski season. Until a lift is built to the summit, snowcats will carry skiers to the top for full-length descents. The infrastructure of the sparsely inhabited area is nearly complete, and the access highways are among the best in Argentina.

Even without the development, Caviahue is the best place for nordic skiing on the continent (outside of Ushuaia). With consistent snow and spectacular scenery, cross-country skiers are already coming from Bariloche and San Martín. Great backcountry skiing is also abundant in the region, and an epic trip through the Copahue Pass to the Biobío River and Lonquimay in Chile could begin here. As yet, there is no public transportation to Caviahue, but check in Zapala. In the meantime, rent a car to enjoy the unique scenery of the last 50km (31 miles) from Loncopue. For further information, write: Parque Caviahue, Paraguay 416, Planta Baja "H", (1057) Buenos Aires, Argentina.

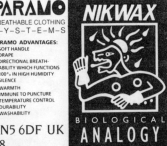

Chapter 28

Primeros Piños

Ski Area Facts and Figures
Base Elevation: 1,500m; 4,920ft.
Vertical Drop: 50m; 165ft.
Season: Early July to Mid September.
Lifts: 3 Portable Surface Tows
Runs: 5, 100% Beginner

Introduction

The management at Primeros Piños prefers to call the operation a *Parque de Nieve* (Snow Park) rather than a ski area. There has been little ski activity in the years since its founding because the slopes lie in a wind corridor in which storms produce a *viento blanco,* (white wind). A passing system can either bury the lifts or strip all snow from the trails.

Two base areas were developed. At the main base, located at the end of the paved road in possibly the easternmost natural grove of araucaria trees on the continent, a modern lodge was built to service two small runs. The other base, 5km (3 miles) farther up the road at Quelli Mahuida, has rarely hosted skiers.

History

There have been three good seasons at Primeros Piños since the first lifts were installed in 1982. The "glory years" of Primeros Piños were the 1984 and 1985 seasons. Perfect weather and the capable management of Miguel Altamira (now at Perito Moreno) and Hector Giovachini (teaching at Chapelco) combined to bring to fruition the dreams of Dr Eduardo Zinni and his brothers. The following seasons were ruined by uncooperative weather, and despite a few good weeks in 1989, Dr Zinni surrendered his concession due to the impossible conditions.

Geography
Primeros Piños is located at the northern end of the Sierra de Catan at the base of Cerro Las Lajas (2,650m; 8,700ft). The *Area Superior* at Quelli Mahuida is at 1,800m (5,900ft) elevation, and the run reaches 1,915m (6,285ft). The harsh storms and prevailing winds originate in the Pacific and pass Llaima due west. The season is inconsistent, with August and September the most likely months to find lifts running.

Skiing Tips
The area operates as a snow park for the families and couples that come from the provincial capital of Neuquén. Sleds rent more than skis, and the real novelty is snow, not skiing. Great nordic skiing can be enjoyed in the area though, and the Argentine military has a small training camp near the lodge. The eroded terrain is more conducive to touring than adventure skiing, although a good run on the east face of Las Lajas could be reached with a two-and-a-half hour hike.

Base Facilities
There is a modern lodge at the base which serves good food and has a few rooms to rent. It is likely to be deserted when the ski area is closed but is quite busy when there's skiing. A "ski bar" serving simple food and a rudimentary rental shop complete the array of structures at the base. Up at Quelli Mahuida, a modern A-frame cafeteria provides shelter.

Getting There

From Zapala
Via Private Auto:
Hwy22 to Hwy13: 1km.
Hwy13: 50km (31 miles), 45min, paved, poorly maintained.

Primeros Piños

Argentina: Caviahue to Zapala

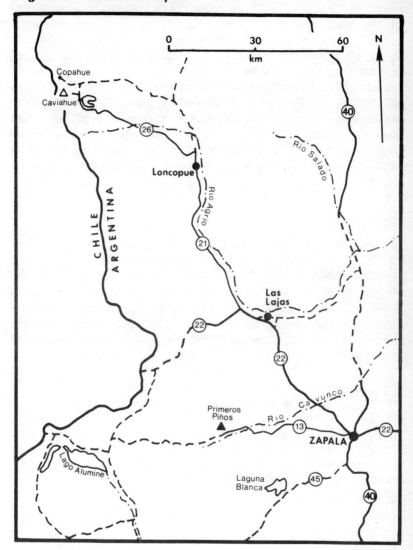

Further Information
Dirección Provincial de Turismo
Provincia de Neuquén, Neuquén, Argentina

ZAPALA

The town of Zapala was founded with the arrival of the General Roca rail line on June 12 1913. The town has a population of about 8,000, and it is generally uninteresting but friendly. The city's economic base is the variety of minerals found in the surrounding foothills and the natural gas fields that lie underneath. Zapala is home to one of South America's best rock and fossil collections, and there is a famous school of ceramics. It is also a fairly important transportation hub for summer tourists visiting the hot springs at Copahue or the lakes and rivers around Aluminé to the east. Many restaurants and hotels are closed in the winter. If driving, don't miss the pink flamingoes and black-necked swans at the Laguna Blanca, a national park oasis in the middle of the otherwise desolate landscape of the Argentine *pampa*.

Transportation

From Bariloche and San Martín
Via Private Auto:
Bariloche-Collón Curá: Hwy237, 132km (82 miles), 1½hr, paved.
Collón Curá-Rinconada: Hwy40, 60km (37 miles), 45min, paved.
San Martín-Rinconada: Hwy234, 74km (46 miles), 1hr, paved.
Rinconada-Zapala: Hwy40, 166km (103 miles), 2hr, paved.
Via Bus:
from Bariloche: TAC, 3/wk, 5½hr, US$18.
from San Martín: El Petroleo, daily, 4hr, US$10.
Via Air:
from San Martín: TAN, 2/wk, ½hr, US$21.

From Neuquén
Via Private Auto:
Neuquén-Challaco: Hwy237, 50km (31 miles), ½hr, paved.
Challaco-Zapala: Hwy22, 135km (84 miles), 1½hr, paved.
Via Bus:
El Valle, Mercedes, and El Petroleo: several daily, 4hr, US$12.
Via Air:
TAN: 2/wk, ½hr, US$21.
Via Train:
Gral Roca, 4hr, Pullman:US$6.
from Buenos Aires, 16hr, Pullman:US$37, Bed:US$49.

Primeros Piños

From Caviahue
Via Private Auto:
Caviahue-Loncopué: Hwy26, 69km (43 miles), 1½hr, paved.
Loncopué-Zapala: Hwy21, 121km (75 miles), 1½hr, paved.

From Mendoza and Malargüe
Via Private Auto:
from Mendoza: Hwy 40, 956km (594 miles); fm San Rafael, 724km (450 miles).
from Malargüe: 535km (332 miles).
Via Bus:
from Mendoza: TAC, 3/wk, 18hr, US$39.

Hotels
First Class:
Huemelen: 929 Brown, Sgl:US$21, Dbl:US$30, best in town, clean, comfortable, good restaurant.
Moderate:
Nuevo Pehuen: Etcheluz w/Vidal, Sgl:US$10, Dbl:US$16, close to bus terminal, slow in winter.
Huencul: 311 Roca, Sgl:US$10, Dbl:US$16, popular, warm, several blocks from center.

Restaurants
Familiar: 139 Italia, basic but popular.
Most closed in winter, dine at hotel.

Important Addresses
Foreign Exchange: Change in Neuquén or Bariloche.
Post Office: San Martín w/Torres.
Telephone: 248 Italia.
Airlines: TAN, San Martín and Cháneton; LADE, Uriburu and Etcheluz.
Bus Terminal: Uribu and Etcheluz.
Train Station: San Martín and Avellaneda.
Cinema: 235 San Martín.
Museum: Museo Profesor Olsacher, 421 Olascoaga.
Ski Shop: El Ciervo Rojo, 342 Brown; Tassone, Houssay w/Chile.

Chapelco ski trails

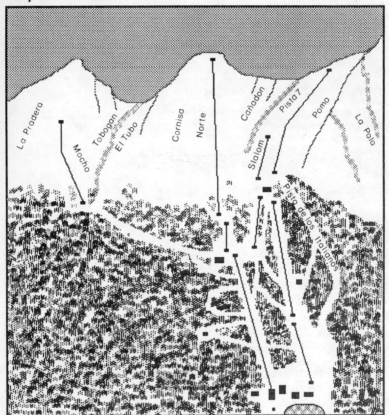

Chapter 29

Chapelco

Ski Area Facts and Figures

Elevation: Top: 1,970m; 6,463ft.
 Bottom: 1,250m; 4,100ft.
Vertical Drop: 720m; 2,363ft.
Season: Early July to Late September.
Lifts: 10:
 1 Gondola, 2 Quad Chairs, 1 Triple Chair, 2 Double Chairs, 1 T-Bar, 2 Poma Lifts, 1 Surface Tow
Runs: 35:
 40% Beginner, 30% Intermediate, 15% Advanced, 15% Expert
Ticket Prices, 1990:
 US$14-26 Adults Full Day, US$10-18 Children under 11; US$ 9-17 Adults Half Day, US$ 7-12 Children.

Introduction

Edmundo Chanel, the former general manager of Chapelco, once said, "we are looking for the skier committed to the concept of skiing as a sport, as an adventure; already we consider the skier of Chapelco the authentic lover of skiing... For this reason, we are not particularly interested in the 'jet-set,' although we are happy to receive them." Apparently, Bolland y Compañia is interested in the "jet-set" because Señor Chanel is no longer with the company.

The only problem with this popular approach is that all the new lifts serve advanced terrain, and the "jet-set" complains about the lack of snow on the beginner runs below treeline. Advanced skiers delight in the deserted upper slopes, but skiers from Buenos Aires remain confused because Chapelco was widely known for its gentle, tree-lined runs.

Chapelco resembles Mad River Glen in Vermont as a friendly, low-key resort favored by the local ski bums. It promises to become a smaller, quieter Vail, with most skiing on the front side and advanced adventure skiing in the back bowls. Although famous for the forested slopes, only the lower trails are wooded, and the vegetation is too thick for tree skiing.

History

Chapelco was first developed commercially in 1978 by Lagos del Sur, a division of Sol Jet who also operated Catedral, the Sol chain of hotels, ferries on Lake Nahuel Huapi, and Austral airlines. Financial difficulties forced the company to divest, and in 1984, the provincial government took control.

After three years of stagnation and mismanagement, an Argentine petroleum company called Bolland y Compañia purchased a 15-year concession to run the resort. Bolland has spent over US$4 million since 1987 to upgrade and build new lifts and facilities at Chapelco. The previously undeveloped north face was opened in 1987, and a hotel complex is scheduled for construction at the base.

Geography

Chapelco is located 120km (75 miles) north of Bariloche. It sits in the middle of the short Cordón Chapelco, one of the few east-west ranges near the Andes. The ski area is set 13km (8 miles) above San Martín de Los Andes, a small village nestled in a valley at the eastern tip of the finger lake Lacar.

About two-thirds of the ski area lies below treeline. The vegetation is typical of the deciduous rain forest native to the Lakes Regions of Argentina and Chile where *lenga* trees predominate. In spring, all skiing takes place above the top of the gondola. Though snow is nearly always thin around the base, it improves considerably on the upper slopes where all the advanced runs lie. It is important to ski early in the mornings, as Chapelco has Argentina's only developed north-facing slopes.

Temperatures at Chapelco are rarely harsh, and rain is common on the lower slopes in the winter season. Though the weather may be damp in town, the upper slopes often remain clear and sunny. Storms can approach heavily laden from the Pacific, but it is far more common that they swirl up meekly from the drier southeast.

Skiing Tips

The gondola, the only six-passenger lift for skiers in South America, carries skiers to the 1,500m treeline. Beginners can enjoy the wide variety of lifts and runs below this point. Intermediate skiers descend the Mocho bowl to ski the T-Bar or the short, mogulled chutes of El Tubo. Advanced skiers might try the hidden ridge system called Norte. Though difficult to find, it keeps adventurous skiers occupied for hours with its varied aspects and snow types. Or, try the marked runs to the immediate right of Del Mallin which are long, consistent, and especially exciting when thin or hard snow provides an added challenge.

The advanced runs accessed from both summit lifts are nearly always deserted. Fresh tracks can always be made with minimal searching. One note of caution: the summit ridge drops precipitously on the back (south) side of both lifts into rocky cliffs and near-vertical chutes. On days when the fog reaches the top, be sure not to stray over the edge.

Adventure Skiing

The most accessible extreme skiing at Chapelco is at La Pala (The Shovel), the long bowl and chute system on the west side of the ski area. It is considered out-of-bounds because it is quite avalanche prone and the exit route at the bottom is extremely flat and heavily wooded. It is never open to the public unless permission is secured from the patrollers who are likely to send skiers with a guide/instructor for their first descent.

There is also a series of extreme chutes and bowls on the south face, some of which seem too vertical to hold snow even though they do. All empty into the basin of the Laguna Verde. This area offers some of South America's best skiing, but it won't be developed until a road is built into the site. A simple chairlift to retrieve skiers could do the trick, but there is already an abundance of under-utilized, advanced terrain.... In the meantime, check at the ski school desk to arrange helicopter pickups in the area, or hike out.

Nordic Skiing

Chapelco has several kilometers of cross-country skiing trails at the 1,500m level of the mountain. Nordic equipment is also available for rent in the shop at the base of Chapelco. Unfortunately, poor snow conditions frequently close the trail, and the northern aspect of the slope means slow, slushy snow.

Skier Services

Chapelco has the most prestigious ski school in South America. It is led by Alfred Auer, an Austrian who also writes the weekly ski tip in the Buenos Aires daily *La Nación*. Chapelco is the ski area of choice for Argentina's first-time skiers because of the reputation of his program. It is estimated that one of every three skiers at Chapelco enrolls in a class. The ski school is completely modern, with video teaching techniques in the advanced clinics and a Junior Academy program for kids 5 to 15 years old. Prices run from US$19 for a private lesson to US$9 for a group class. Nordic technique is also taught, and prices range from US$14 for a private to US$7 for a collective lesson.

There is a professional ski patrol comprised of 17 young skiers recruited locally. No avalanche control techniques are undertaken on the mountain, but the staff is fully trained in trail safety and first aid. A first aid clinic is located at the base of the mountain, and ambulances are always on hand to carry injured skiers to the modern hospital in San Martín.

Base Facilities

The complex at the base of the ski area is complete with (from left to right) the gondola building, a large cafeteria, and the ski school office. The day care facility is found underneath the rental shop, and the medical clinic is in the building farthest right.

Tickets, Storage, and Rentals

Tickets are purchased at the small square hut in front of the gondola building. Ticket and rental prices vary depending on the time of year. Hotel packages include lifts, and discounts are given for 3, 4, and 7 day tickets. Lifts operate from 9.00am to 5.30pm daily, and half-day begins at 1.00pm.

There is a convenient basket and ski check (US$0.65) and changing area underneath the gondola. From the ticket booth, proceed to the middle door right of the gondola line. Another *guardería* is located next to the rental shop.

The ski rental shop is adjacent to the ski school office to the right of the cafeteria. There are also several rental shops in San Martín. It may be worth investigating to find who currently rents the best equipment at the lowest prices. Ski area rental fees wavered between US$8 and US$10. A full nordic setup rented for US$5-6. Sleds and ski locks are also available.

Dining

Three dining facilities are located on the slopes. The **Rancho Manolo** was recently refurbished and has a European ambience with a central fireplace and carved wooden floors, walls, and ceilings. It is located low on the mountain at the 1,370m level beside the Pista de Los Italianos.

The **Antulaquen** cafeteria (at the top of the gondola) serves typical luncheon fare of sandwiches and pastries. The **Refugio Graef** is a convenient but minimal snack bar at the base of Filo. The cafeteria at the base serves the widest variety of food, but the location is impractical for skiers who prefer to avoid the thin snow on the lower mountain.

The Hotel

The 5-star **Club Hotel Sol de Los Andes** is owned and operated by the owners of Chapelco and serves as the ski resort's full-service hotel. It is located in an exclusive position 2km from and overlooking the town of Chapelco. It is a resort unto itself with an elegant restaurant, a heated pool and sauna, a gambling casino, and the town's hottest disco. Prices are excessive in comparison to the rest of the town, and the location prohibits exploration of the picturesque community.

Getting There

From San Martín de Los Andes

The route to Chapelco from San Martín circles from the highway that leads to Villa La Angostura via the Siete Lagos. The road becomes one-way from Highway 19 with descending traffic following a more direct route back to San Martín. Chains are never required because the normal snowline is right at the base of the ski area. The wet mud is slippery however, and cattle and goats frequently block the road.

Via Private Auto:
Hwy234-Hwy19: 5km (3 miles), 10min, unpaved.
Hwy19-Chapelco: 14km (9 miles), 20min, unpaved.
Chapelco-San Martín: 11km (7 miles), 20min, unpaved.

Via Bus:
Check at Bus Terminal: every hour on the hour, 45min, US$2.

Further Information and Reservations

Cumbres de Chapelco
233 Suipacha, Loc 20, (1008) Buenos Aires, Argentina. Tel: 35-0021, FAX: 35-6620, Telex: 02-1611

SAN MARTÍN DE LOS ANDES

Perhaps the greatest pleasure of skiing at Chapelco is the friendly, picturesque, and uncrowded town of San Martín de Los Andes. The quiet tranquillity and surprising lack of "touristiness" is in sharp contrast to the intensity of Bariloche and the haughtiness of Las Leñas. The town sits in a flat valley at the eastern foot of Lago Lacar and is oriented not to the lake front, but to the geographic center of the valley. It occupies the clearly defined square mile of the valley floor and then stretches eastward. The town seems generally underdeveloped but well-planned with streets laid out in a typical grid. The center is reserved for the Swiss-style government offices and araucaria-filled public parks and squares.

San Martín de Los Andes was founded in 1898 as a frontier town to secure Argentine sovereignty near the disputed border with Chile. For many years it was a remote outpost, but was later developed as a haven for sports enthusiasts. Primary economic activities include ranching, timber, and tourism.

San Martín is at least as popular in the summer as it is in winter. It serves as the gateway to the Lanín National Park whose many finger lakes contain large schools of giant brook, brown, and rainbow trout, as well as landlocked salmon. The park is a playground for climbers, campers, and explorers, and the dense forests are home to red deer and wild boar. Much of the parkland is also grazed by goats, sheep, and cattle.

The town has about 17,000 inhabitants, most of whom live on the north side of the River Calbuco which cuts through the center of the valley. The south side of town is filled with many quality hotels and restaurants. The main street is **San Martín**, and addresses are difficult to find due to the lack of street signs. The restaurants specialize in local trout (*trucha*), deer (*ciervo*), and boar (*jabalí*). Many hotels have been converted into pleasant, homey *hosterías*. Most of the cabins and lakeshore hotels are closed in the winter.

Transportation

San Martín's airport, also called Chapelco, lies about 8km (5 miles) east of the town in a beautiful meadow with clear views of the snow-capped Lanín volcano (taxi:US$5). The bus station is modern and clean, and is located six blocks from the center of San Martín and one block from the lakeshore. None of the lake's ferries operate in the winter season.

The drive to San Martín from Bariloche is spectacular, and skiers should try to follow the circular route if possible. Regular buses ply the stark canyon-country of the Río Limay along Hwy 237. The Confluencia area of the Valle Encantado is a particularly pristine spot, and the best seats are on the east side of the bus. This route is completely paved and should be followed in case of foul weather. The other route takes a more westerly course along the *Siete Lagos* and Villa La Angostura through thick rain forest. The isthmus between Lakes Villarino and Faulkner is an outstanding spot for a leisurely picnic. The road is deserted and muddy in winter, so be well prepared.

From Bariloche
Via Private Auto:
Bariloche-Collón Curá: Hwy237, 132km (82 miles), 1½hr, paved.
Collón Curá-Rinconada: Hwy40, 60km (37 miles), 45min, paved.
Rinconada-San Martín: Hwy 234, 74km (46 miles), 1hr, paved.
Siete Lagos Route:
Bariloche-Chacabuco: Hwy237, 20km (12 miles), 15min, paved.
Chacabuco-Correntoso: Hwy 231, 75km (47 miles), 1¼hr, paved.
Correntoso-San Martín: Hwy 234, 98km (61 miles), 2hr, unpaved.
Via Bus:
Mercedes, El Valle (not recommended), Koko: daily, 5hr, US$16.
Via Air:
Aerolíneas Argentinas: 5/wk, 30min, US$20.
TAN: 4/wk, 30min, US$17.

From Zapala
Via Private Auto:
Zapala-Rinconada: Hwy40, 166km (103 miles), 2hr, paved.
Rinconada-San Martín: Hwy234, 74km (46 miles), 1hr, paved.
Via Bus:
El Petroleo: daily, 4hr, US$10.
Via Air:
TAN: 2/wk, 30min, US$21.

Hotels
First Class:
Le Cheminee: Moreno w/Roca, Dbl:US$120, super elegant, best in town.
Le Village: Drury w/Roca, Sgl:US$45, Dbl:US$60, clean and homey.
Caupolican: 969 San Martín, Sgl:US$:42, Dbl:US$56, German management, very good, exquisite bar.
Moderate:
Tunqueley: Belgrano w/Roca, Sgl:US$30, Dbl:US$40, clean, polite, good value.

La Masia: 811 Obeid, Sgl:US$30, Dbl:US$40, nice.
Del Chapelco: 297 Brown, Sgl:US$18, Dbl:US$24, old but friendly.
Budget:
Curruhuinca: 686 Rivadavia, Sgl:US$10, Dbl:US$20, best value.
Berna: 1127 Peréz, US$10 each, basic.
Turismo: 517 Mascardi, US$9 each.

Restaurants
Typical:
Pisces: Villegas w/Moreno, outstanding.
Mi Viejo Pepe: 725 Villegas, Trattoria, homemade pasta.
Mendieta: 715 San Martín.
Budget:
El Jockey: 657 Villegas, very popular.
Pocha's: 788 Villegas, pizza and *empanadas*.

Important Addresses
Foreign Exchange: Andina Internacional, 876 San Martín; ask hotel for others, much better rates in Bariloche.
Post Office: Encotel, 690 Roca (at Peréz).
Telephone: Cooperativa Telefónica, 761 Drury.
Tourist Office: San Martín w/Rosas.
Airlines: LADE, TAN, 915 San Martín; Aerolíneas, San Martín and Belgrano.
Car Rental: Avis, Elordi w/San Martín.
Bus Terminal: Villegas w/Costanera.
Newsstand: Athos, 940 San Martín for Buenos Aires Herald and magazines.
Laundromat: Laverap, 986 Villegas, 878 Drury.
Cinema: Amankay, 1154 Roca.
Ice Rink: Traful On-Ice, Fosbury w/Peréz.
Ski Shop: Wedeln, 547 Brown; Chapelco Sport, 1017 San Martín; several others.
Ski Area Office: San Martín w/Elordi.

Chapter 30

Cerro Bayo

Ski Area Facts and Figures

Elevation: Top: 1,730m; 5,675ft.
             Bottom: 1,010m; 3,315ft.
Vertical Drop: 720m; 2,360ft.
Season: Mid July to Late September.
Lifts: 5:
             1 Double Chair, 1 T-Bar, 2 Poma Lifts, 1 Surface Tow
Runs: 8:
             20% Beginner, 50% Intermediate, 20% Advanced, 10% Expert
Ticket Prices, 1990:
  US$9-14 Adults Full Day, US$6-9 Children 6-12; US$6-10 Adults Half Day, US$4-6 Children.

Introduction

Cerro Bayo is typical of the resorts in the Lakes District. Like the others, a chairlift is often required to carry skiers from the low base to the treeline from where consistent skiing can be enjoyed throughout the season. This crucial lift was operational at Cerro Bayo for the 1989 season and replaces the poma beside it. Above the top of the chair, at the 1,500m (4,920ft) level, there is great skiing on a protected ridge and in a plunging, south-facing bowl.

The chairlift is hardly the only new improvement at Cerro Bayo. The summit was recently reached for the first time by the new T-Bar which retrieves skiers from the basin at the bottom of the bowl. The old wooden poles of the upper poma lift have been replaced with modern steel towers, and the rickety baskets of boulders have been restored with new cement counterweights. In fact, Cerro Bayo saw more improvements in the end of the decade than any other ski area in Argentina.

Argentina: San Martín to Bariloche

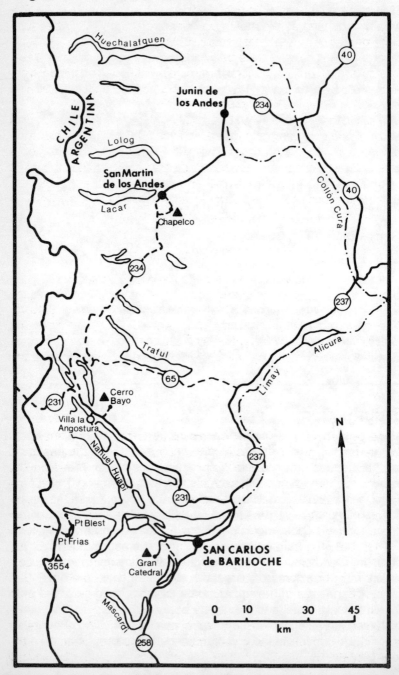

Cerro Bayo

History

Jean Pierre Raemdonck (see Box) arrived in Villa La Angostura in 1961 and began skiing the upper slopes of Cerro Bayo in 1976. The area was chosen as the most appropriate place for skiing because of its proximity to the tourist center of Villa La Angostura. The only other area which might have been appropriate is the Puyehue Pass. Customs and border concerns and the excessive distance from Angostura favored Cerro Bayo, so named for its color (bay, as in a bay horse, or as they like to say, similar to *té con leche*).

Trail clearing began in 1978, and by 1980 the lower poma lift was hauling skiers. A company called Asociación Cerro Bayo was then formed to manage the private land of the ski area. The upper poma was built with minimum resources in 1984, and the critical chairlift was running in 1989 when Jean Pierre was rewarded with a 35-year operating concession. 1990 saw the construction of a new T-Bar and a beginner tow lift at the mountain's mid-level.

Geography

Cerro Bayo (1,782m, 5,846ft) is the name of the double-summited mountain at the southern end of a short range which includes Cerros Inacayal (1,840m, 6,037ft) and Belvedere (1,192m, 3,911ft). The east and southeast-facing runs are well-protected from the prevailing westerlies which often strip the backside of the mountain. Expansive views of the clear Lake Nahuel Huapi are provided at the top of the T-Bar.

Skiing Tips

None of the runs or lifts are named at Cerro Bayo. Two snowcats can groom most of the runs in the ski area, ascending the face on an access road which is also the only easy way to ski down from the mountain's midpoint. Beginners learn on the tow lift at the top of the chair and then download the *aerosilla* to return safely to the base.

Intermediate skiers tend to ski the upper poma lift which ascends the ridge toward the summit. The trail to the immediate left (south) of the poma is the most popular and serves as the race hill. Advanced and expert skiers enjoy the south and southeast aspects of the main bowl left of the upper poma. From the top of the T-Bar, skiers can descend the left side of the lift track to re-enter the bowl or ski the right side to return to the poma lift.

Adventure skiers should try the chutes and bowls of the other summit of Cerro Bayo which is about 50m (165ft) higher than the one served by the T-Bar. The southeastern aspect has several extreme lines, and easier descents are found in the valley separating the two summits. Be sure not to ski too low to return to the lifts as the woods are impenetrable. Avalanche danger here and in the T-Bar bowl can be serious after big storms or in late spring.

Nordic skiers will find the terrain at Cerro Bayo limited. Try driving up the Puyehue Pass and skiing near the summit where more abundant snow and smooth, rolling terrain is found alongside towering rock formations.

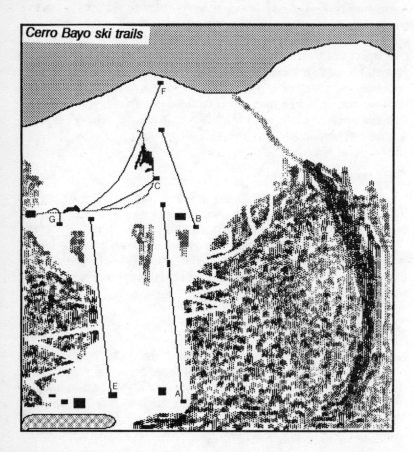

Cerro Bayo ski trails

Skier Services

Cerro Bayo has a small but dedicated group of instructors and patrolmen. Lessons cost about US$5 for a two-hour group lesson, and privates and weekly packages can be arranged. The ski school office is in the small hut next to the rental shop. Villa La Angostura has a small hospital, but serious injuries should go to Bariloche.

Cerro Bayo

Base Facilities

Tickets can be purchased at the bottom of the chairlift. The chair runs year-round, and a single ride sells for US$5. Lift hours are from 9.30am to 5.00pm with half-day rates beginning at 1.30pm. Ticket prices vary with the season.

A cozy *guardería* is located underneath the rental shop (US$0.50, enter from the parking lot side). Rental prices ranged from US$6-10 daily and US$30-50 weekly with a large assortment of adequate equipment available.

Dining

The base cafeteria is the large building closest to the chairlift. Good sandwiches, burgers, and pastries are available, and the young crew is very helpful. It is sometimes dominated by the large student groups which often arrive *en masse*, so it may be better to try one of the *refugios* on the mountain. Left of the top of the chairlift is **Cavla**, and **Isaia** is located between the two poma lifts. Both are leased to competing individuals so the menus vary.

Getting There

From Villa La Angostura

Via Private Auto:
Angostura-Ski Area Rd: Hwy231, 3km (2 miles), 5min, paved.
Hwy231-Cerro Bayo: 7km (4 miles), 15min, unpaved.
Via Bus:
Check at tourist office or with hotel for current service.

From Bariloche

Via Private Auto:
Bariloche-Chacabuco: Hwy237, 20km (12 miles), 15min, paved.
Chacabuco-Ski Area Rd: Hwy231, 59km (37 miles), 1hr, paved.
Hwy231-Cerro Bayo: 7km (4 miles), 15min, unpaved.

Further Information

Papelera San Isidro, SA
456 Corrientes, 1er Piso, (1366) Buenos Aires, Argentina. Tel: 325-6922

VILLA LA ANGOSTURA

Villa la Angostura is a tiny community nestled on a narrow isthmus at the foot of the verdant Quetrihue Peninsula. The town of 3,500 was founded May 15 1932 by Fernando Bustillo, a renowned architect who worked extensively in the area. His churches and chateaus are just some of the countless attractions that lure summer tourists to the area. The difficult highway, which twists around the northeast side of the gigantic Lake Nahuel Huapi from Bariloche, will be completely paved in 1991, and will undoubtedly bring increased tourism to the wealthy village.

Angostura is located in dense forest on the opposite side of the fjord-like lake from Bariloche. Lake Correntoso, which is connected to Nahuel Huapi with a very short river, is behind the village. The town's center is tiny and there are no street addresses. The community is spread out between the center at the El Cruce intersection and the two waterfronts of Nahuel Huapi, both of which have piers to receive ferries in the summer.

Angostura is popular with sports enthusiasts and nature lovers who come to hunt deer, fool trout, pick berries, or harvest mushrooms. Tourism is the only industry, and some of the hotels and restaurants are closed in the slower winter season. Angostura is centrally located in the heart of the southern ski districts of Argentina and Chile with Antillanca (109km, 68 miles), Chapelco (115km, 71 miles), Catedral (115km, 71 miles), and Cerro Bayo all within reasonable driving distances.

Transportation

From Bariloche
Via Private Auto:
Bariloche-Chacabuco: Hwy237, 20km (12 miles), 15min, paved.
Chacabuco-Angostura: Hwy231, 63km (39 miles), 1hr, paved.
Via Bus:
Any Osorno-bound bus: eg:TAS Choapa, 2hr, US$7.

From Osorno, Chile
Via Private Auto:
Osorno-Pajaritos (Chilean customs): Hwy215, 74km (46 miles), 1hr, paved.
Pajaritos-Angostura: Hwy231, 87km (54 miles), 2hr w/customs, mostly unpaved.
Via Bus:
Any Bariloche-bound bus: eg:Bus Norte, 4hr, US$10.

JEAN PIERRE RAEMDONCK

One man is responsible for the proud ski resort at Cerro Bayo. A dedicated skier of Belgian heritage has built the entire lift network and cleared all the trails with a small band of loyal workers. Jean Pierre, as he is respectfully called, is a lanky man with a ruddy face who speaks perfect Spanish with a beautiful Belgian accent. When a problem arises, Jean Pierre is the first to climb the tower, the first to grease the bearings, the first to help the distressed guest. On my first day skiing at Cerro Bayo, there was a local race taking place. Jean Pierre was not only in charge of organizing the event, but was also racing. I'll never forget the image of him leaning over the wooden crossbar of the poma tower in ski boots, wool knickers, and race bib.

The really admirable thing about Jean Pierre's effort is not that he cut all the trails himself. Neither is it that he carried many of the lift parts over his shoulder while riding his motorcycle up the access road (Jean Pierre is also credited with bringing the sport of motocross to Argentina). What's really impressive is that he has been able to construct a modern if modest lift network without begging for foreign capital. While other small resorts complain about the impossibilities of ski area development without outside investment, Jean Pierre has quietly built one of South America's best small ski areas.

Hotels

First Class:
Las Balsas: ½km west of ski area turnoff on lakefront, Dbl:US$100, exclusive, limited rooms.
Moderate:
Lomas del Correntoso: on Hwy234, apart-hotel, prices unavailable.
Correntoso: on Hwy 234, 3km west of town on lakefront, US$25 each w/2 meals, ski programs available, large, transport to hill.
Budget:
Angostura: lakefront by central pier and Chapel La Asunción, Sgl:US$14, Dbl:US$27.
Río Bonito: Topa Topa, Sgl:US$12, Dbl:US$16.
Don Pedro: Belvedere, Sgl:US$10, Dbl:US$13.

Restaurants

Typical:
La Recova: Arrayanes, basic but good.
Cantina de Los Amigos: Los Taiques, good variety, popular.

Pichi Huinca: Arrayanes.
Budget:
Pizza House: Los Taiques w/Belvedere, pizza and pasta, new.
Aproach: in Galería 3 Cerros on Las Frambuesas behind police station, pizza, sandwiches, and ice cream.

Important Addresses
Foreign Exchange: Change in Bariloche.
Post Office: near pier and Hotel Angostura.
Telephone: on Los Lagos.
Tourist Office: on Arrayanes across from ACA.
Bus Terminal: TAS Choapa, Bus Norte, La Union del Sud, in Cantina de Los Amigos; El Rapido Argentino, Lanin, in La Recova.
Ski Shop: Filo Ski, on Arrayanes in center.
Ski Area Office: on Arrayanes, Tel: 94-412.

THE GLOBETROTTERS CLUB
An international club which aims to share information on adventurous budget travel through monthly meetings and *Globe* magazine. Published every two months, *Globe* offers a wealth of information from reports of members' latest adventures to travel bargains and tips, plus the invaluable 'Mutual Aid' column where members can swap a house, sell a camper, find a travel companion or offer information on unusual places or hospitality to visiting members. London meetings are held monthly (Saturdays) and focus on a particular country or continent with illustrated talks.

Enquiries to: Globetrotters Club, BCM/Roving, London WC1N 3XX.

Chapter 31

Gran Catedral

Ski Area Facts and Figures

Elevation: Top: 2,050m; 6,725ft.
Bottom: 1,050m; 3,445ft.
Vertical Drop: 1,000m; 3,280ft.
Season: Early June to Early October.
Lifts: 32:
1 Aerial Tramway (25 Passengers), 9 Double Chairlifts, 2 T-Bars, 9 Poma Lifts, 11 Surface Tows
Runs: 50:
15% Beginner, 60% Intermediate, 20% Advanced, 5% Expert
Ticket Prices, 1990:
US$20 Adults Full Day, US$15 Children 6-11.

Introduction

The management at Bariloche's ski area likes to call Catedral "South America's most important ski area." It is certainly the biggest with some 67km (42 miles) of trails accessed by 27 major lifts with a capacity of nearly 20,000 skiers/hour. Gran Catedral incorporates the competing lift operators of Lado Bueno and Robles and includes the cable car company, the independent Lynch chairlift, and the three rival ski schools of Robles Catedral, Ski Total, and Catedral. The mountain was finally integrated with one lift ticket in 1986.

The reason Catedral is so popular is not the quality of the snow. In fact, it is possible to ski to the base only about 30% of the season as the hill faces east and the summit is at a very low elevation. A strong effort is made to keep at least a portion of the mountain open so that there is always some skiing somewhere on the mountain from June through October. Skiers are attracted to Catedral because over half of the runs are rated intermediate, and the days become warm well before most skiers approach the upper slopes.

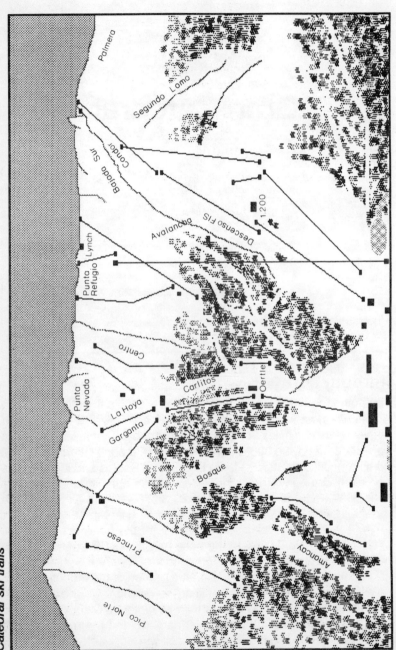

Gran Catedral

History

Cerro Catedral is legitimately called the national *cuña*, or cradle, of skiing. While skiing in the region actually began at Cerro Otto, Catedral was the first place in Argentina to have mechanized ski lifts. In the late 1930s, the focus of skiing in Bariloche moved away from the city after Hans Nöbel, an Austrian hired by the National Park Service for the purpose, identified Catedral as the having the best potential for future alpine ski activities.

In 1939, the order was placed with an Italian lift manufacturer for Argentina's first aerial lift. But the tramway sank to the bottom of the Atlantic Ocean when the cargo ship was destroyed as a consequence of World War II. The tram was reordered and it finally opened on November 28 1950.

Surface lifts were added slowly throughout the 1940s, '50s, and '60s by the Dirección de Parques Nacionales. In 1967, the government finally allowed private bidders to compete for the right to construct a modern ski area on Catedral. Lagos del Sur, the same company that later bought Chapelco and owned Austral Airlines, won the bidding and had new lifts in place for the 1968 season. By 1970, the ridge at Piedra del Condor was accessed with a new chairlift.

A decade later, the government again decided to allow further development of the mountain, this time on the north side of Catedral adjacent to and bordering the existing area. This bidding was won by Vicente Robles who headed a huge construction company in Buenos Aires. He was a frequent visitor to the area and gave the primary management duties to his wife, Graciela. By 1980, after three years of labor, they had built most of the lifts operating today.

For political reasons, Lagos del Sur suffered severe financial setbacks, and in the mid-1980s the government took control of their ski area operations. Like Chapelco, Catedral was mismanaged and a new solicitation was put out for the operation of the "right" side of Cerro Catedral. The property was purchased by Juan Cruz Varela who immediately named the area Lado Bueno, or the Good Side. By 1986, Lado Bueno and Robles had tired of their long competition and united under the banner of Gran Catedral.

Immediate plans for the future call for a greater consolidation of the administrative operations. This will take place with continued lift and run improvement. Future lift plans include the development of Pico Norte. There are also plans for modernistic development of the base area, including a monorail or some other transportation system to move skiers around the base village.

Geography

Gran Catedral is located on the northern end of a range which extends from Lake Mascardi in the south to Lake Nahuel Huapi. The majority of the runs face east, and all other slope aspects are stripped clean by the prevailing westerlies of the region. The normal snowline seems to have ascended to the 1,200m (3,940ft) level in recent years, and skiing to the base is becoming a rarer privilege.

In a five-month season, expect to have good skiing to the bottom of the mountain for one to two months. The snow is typically heavy and soft, and unseasonably warm temperatures or rain often destroy a good mid-season snowpack. Average annual snowfall is 0.4m (16in) at the base, 2m (6.5ft) at the Piedra del Condor, and 5m (16ft) at La Hoya.

Skiing Tips

Three summit areas at Catedral define the ski area. The southernmost is the Piedra del Condor located at the top of Lado Bueno's three Condor chairlifts at 1,785m (5,855ft). In the center is the Punta Nevada whose 2,090m (6,855ft) summit is not quite reached with a lift. On the north side of the ski area, Punta Princesa is at the end of the Robles chain of chairlifts. This area receives the most snow and is well protected for good intermediate skiing all season long. The lifts are color coded, and from the base the red Robles line is on the left, the yellow Lado Bueno lifts are on the right, and the *Cable Carríl* and the green Lynch chair are in the center.

The tram is the oldest lift on the mountain but the cars were replaced recently. Its utility is limited to the first ascent because the location of the bottom station on a hill above and behind the base of the ski area makes the access impractical to skiers. When choosing an ascent route, look to see which side is currently loading pedestrians, then choose the other to avoid long lift lines (although preference is given to skiers).

Beginner skiers have several lifts at the base of Robles set aside for their use. If these are crowded, try the Plaza poma at the top of the Plaza chairlift. Intermediates have a great variety of runs to choose from and can freely ride any lift on the mountain without concern. One of the best intermediate runs is alongside the Condor III chairlift at the top of Lado Bueno.

Advanced skiers will thrill to the high-speed cruising offered by Catedral's upper slopes. For increased steepness, try the runs around the Lado Bueno's Condor II chair and Largo T-Bar. Expert skiers will want to hike or traverse into the beautiful chutes and bowls of Punta Nevada. Most people ascend on a traverse from the Nubes poma, but an easy 15-minute hike from either this lift or the

La Hoya poma accesses the area.

The best mogul runs are Carlitos and La Hoya, both steep trails that start just below treeline. For powder, try a high traverse along the ridge south (right) from the Filo chairlift. The glades of Catedral are dense and thinly covered with snow making most tree skiing hazardous.

Racing

Catedral, Argentina's ski racing capital, is home to many famous and successful ski racing families. Bariloche has a large skiing population and a proud racing tradition. On any given day, there will be several groups of local youngsters practicing on the La Hoya and Nubes pomas or on the Largo T-Bar. Catedral hosts more national and regional races than any other resort in South America on its eight FIS homologated runs.

Adventure Skiing

Adventurers will find ample space at Catedral if they are lucky enough to be there when there is good snow to the bottom. Try the Segundo Lomo and Palmera runs to the south of the Piedra del Condor. These areas are the obvious snowfields widely visible during the drive to the ski area. They offer the continent's best tree skiing, and there are several long roads at the bottom which lead back to the ski area. Wet afternoon snow and thick bushes near the bottom present some difficulties but should not deter expert skiers. The only other possibility is in the Pico Norte. This area is skiable only after considerable hiking, but the new Luipe poma has made it easier to return to the ski area. There is little avalanche danger on the mountain due to high winds that strip the most dangerous slopes.

Nordic Skiing

Not since 1985 has a track been laid in the valley at the bottom of Cerro Catedral. Due to lack of snow, plans to develop cross-country skiing at the area have been put aside. The site would be perfect, as it somewhat resembles the flat meadows of Squaw Valley, but the snowline continues to ascend Catedral each season. With an elevation between 1,000 and 1,200m (3,280-3,940ft), it is impossible to schedule events and races in the area. In exceptional snow years however, expect to find better skiing and more skiers here than at Cerro Otto. Check with the CAB for rentals, lessons, and information.

Skier Services

There are three major ski schools at Catedral, and several ski clubs and individuals in Bariloche offer lessons. The choice between the Catedral, Robles, and Ski Total ski schools depends on a skier's specific needs. Anyone interested in taking lessons should check with each to compare current programs and prices. All have offices in the base village.

The ski patrols at Catedral have a combined total of about 50 professional patrollers. The main clinic is located at the southern end of the base complex near the Lado Bueno ticket office. The clinic and ambulance service is a private concession run by Medicare of Bariloche. Skier insurance is available in the base village.

Base Facilities

Catedral has the best base complex of any ski area in South America. Villa Catedral boasts a great variety of competitive services from ski shops and restaurants to day care centers and *guarderías*. A bank, police station, and ski club facilities are a few of the other facilities in the village. Two information booths are strategically located to assist confused visitors who find the partial description below inadequate.

Tickets, Storage, and Rentals

Lift tickets can be purchased at either the Robles or Lado Bueno ticket offices which are located at the bottom of their respective lifts. All ticket prices vary with the season, and weekly, 15-day, month-long, and season passes are also available. There are also a variety of packages for beginners that include lifts, classes, and/or equipment to make skiing more economical at the entry level. Lift hours are 9.00am to 5.00pm.

There are several equipment storage facilities at the base. American Express cardholders can enjoy this service with no charge at their facility in the Snow Center building located close to the slopes between Robles and Lado Bueno. The Ski Club Bariloche and several of the ski shops also operate *guarderías* which are all economical and provide a warm place to change and boot-up.

Villa Catedral has at least seven different rental and repair shops. Also, several stores in town rent not only ski equipment but ski clothing as well. Skiers can arrive in Bariloche with no ski equipment and still enjoy skiing if they're not too particular. Shop around to find the best prices and equipment.

Dining

Catedral has a great variety of dining options both on the slopes and at the base of the ski area. All the dining facilities are leased in concession to private operators. The restaurants run the gamut from trendy snack bars where the music is loud and the seating outdoors, to fancy tablecloth service with waiters, European dishes, and old-world ambience. On the hill, there is food service at nearly every transition point between lifts. At the base, restaurants, cafeterias, and snack bars are everywhere. This review does not exhaust all the options, but it should be noted that eating is an important part of the ski experience at Catedral.

Beginning on the mountain where dining is both more convenient and enjoyable, there are two exceptional restaurants which deserve special mention. **Piedra Blanca** is located at the top of the Condor III chairlift. It is a large, new, and immaculate restaurant with Catedral's most extensive menu. In addition to the regular selection of sandwiches, dishes like goulash, milanesa, pasta, and polenta are also available. A wide selection of hot and cold appetizers and fresh salads is also offered.

The best views are at the **Refugio Lynch**, the oldest and most formal of all the restaurants on the mountain. The food is more of a mix of typical European and Argentine dishes, and this is the favorite of the families who have been skiing Catedral for generations. The Refugio Lynch is located at the top of Lynch chairlift and can be accessed in combination with the tram by non-skiers.

The other summit restaurant is at Punta Princesa and is called **Salon Los Robles**. The menu here is also a bit more upscale with typical Argentine dishes like *mayonesa de pollo* and *milanesas* as well as sandwiches and burgers. The unique feature here is the cozy bar in the corner that surrounds two fireplaces and offers real coffee and rich cappuccino.

At the base of the Punta Princesa chairlift is the **Tage** cafeteria. *Empanadas* are the specialty here, but the real treat is a chunk of outstanding apple strudel with a spoonful of fresh whipped cream. Other basic cafeterias on the mountain that serve mostly sandwiches and burgers include the **Plaza Confitería** at Plaza Oertle, and the **Platforma 1,200** on Lado Bueno, easily the largest dining facility at Catedral. It features a crepereé, kiosk, and coffee bar in addition to the regular cafeteria service.

At **Las Nubes**, *lomitos*, pizza, and burgers are offered, and **Barrilete**, at the base of the Punta Nevada T-Bar, serves burgers and broiled *chorizos*. Both are very small with most of the seating outside on the decks and on the snow. With seating for 10 inside and blaring music outside, Barrilete is Catedral's most popular dining establishment.

At the base there is even a greater selection of cafeterias and restaurants. Suffice it to say that the most formal luncheon can be leisurely enjoyed in the dining room of the **Hotel Catedral**, while a cup of yogurt can be purchased at the kiosk of the Club Andino Bariloche. In between, there are pizza places, burger barns, and entree eateries of all types. All are relatively expensive, but the quality of the food is high.

Lodging

The **Hotel Catedral**, also known as the Catedral Ski Hotel, serves as the first-class lodge at the base of the ski area. The hotel is a grand, old lodge with wooden floors and ceilings contributing to the alpine ambience of the spacious rooms. Prices are comparable to the better hotels of Bariloche, and range around US$50 each based on double occupancy with two meals. Ski weeks are also available.

There are a few other lodges and several private homes in Villa Catedral. The **Hostería del Cerro** and **Hotel Dhala Ghuri** are a couple of options. The cheapest might be the **Refugio Knapp** of the Club Andino Bariloche. Check at the tourist office in Bariloche to discover other possibilities. Lodging here is a good way to avoid the faster lifestyle of Bariloche but is inconvenient for those who desire to enjoy the fine restaurants and other services of the nearby city.

Getting There

From Bariloche

Via Private Auto:
Bariloche-Puerto Playa Bonita: Ave Bustillo, 8.5km (5 miles), 10min, paved.
Playa Bonita-Catedral: 3.5km (2 miles), 10min, paved, well-signed.
Via Bus:
TA Mercedes: every ½ from office on Mitre, US$4rt, also stops along Bustillo.

Further Information and Reservations

Gran Catedral
Paraguay 783, P9, "B", (1047) Buenos Aires, Tel: 312-2420.
In Bariloche:
Moreno 69, Loc 6, (8400) San Carlos de Bariloche. Tel: (0944)25-348
Hotel Catedral
Farellones SA, Lavalle 482, P5, Der, (1047)Buenos Aires. Tel: 393-9048; 60-006 in Villa Catedral.

Chapter 32

Bariloche's Other Ski Areas

Cerro Catedral is not the only place to ski in Bariloche, but the other ski areas might be considered insignificant to skiers seeking international standards. Options do exist though, and a visit to any of these places would provide an interesting and fun diversion for many skiers.

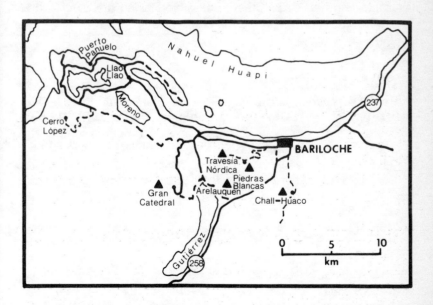

The *Refugios*

There are about 10 mountain huts in the area around Bariloche, and most are owned and operated by the Club Andino Bariloche (CAB). Most *refugios* are reached with a hike of several kilometers, and some are closed in the winter. The highest and best for winter sports enthusiasts is **Otto Meiling** located at 2,000m (6,560ft) on the east side of Tronador, southern Argentina's highest peak. Spring skiing is a popular activity at the **Refugio López**, the largest and oldest lodge in the area.

A few of the *refugios* are located roadside and thus operate as hotels or hostels. Such is the case with **Refugio Knapp** at Villa Catedral and **Refugio Neumayer** in the Valley of Chall-Huaco. Information and reservations for these and several others can be obtained in the CAB office in Bariloche.

Nordic Skiing

There are two principal areas for nordic skiing in the Bariloche area. The first, and most important, is on Cerro Otto. There is also a trail network at the base of Catedral, but it has not been skied for the last several years due to lack of snow (see *Chapter 31*). Chall-Huaco also has a few trails and a good stock of rental equipment. Lessons are available from the CAB. Other accessible touring areas are found around Cerro López or in the Puyehue Pass.

Cerro Otto

Travesía Nódica is a cross-country skiing resort of sorts operating on the slopes between and around Piedras Blancas and Cerro Otto. There are about 15km of trails centered around the **Refugio Tronador**, one of Argentina's oldest and best mountain huts. The *refugio* was the home of Otto Meiling, a local ski pioneer, until his death in 1989. In 1980, he donated all of his property on Cerro Otto to the CAB who will convert the *refugio* into South America's first and only ski museum. Cerro Otto is named for Otto Weiskoff who operated his early climbing school on the mountain.

The ski trails lie at an elevation between 1,200 and 1,400 meters (3,950-4,600ft) and thus are skiable for a very short period of the season. A 10km FIS homologated trail, the only one in South America outside of Ushuaia, is located within the network. The trails are actually maintained by the Escuela Militar de Montaña who train their mountain warfare units in the area. If there is sufficient snow for skiing, it is not possible to ascend to the site in a normal vehicle. Contact the people at Mutasia Viajes or the CAB who share several strong four-wheel drive vehicles. Either can arrange for guides, instructors, and rental equipment and can be contacted for more details.

Alpine Skiing

Around the city of Bariloche, three minor resorts offer alpine skiing. All have just one or two lifts serving intermediate terrain and are designed to receive student groups and large parties. They do welcome the public but are difficult to find. None would be appropriate for advanced skiers but should be sought by beginning and intermediate skiers looking for a low-key ski experience.

Other lifts operate in the area but none for skiers (eg: Cerro Otto, Cerro Campanario). Another lift operates along Hwy258 on the eastern shore of Lake Gutiérrez for summer grass skiing. To clarify confusing reports, Cerro López has good spring skiing but no mechanized lifts. Below is a complete list of all the other lifts in the region.

Piedras Blancas

Piedras Blancas is located on the eastern shoulder of Cerro Otto with the main trail facing east toward Cerros Ñireco and Carbón. Built in 1984 by Guiñazú of Mendoza, the single chairlift has three towers and is about 240m (790ft) long. The ski run descends between the chairline and the parallel sled run in front of the lodge. The chairlift is thus used by skiers and sledders equally. There is also a short rope tow on a flat ridge above the main run.

The trail is sufficiently steep to keep all sorts of winter enthusiasts busy for at least a half-day. Other activities include tobogganing on the fast bobsled-like track, snowmobiling on Arctic Cat Cheetahs, and skibobbing on *bicicletas de ski*. There is also a 10-passenger snow cat for tours of the area. Lift tickets cost US$6 in 1990 with operating hours from 9.00am to 6.00pm. Rental equipment is available but in poor condition. There is a good cafeteria facility at the run's midpoint.

Valle de Chall-Huaco

The Valle de Chall-Huaco, which translates in the Araucana language to "Valley of the Fisherman's Brook," encompasses two small ski hills on opposite sides of a reforested valley. It is the most modern and would be the best destination of the three alpine areas. Built in 1985, Chall-Huaco is a popular summer resort offering horseback riding, hiking, swimming and other activities. In the winter, they operate two surface lifts of about 400m (1,300ft) length each.

The hotel and cafeteria complex is built at the base of Cerro Ñireco at about 850m (2,790ft) elevation. A portable lift can also be installed at Cerro Carbón whose base is about 100m higher.

At Ñireco, the run is on the left side of the simple tow lift that ascends a short portion of the forested slope at the northern base of the 2,200m (7,220ft) mountain. Cerro Carbón has better skiing not only because the run is higher but also because it faces southwest. There is a simple *refugio* at Carbón, and all skiers should first check at the entrance gate of the resort complex before driving the additional kilometer. If there is sufficient snow, the Valle de Chall-Huaco would be a good area to base off-piste touring and alpine ski adventures.

There are four rooms for 15 guests inside the new lodge. The rental equipment (both nordic and alpine) appears to be new and may be the best in the Bariloche area.

Villa Arelauquen

Villa Arelauquen is Bariloche's main golf resort. Located on the northern shore of Lake Gutiérrez, a 450m-long (1,500ft) surface lift was added in 1981 to provide some skiing. The southeast-facing trail descends the right side of the lift and is fairly steep with good terrain variations. On the far right side of the run, near the top, is the beautiful creekside cafeteria. Inside, skiers can arrange lessons or rent equipment. There is also a large assortment of condominiums and apartments available at the resort.

Getting There

To Piedras Blancas and Cerro Otto
Via Private Auto:
Start on Ave de los Pioneros, take 2nd right, look for sign "Acceso a Cerro Otto," go left, drive 1 block, go right on dirt road, 6km (4 miles) to Piedras Blancas; 8km (5 miles) to Cerro Otto, unpaved, very poorly signed, carry chains.
Via Bus
Check at Mutasia Viajes, Alumine Deportes, or CAB.

To Villa Arelauquen
Via Private Auto:
Bariloche-Puerto Playa Bonita: Ave Bustillo, 8.5km (5 miles), 10min, paved.
Puerto Playa Bonita-Villa Arelauquen: Catedral access road, go

Bariloche's other ski areas

staight toward Hwy258 and El Bolsón, 7km (4 miles), paved, (2km unpaved past Catedral road), 15min, poorly signed.
Villa Arelauquen-Ski Hill: enter through gate to traffic circle before golf course, turn left (at sign), 2.5km (1.5 miles), 5min, unpaved, poorly signed.

Via Bus:
Bus 3 de Mayo, No 50: from Moreno w/Rolando, every 20min, US$1.

To Valle de Chall-Huaco

Via Private Auto:
Bariloche-Chall-Huaco Rd: Onelli to Hwy258, 4.5km (3 miles), 5min, paved.
Hwy258-Cerro Ñireco: 4.3km (2.5 miles), 10min, unpaved, well-signed.
Cerro Ñireco-Cerro Carbón: follow road up valley, 1.25km, 5min, unpaved.

Further Information

Refugio López: 1323 Antártida Argentina.
Travesía Nórdica: at Mutasia Viajes, 244 Roland, Loc 9.
Piedras Blancas: write CC301, Tel: 25-720.
Valle de Chall-Huaco: 482 San Martín, P8, "A", (1047) Buenos Aires, Tel: 22-181 in Bariloche.
Villa Arelauquen: write CC582 or 952, Tel: 61-037.

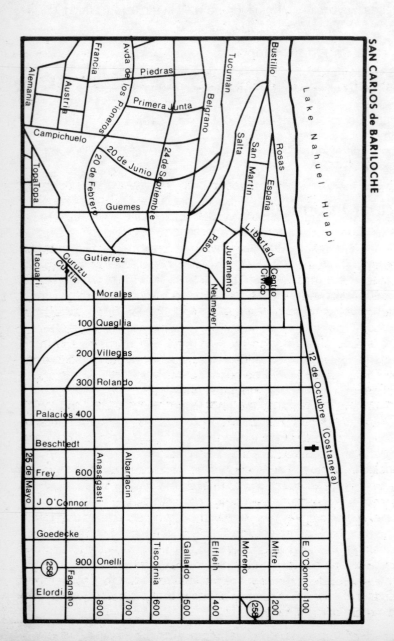

Chapter 33

San Carlos de Bariloche

Introduction

Bariloche is ski town, South America. It is the only community on the continent with a ski culture. With Swiss-style architecture, chocolate shops, and skiing promotion visible all over town, skiers really belong. There are more local skiers and more good skiers in Bariloche than at any other ski resort in South America. Three ski clubs operate from the city with the Club Andino Bariloche, or CAB, the oldest and most active. The Club Argentino de Ski (based in Buenos Aires), and Ski Club Bariloche also promote local skiing.

Bariloche is a town for the upper-middle classes with modest but successful merchants catering to the once-wealthy of Buenos Aires. But it is also accessible to the less fortunate who arrive in large groups to enjoy South America's most popular winter vacation spot. They come not to ski and be seen, but merely to frolic in the snow, novel enough in the alien mountain environment.

There is a downside to the show, and many visitors and locals alike have denounced the city's "progress." Noisy traffic and extreme overcommercialization have all but destroyed the alpine ambience that the *Barilochenses* have tried to create. There are over 50 tourist agencies in Bariloche competing to fill their tour buses with anyone they can entice with pictures or prices. The visiting student groups dominate the streets of the community with their graffiti, cheering, and get-out-of-our-way attitude. With vacation schedules that rotate throughout the year, no season is safe from the hordes. Traffic clogs the main streets and aggressive drivers don't hesitate to express anger with their horns. Marginal *barrios*, largely hidden from tourists on the south side of the city, are the final reminder that some forms of tourism are not the economic panacea that promoters would have government officials believe.

History

San Carlos de Bariloche was founded on May 3 1902 after the German brothers Wiederhold started trading with other Germans on the Chilean side of the border. The name "Bariloche" comes from the nearby Vuriloche Pass which was the most frequently used Trans-Andean corridor of the local Araucano population. In their dialect, Vuriloche means "The People from Behind the Mountains."

Early immigrants to the area included German, Spanish, Basque, French, Italian; and Swiss colonists who sought a terrain and lifestyle similar to that of their own in Europe. Early industries included sheep ranching, timber harvesting, and commerce with Chile as all the major southern passes (Peréz Rosales, Puyehue, and Vuriloche) are within a short distance.

Geography

Bariloche is located in a narrow transition zone between the thick *Bosque Andino Patagónico*, as they call the rain-soaked deciduous forests to the west, and the semi-arid Patagonian plain to the east. The city averages about 800mm (31in) of rain per year, Catedral receives about 2,000mm (79in), and Tronador, in the center of the *Selva Valdiviana*, receives some 4,000mm (157in) of precipitation annually.

Bariloche sits at the southeast end of the 96km-long (60 mile) Lake Nahuel Huapi (Nah-well Wah-pee) near its outlet at the Río Limay. The lake is deep and clear, and several large islands and peninsulas split it into long, fjord-like arms. The lake is situated at 765m (2,510ft) above sea level in the huge Nahuel Huapi National Park. Although the lake's surface is often whipped into a Patagonian frenzy by strong winds from Chile, it is very popular for fishing and other sports in the summer months. The lake is also important as a transportation route, and a variety of ferries cross it even in winter.

Wildlife in the area includes red and axis deer, pudu, *jabalí* (wild boar), *huemul* (a type of deer), red fox, and pumas (cougars). Although most mammals are rarely seen by the casual visitor, some of the huge variety of birds that live in and migrate through the area are frequently spotted. The best flora and fauna can be seen on the nature reserve on the lake's Isla Victoria.

The City

The Bariloche region has about 70,000 inhabitants many of whom are German speaking. The city is built along the waterfront with the main street, **Mitre**, one block from and parallel to the shore. **Bustillo**

San Carlos de Bariloche

follows the lakefront from the train station east of town past Llao Llao some 24km (15 miles) west of the city. It is dotted with all sorts of hotels and restaurants. The downtown area is best defined as the area between the Civic Center to the west, the main cathedral on Beschtedt to the east, and Elflein to the south.

The community spreads westward along the lake to the once-grand but now-condemned hotel at Llao Llao. The lakefront is the focus of summer activities while winter tourism is more concentrated at the ski resort. Many of the beautiful lakefront hotels along Bustillo are closed in the winter season.

Things to See and Do

There are all sorts of organized tours which can be both interesting and economical. The best of these is the *Cruce de Los Lagos* to Puerto Montt in Chile (see *Chapter 6*). Other popular excursions include the *Circuito Chico* (to Llao Llao and Cerro López), the *Circuito Grande* to San Martín via the Siete Lagos, and the ferry trip to Victoria Island and its amazing groves of web-like arrayanes trees.

Skiers intent on riding all the lifts in the Bariloche area will want to ride the modern gondola at Cerro Otto. The four-passenger cars take about 12 minutes to climb to the 1,405m (4,610ft) summit where there is an expensive cafeteria and extensive views. The gondola on Cerro Otto is unrelated to any skiing activity, and all proceeds go to a private foundation that operates hospitals in Buenos Aires and Bariloche. A double chairlift also operates most days at Cerro Campanario for sightseers (Km17 of Bustillo).

Transportation

Since most people arrive at Bariloche in private groups or cars, the town has yet to develop a central bus terminal. Several of the companies have combined offices and all are located in the center of the city. From Buenos Aires, the Club Argentino de Ski has a good weekend ski bus, and many load their car on the train in order to enjoy a safer and more relaxing, if slower, trip to Bariloche.

The main port facility is located about 30km (20 miles) from Bariloche, but there are plans to build a much-needed modern port in front of the Civic Center. The airport is modern but without a public bus service. Taxis will cost US$10 into Bariloche and are widely available in the city.

From Buenos Aires
Via Bus:
Mercedes, La Estrella del Sur, Chevalier, El Valle: daily, 22hrs, US$78, watch for specials.
Via Air:
CATA: 4/wk, 3hr, US$107.
Aerolíneas Argentinas: 3/day, 2hr, US$234rt.
Austral: 10/wk, 2hr, US$125.
Via Train:
Linea Roca: from Constitución, 2/wk, 38hr, Sleeper:US$63, Pullman:US$50, First:US$40, Car:US$94-140.

From El Bolsón
Via Private Auto:
El Bolsón-Bariloche: Hwy258, 129km (80 miles), 2½hr, paving in progress.
Via Bus:
Mercedes: daily, 3½hr, US$9.
Don Otto: 2/wk, 3½hr, US$8.
Charter SRL: 2/day, 3½hr, US$9.

From San Martín de Los Andes
Via Private Auto:
San Martín-Rinconada: Hwy 234, 74km (46 miles), 1hr, paved.
Rinconada-Collón Curá: Hwy40, 60km (37 miles), 45min, paved.
Collón Curá-Bariloche: Hwy237, 132km (82 miles), 1½hr, paved.
Via Bus:
Mercedes, El Valle (not recommended), Koko: daily, 5hr, US$16.
Via Air:
Aerolíneas Argentinas: 5/wk, 30min, US$20.
TAN: 4/wk, 30min, US$17.

Hotels
According to one list, there are 57 hotels, 49 *hosterías*, 53 *residenciales*, and 28 cabin resorts in the Bariloche area not including those at Catedral. Many of these are located along the lakeshore outside of the city and some are closed in the winter. Many book student groups and can be loud in the evenings. If arriving in season (late July), reservations are mandatory and prices are triple. Out of season (September), take your pick and discover very reasonable rates. All of the hotels listed below are located near

San Carlos de Bariloche

the center of town and none accepts student groups. Prices shown reflect 1990 mid-season rates.
Deluxe:
Edelweiss: 202 San Martín, Sgl:US$80, Dbl:US$90, Suite:US$142, best in Bariloche, lake views, some cheaper rooms off season.
Panamericano: 536 San Martín, Sgl:US$102, Dbl:US$113, huge, new, several restaurants.
Sol Bariloche: 212 Mitre, Dbl:US$60, Suite:US$90, central, snooty.
First Class:
Tres Reyes: 135 12 de Octubre, Sgl:US$40, Dbl:US$50, low-key, an old classic, lakefront.
Bella Vista: 351 Rolando, Sgl:US$62, Dbl:US$72, green grounds, overlooks Bariloche and lake, very comfortable, busy.
Bariloche Ski: 663 San Martín, Sgl:US$50, Dbl:US$65, good.
Moderate:
Slalom: 194 Salta, Sgl:US$26, Dbl:US$40, best deal in Bariloche.
El Candíl: 150 Rosas, Sgl:US$30, Dbl:US$40, lakefront, central.
Internacional: 171 Mitre, Sgl:US$30, Dbl:US$40, closest to Catedral bus, central and loud.
Budget:
La Paleta del Pintor: 630 20 de Febrero, Sgl:US$8, Dbl:US$12, best for budget travellers, kind owner, outdoor entrances.
Roshec: 533 Elflein, Sgl:US$15, Dbl:US$20, cheaper for longer stays.
Zagreb: 526 Quaglia, Dbl:US$15, homey *residencial*, good.

Restaurants

Bariloche has more good restaurants than any other city listed in this guide. Many are expensive by South American standards, and reservations are needed at the top spots, even out-of-season. Local specialties include fondue, trout, and smoked meats. There are also many inexpensive locals' places. Try some of the *rotisierres*, especially on 20 de Febrero, for savory *empanadas*, chicken, and other carry-out, hot dishes.
International:
Caza Mayor: 96 Elflein, excellent, local specialties, formal.
Casita Suiza: 342 Quaglia, outstanding, best in Lakes District.
La Chiminée: 351 Rolando (in Hotel Bella Vista), continental cuisine.
Typical:
1810: 167 Elflein, popular *parrilla*, big steaks.
Kandahar: 698 20 de Febrero, homey and warm, great food.
Villegas: 362 Villegas, trout, 15 ways.
Budget:
Mangiare: 150 Palacios, good pizza and pasta.
Pin 9: Rolando w/O'Connor, best pizzas in Bariloche.

Simoca: 264 Palacios, great *empanadas*, try *locro* or *humita*, best value.
Locals' Favorite:
Friends: Rolando w/Mitre, good sandwiches and juices.
La Andinita: 56 Mitre, pizza and *empanadas*.
Weiss: 167 Palacios, smoked meats, fish, and cheeses, don't miss.
Vegetarian:
La Huerta: 362 Morales, good Indian-style food.
Bakery:
La Boutique del Pan: 64 Mitre, great *empanadas*, pastries, rolls.
Outside of City:
Del Viejo Molino: Km6.4 Bustillo, outstanding, expensive.
Il Cabbiano: 24 Bustillo, small, unique Italian-style food.
El Boliche de Alberto: Hwy237 N to police checkpoint, huge Argentine *parrilla*.

Important Addresses

Foreign Exchange: Banco Provincia de Rio Negro, Moreno w/Quaglia; Casa Piano, 131 Mitre; Exchange Turismo, 292 Villegas, best.
Post Office: Centro Civico.
Telephones: 554 Elflein, 127 and 470 San Martín; Quaglia w/Mitre.
Consulates: Chile, 313 Rolando, P7; Germany, 19 Moreno; Italy, 237 Villegas; Spain, 268 Rolando.
Tourist Office: Centro Civico.
Travel Agents: Diner's Club, 166 Quaglia, American Express, 139 Mitre; Visa, 627 O'Connor; Travel Service, 265 Mitre; Mutasia Viajes, 244 Rolando, Loc 9; Alun-Co Turismo, 76 Mitre.
Airlines: Austral, 127 Rolando; Varig, 127 San Martín No 6; CATA, 126 Palacios; LADE, 199 Mitre; Aerolíneas Argentinas, 199 Mitre; TAN, 28 Mitre.
Car Rentals: Avis, 124 Libertad; National, 114 Libertad; Hertz, 295 San Martín; Al, 242 Quaglia; Carro's, 26 Mitre; Budget, 46 Moreno; others, shop around.
Bus Terminal: Don Otto, Carter SRL, TAC, El Valle, Bus Norte, La Puntual, 283 San Martín; TAS Choapa, 459 San Martín; TA Mercedes, 161 Mitre; Chevalier, Koko, 107 Moreno; La Estrella del Sur, 246 Palacios.
Train Station: On Hwy237, 5km from center, tickets at 127 San Martín.
Newstand: Casa Raul, 369 Mitre, *Buenos Aires Herald* and magazines.
Books: Buho, 641 Mitre, English and French; Mileno, 262 Quaglia, Loc 19, mostly German, some English and magazines; Victoria

San Carlos de Bariloche

Ocampo, 163 Mitre; Cultura, 78 Eiflen.
Laundromats: Marva, 474 San Martín, 176 Beschtedt; El Lavadero, 578 San Matín; Brujitas, 93 Belgrano; Lavematic, 258 Villegas.
Art and Handicrafts: Moreno w/Villegas.
Cinemas: Arrayanes, 21 Moreno; Coliseo, 281 Mitre.
Ice Rink: Skating, 742 Mitre.
Cerro Otto Gondola: Km5 Pioneros; public transport at San Martín w/Independencia, US$8.
Ski Shops: Baruzzi, 250 Urquiza, good shop; Alumine, 60 Neumayer, clothes and shoes; Roskenjer, 91 Mitre, sweaters and shirts; Runge Sports, 838 Bustillo, biggest store, good rentals and repair shop, good used selection; also at Catedral base.
Ski Area Offices:
Gran Catedral, 69 Moreno Loc 6, or at Catedral.
Other Ski Related Addresses:
Club Andino Bariloche, 30 20 de Febrero (at Neumayer).
Ski Club Bariloche, 104 Curuzu Cuatia (in Gimnasio SAC).

Chapter 34

Perito Moreno

Ski Area Facts and Figures
Elevation:	Top:	1,450m; 4,755ft.
		Bottom: 1,000m; 3,280ft.
Vertical Drop:	450m; 1,475ft.
Season:	Mid July to Late September.
Lifts:	5:
		1 T-Bar, 4 Surface Tows
Runs:	2:
		20% Beginner, 60% Intermediate, 20% Advanced
T-Bar Prices, 1990:
  US$8 Adults Full Day, US$6 Children; US$5 Adults Half Day, US$3 Children.

Introduction

Perito Moreno is a small ski area owned and operated by the Club Andino Piltriquitrón 25km (15 miles) northwest of El Bolsón. Four short tow lifts have been installed alongside the tidy main run for beginner and intermediate skiers. A modern Doppelmayr T-Bar then hauls skiers from the top of the highest tow to a point well below the rounded summit of the Pico Mayor. The thickly wooded, east-facing hill has not received an abundance of snow in the last several years, but little is needed to cover the short grass and bamboo-like *caña* shoots that grow on the rock-free runs. The ski area is named in honor of Francisco "Perito" Moreno, an early surveyor of the nearby borders whose profession demanded that he become one of the first Argentine skiers.

History

After the club's founding on April 10 1946, members began skiing in the higher Cordón Piltriquitrón southeast of El Bolsón. They even built a 100m-long, five-tower tow lift above their ample *refugio* at "Piltri," as the locals call it. The remote location, lack of a good water source, and the poor northwestern exposure of the ski run were daunting obstacles, though. The hut was located at the top of a steep trail 2km from the closest road. All equipment, including gasoline for the lift, had to be hauled up to the ski run which was another 1km above the *refugio*. This was sometimes accomplished with mules, but club members were the more common beasts of burden.

Therefore, in 1978, the club began working in the Pampa de Luden to build a new base at Perito Moreno. Each summer, trail clearing and lodge construction by members improved the site. The club's skiing activities were officially transferred from Piltriquitrón in the early 1980s when the first tow lifts were introduced. The T-Bar was purchased in 1980, but it could not be installed for financial and technical reasons until 1986. To help defray the costs of installation, a local construction company offered to assemble the lift in exchange for a 10-year concession to operate it.

Geography

Perito Moreno climbs the eastern slope of the Pico Mayor (2,200m; 7,220ft) which lies between the Valle del Encanto and the Arroyo Perezoso. Storms approach from the west, and the ski run is set in the east-facing lee of the prevailing winds.

Skiing Tips

The tow lifts ascend the sides of the only run from the parking lot to the T-Bar. The first two ascend the left side of the tree-lined trail and carry skiers high enough to reach the *refugio*. The third lift, the longest of the four, ascends the right side of the run from the front of the lodge. Skiers must then skate back across the trail to reach the fourth and final tow lift which accesses the T-Bar.

The T-Bar serves the Pista de Mario, dedicated to the memory of Mario Marqués, a Club secretary for 30 years. Skiers can unload at Towers 4 or 5 and follow a road through the forest to reach the main run. The area around the T-Bar track is cleared of trees, but tall *caña* bushes prohibit serious skiing alongside the lift (although there is enough room to sideslip down if a skier falls). The glade areas are generally unskiable unless there is a great amount of snow. A new run is being cleared from the bottom of the Pista de Mario on the left (south) side of the lower run and lifts. A half-day of skiing should be plenty of time for experienced skiers.

Perito Moreno ski trails

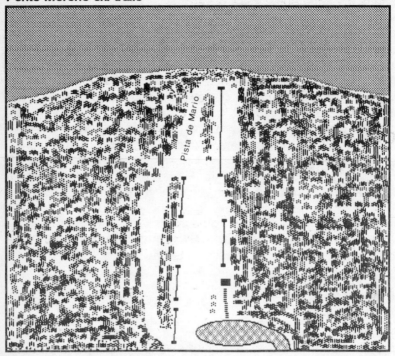

Adventure Skiing

There is no good off-piste skiing at Perito Moreno due to the thickness of the surrounding forest. Adventure skiers should hike to the *refugio* at Piltriquitrón and begin excursions from there. Ice climbers will find a 100m-long frozen waterfall in front of the hut for climbing adventures. The hike to the *refugio* is 2km of very pretty trail and offers great views of El Bolsón and the wide Valle Nuevo below. It should take no more than 30 minutes unencumbered. The Club has four other *refugios* in the region (the best on Cerro Lindo) which are maintained even in winter. Check at the tourist office for current information.

Skier Services

Ski school prices begin at US$2.50 for a group lesson and range as high as US$6.50 for a one-person private. Arrange lessons with Miguel Altamira inside the Club's *refugio*.

Base Facilities

Lift hours are from 11.00am to 5.00pm daily, and half day prices begin at 2.30pm. Tickets can be purchased at the base of the T-Bar.

Use of the other surface lifts is free.
  The lodge is accessed by either climbing the long, sturdy, staircase from the parking lot or by riding the first two lifts. Inside, the bar and cafeteria are modern and comfortable. There are seats for 150 inside, and 70 bunks occupy five rooms upstairs. The *refugio*, always open no matter the snow conditions, is worth a visit. Beds rent for US$2.50 per night, and the food is basic and inexpensive.

Getting There

From El Bolsón
To Perito Moreno
Via Private Auto:
El Bolsón to Tenis Center: Hwy258 north, 5km (3 miles), paved.
Tenis Center-Perito Moreno: Mallin Ahogado Road, 19km (12 miles), 25min, unpaved.
Via Bus:
Check at tourist office for current schedule.

To Piltriquitrón
Via Private Auto:
El Bolsón to Villa Turismo: Hwy258 south, 2km (1 mile), 5min, paved.
Villa Turismo-Piltriquitrón parking area (signed): 13km (8 miles), 30min, steep, unpaved.
Parking area-Refugio Piltriquitrón: 2.5km, 30min, well-maintained hiking trail.

Further Information
Club Andino Piltriquitrón
Casilla 127, (8430) El Bolsón. Tel: (0944) 92-600

EL BOLSÓN

El Bolsón is a small community located at 280m (920ft) above sea level in the middle of the fertile Valle Nuevo, a wide and flat valley that runs north-south. It is the center of a rich agricultural district specializing in fruits and berries. Rich liqueurs, fruity jams, and sweet jellies are the specialties of the region. Local hops account for about 75% of Argentina's hop production. The other important economic activity is tourism with great hunting, fishing, and hiking in the area.
  El Bolsón was founded in 1933 and was incorporated in 1957. Before 1902, the valley was actually a part of Chile but was ceded

to Argentina after the adjudication of King Edward VII of Great Britain. The region is populated with many descendants of immigrants from Eastern and Western Europe with the Welsh influence particularly strong.

The town now boasts about 8,000 permanent residents, but this number swells considerably in the summer months. The center is at the Plaza Pagano with **Sarmiento, Belgrano**, and **San Martín** the main streets. The village is particularly un-South American as development is spread along the highway to Lake Puelo, 18km (11 miles) south. It is thus not nearly as conducive to walking as are most towns in Argentina, and many of the businesses and hotels are closed in the winter season.

Transportation

There is a small airport several kilometers outside of town but only LADE has flights. With the spectacular scenery, travel via the new road is recommended. It should be finished by the 1991 season and will open El Bolsón and Esquel to increased tourism. The drive and bus trips should be shortened by at least an hour by the new road.

From Bariloche
Via Private Auto:
Bariloche-El Bolsón: Hwy258, 129km (80 miles), 2½hr, half paved.
Via Bus:
Mercedes: daily, 3½hr, US$9.
Don Otto: 2/wk, 3½hr, US$8.
Charter SRL: 2/day, 3½hr, US$9.

From Esquel
Via Private Auto:
Esquel-El Bolsón: Hwy259 to Hwy40 to Hwy258, 170km (106 miles), 2½hr, mostly paved.
Via Bus:
Don Otto: daily Mon-Fri, US$9, 5hr.
Mercedes: 5/wk, US$14, 4hr.

Hotels
Moderate:
Cordillera: 3210 San Martín, Sgl:US$18, Dbl:US$26, clean, modern, helpful.
Amancay: 3217 San Martín, Sgl:US$12, Dbl:US$22, warm, friendly.

Perito Moreno

Budget:
Hostería Steiner: 900 San Martín, US$4 each, 2km from center, difficult to find, great food, very hospitable.
Hostería Edelweiss: 364 Angel de Agua, US$4 each, basic.

Restaurants
Typical:
El Viejo Maitén: 359 Roca, outstanding local specialties, clean, friendly, best in town.
Don Diego: 3217 San Martín, very good, in Amancay.
El Candíl: Sarmiento w/Belgrano (across from ACA), good *parrilla*.
La Posta del Indio: 2469 Sarmiento, good and inexpensive.

Important Addresses
Foreign Exchange: Change in Bariloche.
Post Office: 2306 San Martín.
Telephone: San Martín w/Pellegrini.
Tourist Office: San Martín w/Pellegrini, very helpful.
Bus Terminal: Don Otto w/Mercedes, 2377 Perito Moreno; Charter SRL, 2524 San Martín.
Cinema: Amancay, 2528 San Martín.

SKI NUKE FREE

When I finally found the ski area at El Bolsón, I couldn't believe that there was no fee to use the Club Andino's ski lifts. Their discovery was hampered because each of my road maps had the little red skier printed in different spots around the small town. In addition, a variety of road signs in El Bolsón indicate that the route to the ski area is both north and south of the community. Although I got to know the town quite well, it was not until my third trip through the area that I finally located the lifts and runs of Perito Moreno.

El Bolsón is an agricultural community two hours south of Bariloche. Due to the poor road, mass tourism has yet to spoil the town which has become famous as a haven for Argentina's hippie youth. These peace-loving, nature-seeking inhabitants have declared the entire valley a *Zona No Nuclear*. In the summer, they sell their handicrafts and artwork at a twice-weekly bazaar in the central plaza. In the winter, most return to school or to their warmer hometowns leaving El Bolsón to the very few who can appreciate the humanity of free skiing in a nuclear-free zone.

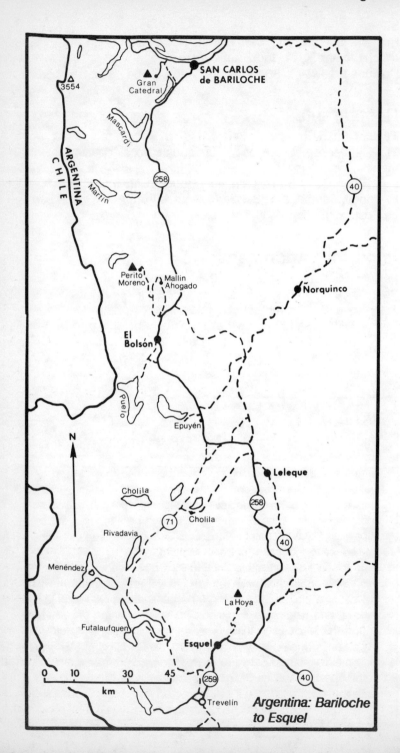

Chapter 35

La Hoya

Ski Area Facts and Figures

Elevation: Top: 1,850m; 6,070ft.
               Bottom: 1,350m; 4,430ft.
Vertical Drop: 500m; 1,640ft.
Season: Early July to Late October.
Lifts: 5:
               1 Double Chairlift, 1 T-Bar/Single Chairlift, 3 Poma Lifts
Runs: 7:
               20% Beginner, 30% Intermediate, 40% Advanced, 10% Expert
Ticket Prices, 1990:
    US$17 Adults Full Day, US$8 Children; US$13 Adults Half Day, US$4 Children.

Introduction

La Hoya is the mid-sized ski area located about 15km (9 miles) from the tranquil town of Esquel. It can be viewed as the southernmost ski area in the Lakes District or as the most northerly in Patagonia. La Hoya is set above the treeline in the middle of a wide, south-facing, circular basin and boasts good skiing later than the other ski areas of the region.

In spite of good, consistent skiing, La Hoya has been known as a regional center attracting skiers from Rawson, Comodoro Rivadavia, and other Patagonian cities. Anyone from the north skis at Bariloche because it is a bigger resort with easier access. Two factors are easing La Hoya's isolation. The first is the completion of a direct, paved route between Bariloche and Esquel. The other is the recent privatization, on May 9 1990, of the provincially owned resort.

History

La Hoya was first skied in the 1930s by enthusiasts who learned of the sport in Bariloche. In the 1940s, the military garrison stationed in Esquel began winter training in the valley. They changed the name from *Pirrén Challá*, as it was known to the local Indians, to La Hoya (The Basin). Their *refugio* was soon augmented by that of the Club Andino Esquel which was formed in the 1950s.

The first lifts were constructed in 1974 by the provincial government. The double chair and T-Bar were joined by two portable tows in 1978 and the upper poma lift in 1980. The ski area was managed as a private club for government bigwigs and their pals who had little, if any, interest or incentive to commercialize the site. The privatization was the result of strong, nationwide political pressures to sell the inefficient enterprises of the bloated Argentine government. A Buenos Aires construction firm named Vialco, SA obtained a 40-year lease just before the 1990 season. Vialco had been active in the region as the principal contractor of the hydroelectric project at Futaleufu, about 50km from Esquel. Vialco joined with Turismo Lago Traful, a Buenos Aires travel agency, to form La Hoya Ski, the new operator of La Hoya.

Plans call for developing La Hoya's upper slopes and building hotels at the base of the ski area and in Esquel. Extensive trail improvement will complement the five or six new lifts due to be built over the course of the next four to five years.

Geography

La Hoya is positioned in the middle of the Cordón de Esquel which reaches 2,093m (6,867ft) at its highest point. The north-south range is about 70km (43 miles) east of the *Cordillera* and the border with Chile. About 30% of the available skiing terrain is now serviced by lifts. The ski area is divided into La Hoya Inferior (all the terrain below the top of the "T-Chair"), and La Hoya Superior.

In spite of its low elevation, La Hoya has a long season because a warm sun never hits the south-facing slopes. The bottom chairlift runs alongside a creek that drains the basin in a deep valley much like Venus at Las Leñas. Treeline is reached just before the top of this lift, and the trail is skiable about half of the season.

Skiing Tips

Description of the five main runs at La Hoya is difficult because none are named. Snow conditions are often icy on the main runs but can soften into corn in the spring afternoons.

Beginner skiers practice on the tow lifts in front of the mid-station

La Hoya

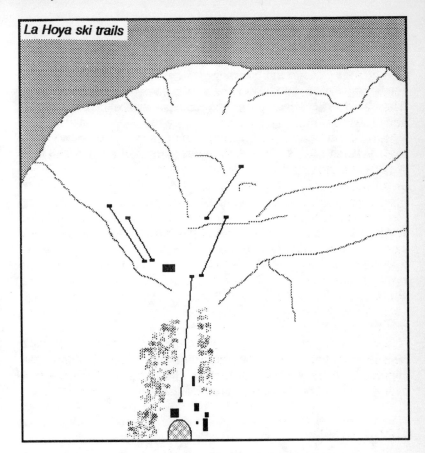

La Hoya ski trails

cafeteria. Intermediates prefer the two variations of the run on the left (east) of the upper poma. Advanced skiers can find four excellent bowls to the right of the T-Chair (the middle lift). The bowl closest to the lift is the most popular and is often heavily mogulled. Expert skiers will find some steep — if somewhat narrow and rocky — chutes on the right side of the T-Chair. Four separate runs on the main face have been certified by the FIS for slalom and GS races.

Adventure Skiing

What really makes La Hoya special is the vast amount of expert terrain within easy reach of the ski lifts. The easiest and best is the snow-filled bowl above the two poma lifts. The corniced ridge is reached with a simple, 15-minute traverse west from the top of the upper poma. Hard chutes empty into the bowl on its left side, while the right side softens earlier than expected due to its more northerly orientation. After a few runs in this area, skiers will want to continue past this bowl to reach the top of the long chute system that ends at the midpoint of the lower double chairlift. Scout a route on the first ride in the morning by looking left and up.

Any other ridge in the cirque can be reached with no more than two hours of moderate hiking. Safe ridge lines provide access to six major bowls all of which are clearly visible from the top of the upper poma. Avalanche danger is minimized by the lack of major storms; weakened cornices and unstable spring snowpacks provide the biggest hazards. A week could be easily passed enjoying hikes to the off-piste terrain of La Hoya.

Nordic Skiing

Nordic skiers will find little appropriate terrain at La Hoya. Cross-country enthusiasts should instead seek snow in the Los Alerces National Park, famous for big lakes and tall trees and deserted in the winter season.

Skier Services

The able ski school at La Hoya has several young instructors who specialize in teaching kids. Rates begin at US$6 for a two-hour group lesson with six or more skiers and reach US$13 for a one-hour private. Lessons are arranged at the ski school desk inside the mid-mountain cafeteria. The ski patrol is run by Bill who has five other professionals to maintain the runs and assist distressed skiers. Be sure to inform them of any off-piste skiing plans.

Base Facilities

Lift tickets can be purchased at the base of the chairlift and are included in ski-week packages. Six and seven-day passes are available at a discount. A single chair ride is US$4. Lift hours are 10.00am to 5.00pm, and half-day tickets are sold from 12.30pm.

There is a basket check adjacent to the ski school desk in the mid-station facility. The ski area's rental shop is in the middle building at the base of La Hoya. Good rentals are also available in Esquel, and it would be worthwhile to compare the current variety of equipment and prices.

Dining

Outstanding, home-style fare is served in the **La Piedra** mid-mountain cafeteria. Sandwiches and burgers are also available, but the *Plato del Día* is healthier, tastier, and cheaper. Plan on eating late to avoid the noontime crowd. The cafeteria at the base also has very good food, but it is impractical unless there's sufficient snow to ski to the base.

The Hotel

Rates at the **Mont Blanc** hotel at the base of the ski area were US$33 each including two meals in 1990. Weekly packages are also available. Esquel is close, interesting, and fun, so the strong recommendation is to stay in the city. The ski area books packages for several of Esquel's hotels. Prices listed in the appendix include transportation from Buenos Aires and daily connections to La Hoya. Independent travellers can save US$285 without the transportation and US$68 without rental equipment and classes.

Getting There

From Esquel
Via Private Auto:
Esquel to La Hoya Road: Hwy259, 1km, paved, (turn after bridge and go through military zone).
Hwy259-La Hoya: 13km (8 miles), 20min, unpaved but good, US$2 parking fee at La Hoya.
Via Bus:
Don Otto: 2/day, US$2, check current schedule at terminal.

Further Information and Reservations

La Hoya Ski
Viamonte 377, (1053) Buenos Aires, Argentina. Tel: 311-2164.

ESQUEL

Esquel is a town of about 20,000 inhabitants set in a valley between the Welsh settlements of Trevelín (south) and Leleque (north). The city is known for its summer tourism industry and serves as a transportation hub for the region. Esquel is also the gateway to the Los Alerces National Park which has some of Argentina's best fishing and hunting but is still unknown to the majority of the sports-minded Argentines. Recent forest fires have damaged the eastern edge of the park. The city was founded in 1895 and incorporated in 1946. The population is particularly young, friendly, and dark-skinned.

THE T-CHAIR

The central ski lift at La Hoya connects the bottom part of the ski area to the upper slopes. Without this lift, the mountain would be nothing. Not only does it provide crucial access, but it serves the only advanced runs at La Hoya. Serious problems develop, however, when the T-Bar track becomes too icy or rocky for the beginner skiers who ascend the steep face to access the upper mountain. La Hoya has a unique solution.

In hindsight, this is all quite easy to explain. But, imagine my disappointment when I returned from an exciting run to find that they had closed the T-Bar. When I asked the mechanics for an excuse, they explained that the track was too icy for the *principantes* who were having great difficulties. So, tell them to go home, I thought in muted disgust, and shrugged my shoulders in resigned acceptance of more Latin mismanagement. They suggested that this would be a good time to break for lunch in the nearby cafeteria. Oh, I get it, the snow will soften sufficiently in the next hour to reopen, sure...!

When I returned, the lift had undergone a complete transmutation, a changing of the apparatus, a metamorphosis of iron. It turns out that the able crew has a hidden stash of single chairs available for just such an occasion. They had replaced half of the T's with chairs and were ready to proceed. Loading procedures have to be highly organized because the sitters have to remove and carry their skis. In exchange, they can unload 25m higher on the top ramp. It's really strange to ride the chair and see skiers ascending directly below you on the extended ropes of the T's. It is more distressing to ride the T-Bar with a beginner up above dripping snow (and who knows what else) on your head. This system is probably not unique in the world, but for someone accustomed to detachable quads and protective gondolas, it was astonishing.

Transportation

Esquel is the southern terminus of the near-interconnected South American rail system. The journey from Ingeniero Jacobacci on the narrow-gauge steam train is described in Paul Theroux's *The Old Patagonian Express*. The rail line was finished in 1946, and in spite of its somewhat shabby condition, the train still functions. The airport is about 22km (14 miles) east of town and public transportation meets the commercial flights. Southern bus travel from Esquel is difficult, especially in winter.

La Hoya

If driving, try Route 71 which is a big summer tourist corridor but is absolutely deserted in the winter. This detour begins after Epuyén and increases travel time from El Bolsón by at least an hour. The road passes Lakes Lezana, Rivadavia, Verde, Menéndez, Futalaufquen, and Terraplén, to name just a few. Fill the tank with gas, check the spare tire, and make a day of it.

From El Bolsón
Via Private Auto:
El Bolsón-Esquel: Hwy258 to Hwy40 to Hwy259, 170km (106 miles), 2½hr, mostly paved.
Via Bus:
Don Otto: daily Mon-Fri, US$9, 5hr; from Bariloche, US$17, 11hr.
Mercedes: 5/wk, US$14, 4hr; from Bariloche, US$22, 10hr.

By Air
Aerolíneas Argentinas: from Bariloche, 2/wk, 40min, US$34; from Buenos Aires via Trelew, 4/wk, 3hr, US$234.
LADE: check airport for current flights.
TAN: from Bariloche, 3/wk, 25min, US$28; from Chapelco, weekly, 1½hr, US$42.

By Train
Ferrocarril General Roca: from Jacobacci, US$7, 14hr; from Buenos Aires, Constitución Station, 42hr, Sleeper:US$57, Pullman:US$46.

Hotels
First Class:
Tehuelche: 825 9 de Julio, Sgl:US$40, Dbl:US$45, overrated but under new management.
Sol del Sur: 1096 9 de Julio, Sgl:US$28, Dbl:US$40, small but good.
Moderate:
Hostal La Hoya: 2296 Ameghino, Sgl:US$13, Dbl:US$26, between center and ski area turnoff, new and clean, best for motorists.
Angelina: 758 Alvear, Sgl:US$15, Dbl:US$20, nice, central.
Huemul: Alvear w/25 de Mayo, Sgl:US$13, Dbl:US$16, popular bar, close to bus terminal.
Budget:
Arrayán: 767 Antártida Argentina, Sgl:US$10, Dbl:US$13, best value in town, central, dark.
Huentru Niyeu: 606 Chacabuco, Sgl:US$9, Dbl:US$14.

Hospedaje Argentino: 862 25 de Mayo, US$3.50 each, near bus, good.

Restaurants
Typical:
La Tour D'Argent: 1063 San Martín, a favorite, try the *Arroz a la Cubana*.
Jockey Club: 949 Alvear, popular with tourists, try a *Suprema*.
Vascongada: 9 de Julio w/Mitre, businessmen's favorite, outstanding food and wine, inexpensive.
Budget:
Ashla Wsahla: 1100 San Martín, popular for sandwiches and drinks.
Pub El Correo: 1038 Rivadavia, hamburgers, popular with young crowd.
Bakery:
Confitería Suiza: 569 Antártida Argentina, Welsh tea room with great pastries.

Important Addresses
Foreign Exchange: Change in Bariloche.
Post Office: Fontana w/Alvear.
Telephone: 850 San Martín.
Tourist Office: at bus terminal.
Airlines: LADE, 777 25 de Mayo; Aerolíneas Argentinas, Fontana w/Ameghino.
Bus Terminal: end of Fontana on Alvear.
Train Station: Alberdi w/Roggero.
Laundry: Marva, 823 Rivadavia; Laverap, 543 Mitre.
Cinema: Coliseo, 558 25 de Mayo.
Disco: Ver, 543 25 de Mayo.
Ski Shop: Bad Boys, Rivadavia w/Mitre, basic but nice; Gemelo'sport, 1067 9 de Julio, best in town; Bolsa de Ski, 612 25 de Mayo, good shop and rentals.
Ski Area Office: Viajes Schneider, 1024 Almafuerte.

Chapter 36

Valdelén

Ski Area Facts and Figures
Elevation: Top: 830m; 2,725ft.
Bottom: 580m; 1,900ft.
Vertical Drop: 250m; 825ft.
Season: Mid May through September.
Lifts: 2 Surface Tows
Runs: 3:
30% Beginner, 70% Intermediate
Ticket Prices, 1990:
  Weekends: US$13 Adults Full Day, US$10 Children under 16.
  Weekdays: US$10 Adults Full Day, US$ 6 Children.

Introduction

Valdelén may be the smallest ski area in South America, but it seems to have the highest proportion of skiers to residents on the continent. The slopes become crowded every day around 4.30pm when working parents are free to car-pool their kids up to the ski hill. With night skiing continuing until 9.00 or 10.00pm, everyone can get in their daily turns. Those without transportation take to the steeper streets of snowy Río Turbio with homemade sleds and anything else they can coax to slide.

History

The Club Andino Río Turbio installed its first lift in 1977 in the area known as Mina Uno, so named because this is where the first of many interconnecting coal mines was dug. Throughout the following summer, members worked to clear trees for two new portable tows which were purchased and installed in 1979. The decade of the '80s saw limited construction at the base of the ski area including the *refugio* which was actually built by the Army for the club.

Ongoing projects include the expansion of the small cafeteria at the base. In the next two years, the club hopes to replace the two portable tow lifts with a permanent chairlift. The portables would then be moved to the left side of the existing runs where a *gelandesprung* jump is sometimes erected.

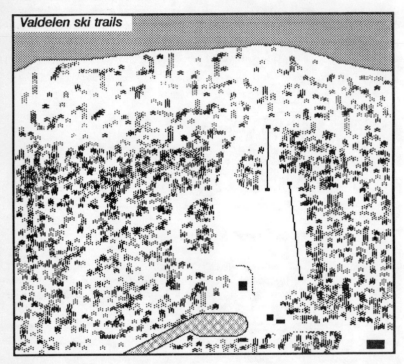

Valdelen ski trails

Geography

Valdelén is located at the weathered end of the Andes on a subrange called the Sierra La Dorotea. The actual hill is properly called either Mina Uno or Mina Arriba and is covered by the *ñire* and *lenga* trees typical of the Patagonia area. It is Argentina's southernmost ski area on the mainland. The Argentine customs house is at the end of Valdelén's parking lot, and the actual border is at the top of the pass, about a mile distant.

In spite of low elevations, Valdelén has one of South America's earliest and longest ski seasons. Storms approach from the southeast, but lingering clouds typically dust the hill every evening. A relatively thin base (40cm, 16in) is sufficient to ensure good skiing because of little melting and the lack of sharp rocks on the eroded and grassy hill.

Skiing Tips

All trails are cut in the forest and tree skiing would be impossible in most of the thick groves. A gully left (west) of the main run provides the only variant from the three trails. There are no snow cats for grooming, but 14 street lamps provide South America's best night skiing.

Both lifts have about 15 handles, and skiers will soon tire if they allow the handle to pull them up by their arms each run. To load, grab a handle as it passes with your right hand. When secure, pull your body forward and place the handle behind your thighs. With your left hand, grasp and support the end of the handle behind your body. Switch your poles to your right hand which should rest on the cable to hold it at a comfortable level.

Adventure Skiing

There's really no good off-piste skiing in the Mina Uno area. Talk to Jerman Gregory about skiing the area called La Meseta del Torre. This is located about 20km from Río Turbio and is reported to have great snow and challenging runs. Otherwise, try the Torres del Paine area north of Puerto Natales. There is no avalanche danger in the region.

Nordic Skiing

The Club Andino maintains about 16km of cross-country trails just east of the ski area. A 10.5km track called Monte Ñire and an 6km track called Monte Lenga are marked. A shooting range alongside the course makes the track appropriate for biathlon training, but the sport is not popular in Río Turbio. About 10 sets of good nordic equipment are available in the rental shop.

Base Facilities

Lift hours are from 11.00am to 11.00pm but skier demand usually shortens these to roughly noon to 9.00pm with longer hours on weekends. Purchase tickets in the rental shack.

Equipment can be safely left in a corner of the cafeteria. Change in town, in the restrooms, or in the changing area of the rental shop. A large but tired collection of old skis and frozen boots is available in the rental shop located adjacent to the cafeteria. Rental prices are the same as lift tickets.

The cafeteria at the base has 10 tables and can accommodate no more than 50 skiers at one time. The lodge is popular with the kids who play cards and listen to loud music. Good sandwiches, pastries, coffee, and liquor are available at the counter at economical prices.

The *Refugio*

The *Municipalidad* of Río Turbio operates the lodge which is located a few hundred meters east of the base of the ski area. It was originally built by the Army for the club, but the new leadership in the higher ranks of the provincial government decided it would be better to give it to the city. At any rate, the lodge is as comfortable as any other in the area and is rarely crowded outside of the holiday periods. There are eight rooms with 36 bunks that sell for US$2 per night. There's no restaurant, but guests may be able to use the modest kitchen facilities. Bring food.

Getting There

From Río Turbio

Via Private Auto:
Hwy40, 4km (2.5 miles), 10min, unpaved and icy, international pass well-maintained, difficult driveway to parking lot, park by customs station.

Via Bus:
Check at tourist office. Otherwise take the Puerto Natales bus for US$2.

From Puerto Natales, Chile

Via Private Auto:
Hwy9: 16km (10 miles), 15min, paved.
Turnoff to Río Turbio: 13km (8 miles), 45min depending on customs, unpaved.

Via Bus:
Río Turbio bus: unload at Argentine customs, 1hr, US$2.

Further Information

Club Andino Río Turbio
Casilla 279. (9407) Río Turbio.

RÍO TURBIO

Río Turbio, a small town of gravel streets and steam locomotives, is located in a winding valley within 5km of the Chilean border. The city was named by the Englishman, William Greenwood, who gave it the label of a nearby rushing creek. The town is affectionately called "Sled City" because of the abundance of kids riding a variety of sledding devices on the steep streets of the village. Río Turbio is atypical because it is one of the few towns on the continent where the population actually lives in the snow for a good portion of the year. In addition, the town stands equally in the main valley and the surrounding hills, creating streets which deviate from the grid pattern so commonly found in nearly all other South American cities.

The story behind the existence of Río Turbio is coal (*carbón*). The black mineral was first discovered in 1887 by Naval Lieutenant Agustín del Castillo. A railroad was built to transport the ore to Río Gallegos and its port at Punta Loyola. It is Argentina's biggest and only active coal field. The industry has brought in workers from Chile, Uruguay, and other South American countries who make up almost 50% of the town's population.

For those with or without interest in the topic, the mine, owned and operated by the state energy company YPF, conducts tours through its Museo y Escuela de Minerolagía. The tour is a hands-on experience with good models of a variety of mining systems and all sorts of functioning drill and hydraulic equipment. The tour is actually required for all workers who enter the shafts and lasts an hour. Arrange the visit at the tourist office in the city (there is no winter schedule). This is a highly recommended activity even for those who won't understand any of the guide's Spanish monologue.

Railroad buffs will be interested in the coal train, which is not only the southernmost railroad in the world but also one of the last that still employs steam locomotives. It is also the only train in Argentina that doesn't connect with Buenos Aires. No passenger cars run on the line, but it may be possible to hitch a ride.

Although the town has a real and severe shortage of hotel and restaurant facilities, hardy tourists should not hesitate to visit. It is easy to imagine yourself in some sort of one-horse, frontier town in Wyoming, and the friendliness and joviality of the population is unmatched by any of South America's other ski towns. For skiers who prefer a more luxurious standard, the tourist-oriented Chilean city of Puerto Natales is just 30km (19 miles) from Valdelén.

Transportation

Río Turbio's airport has a gravel runway and poor connections with the city. In addition, flights are often delayed or canceled due to dangerous weather conditions. The bus, although it arrives after dark and is nearly twice the price, is more reliable and recommended from Río Gallegos. Reports indicate that the coal train may take a few passengers, so it may be worth asking. Transportation is cheaper and easier from Puerto Natales, Chile, so try to plan the approach from the west.

From Río Gallegos
Via Private Auto:
Hwy40: 239km (149 miles), 4hr, unpaved.
Via Bus:
Expresso Pinguino: daily, 8.00am, 8hr, US$15.
Via Air:
LADE: 5 days/week, 1½hr, US$8.

From Puerto Natales, Chile
Don't forget 1hr time change.
Via Private Auto:
34km (21 miles), 1hr w/customs, paved in Chile, gravel in Argentina.
Via Bus:
4/day, last to Puerto Natales at 8.00pm, can load/unload at Argentine customs at ski area, 1hr, US$2.

Hotels
Moderate:
ACA Capipe: Dufour 30, prices unavailable.
Budget:
El Gato Negro: on Laprida, Sgl:US$8, Dbl:US$12.
Azteca: Laprida w/Castiglione, prices unavailable, may be closed in winter.

Important Addresses
Post Office: Castiglione w/Peña.
Telephone: Peña w/Mineros.
Tourist Office: ask for Prof César Cetta, San Martín w/Paso, tel: 91-266.
Bus Terminal: Expresso Pinguino on Borritt; bus stop for Puerto Natales on Castiglione at Borritt.

Chapter 37

Ushuaia's Ski Areas

Introduction

There are five individual ski centers in the Ushuaia area. Since each is quite small, the descriptions deviate from the normal format. The two alpine ski areas, Wolfgang Wallner and Glacier Martial, are located just north of and overlooking Ushuaia. Between the two is the Club Andino's nordic ski area called Francisco Jerman. Several kilometers northeast of the city are two more cross-country ski centers, Tierra Mayor and Las Cotorras. All five are serviced by Ushuaia, the southernmost city in the world.

History

The first skier in the region was Ernesto Krund, a postal carrier who reportedly skied between Ushuaia and Río Grande before the highway was constructed. Organized skiing began in 1956 with the formation of the Club Andino Ushuaia, or CAU, whose purpose was to promote all sorts of adventure tourism in the zone. Founding members had started skiing recreationally in the Martial area in the 1950s. The club's first project was the construction of a small *refugio* alongside the ski run. The structure was repeatedly destroyed by fire and storms, but was rebuilt by club members each time despite the difficult, narrow trail that led from the city to the hut.

The club soon acquired title to a wide, wooded hill on the northwest edge of the city. This site was chosen over Martial because the slope was better protected from the harsh weather by dense trees. The relative ease of access and the more challenging angle of the slope also appealed to members. The first ski lift was a portable tow which arrived in 1973. A second, permanent poma lift was installed in 1978. The Martial chairlift was installed in 1983 by

Tierra del Fuego: Puerto Natales to Ushuaia

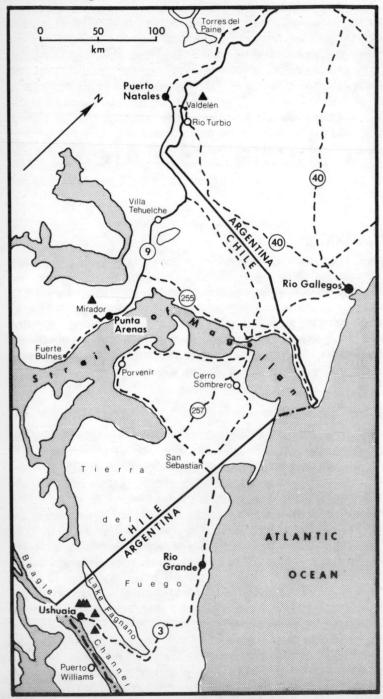

the city government who sought to promote both summer and winter activities in the nearby valley.

Nordic skiing advanced with the arrival in 1975 of Francisco Jerman, Argentina's biggest *protagonista* of nordic skiing. The CAU recruited this dedicated skier from Bariloche in order to develop the sport in Ushuaia which is not only ideally located for the sport, but also has an athletic and enthusiastic population. In 1976, Gustavo Giró, an Antarctic tour operator, opened a nordic ski area in the wide, flat valley of Tierra Mayor. This proved to be a natural complement to his summer operations, and his sons and daughters soon became national ski and biathlon champions. Las Cotorras was one of the huts used by the early mail carriers and developed a small trail network for skiers in the late 1970s. The CAU did not develop its nordic facilities until 1980.

Geography

The ski season around Ushuaia generally lasts from early July to late September. An earlier storm will, however, start the season because short days and low temperatures prevent melting until spring. Destruction of the accumulated snowpack is instead performed by the high-velocity, ground-hugging winds that often roar down the valleys of the region. Storms normally approach from the southwest and will drop 10-15cm of very light, dry snow over their 2-3 day duration.

Alpine Skiing

Two alpine ski areas, each with one principal and one beginner lift, are located very close to Ushuaia. The CAU offers skiing at the northwest edge of the city on a run named Wolfgang Wallner in honor of one of the founding members of the Club. The other ski area, Glacier El Martial, is located above Wallner in the bottom of a narrow valley which leads to the Martial glacier. Wallner is clearly the locals' favorite place to ski.

Glacier El Martial

Martial has the only aerial lift on Tierra del Fuego. The Doppelmayr double chairlift begins at 114m (374ft) above sea level and ascends a deeply carved, but softly inclined valley to the top of the treeline. It lies right (east) of the brook that drains the circular basin above. The prevailing winds blow down the valley making the ride particularly bracing. A second tow lift runs directly underneath the chairline alongside the top two towers.

There are two south-facing runs at Glacier Martial. The main run is 30 meters wide and cuts into the left (west) side of the valley. The run slopes gently with eroding banks on the right side and sudden drops into the forest on the left side. A second run could be described under the chairlift. This trail needs a great deal of snow to facilitate skiing and rates upper intermediate mainly because skiers need to be alert not to hit their heads on the dangling skis of chairlift passengers.

Outstanding backcountry skiing could be enjoyed from the top of the lift, and it may be possible to enlist the assistance of a snowcat. Numerous extreme and avalanche-prone chutes and bowls come into full view after a short hike from the top. A ski adventure here would be a day-long ordeal and should be attempted only by the most experienced ski mountaineers.

At the base is a cafeteria and bar serving good meals and sandwiches in season. Most skiers will ride the chairlift before donning their equipment because the upper lodge has more services. It is located several meters above the top of the chairlift and is thus rather inconvenient. All ski area services such as lessons and rentals are located in this structure which also houses a dining facility. Pristine views of the Beagle Channel and its islands are enjoyed from the top.

About six instructors are available. Their services cost US$3 for a group lesson and US$7 per hour for a private. A few volunteer patrollers, one toboggan, and the hospital in Ushuaia provide medical services. Tickets are purchased at an outdoor window before loading. Ticket prices in 1990 were US$13 with a single ride selling for US$5. A full equipment setup rented for US$8, and the inventory is in fair condition. Plastic sleds are also available. Operating hours are from 10.30am to 6.00pm daily except Monday when the lifts open at 2.00pm. The lift is open year-round regardless of snow conditions.

Wolfgang Wallner

Ushuaia's other alpine ski area, Wolfgang Wallner, is the lowest ski area in South America and the southernmost ski area in the world. Starting from a base altitude of 90m (295ft), the detaching poma lift ascends the left (west) side of the trail. A second tow lift is located on the left side of the base of the poma and ascends to the third tower of the larger lift. The ski area is named in homage to CAU Member No 1 who served as club President for 25 years until his death in 1970.

The main run is rated upper intermediate to advanced. The south-facing trail is frequently mogulled, and the locals like to build jumps

Ushuaia's ski areas

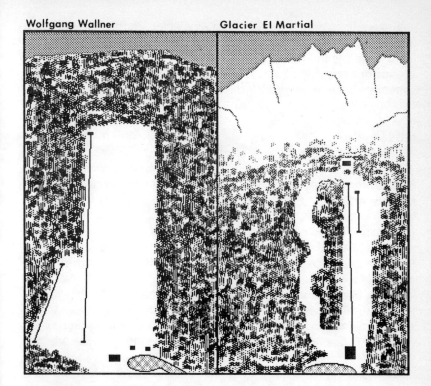

and ramps to add variety to the immaculate and consistent slope. The bordering forest is impenetrably thick and there are no off-piste options.

There are three structures at the base complex which is easiest reached by taxi. The main building is a two-story *refugio* that houses a very basic food service facility and the ticket window. The A-frame structure to its right is the ski school building, and a rental shop is inside the third building. All the facilities are rather rustic and are best viewed as clubhouses rather than lodges.

Rates at Wallner were US$8 for the poma and US$4 for the Bambi lift in 1990. Ski lessons sold for US$7 for a private and US$5 each with a group of four or more. Adventurous night skiing is popular, and each tower has at least one light to illuminate a minimal part of the trail.

Nordic Ski Areas

Ushuaia is, without question, the nordic skiing capital of the continent. Low elevations and cold temperatures combine to make the spot ideal for nordic training, and many international teams come to Ushuaia to train in the off-season. There are about 100km of trails between the three developed ski centers. Jerman is the most wooded of the three, but Tierra Mayor has the best developed trail system and is the most popular. Other possibilities for skiing in the region abound. The best is probably at Lapataia where the CAU maintains a small *refugio*.

Tierra Mayor

Tierra Mayor is the biggest of the three nordic centers with about 50km of trails set in a beautiful sprawling valley between the high peaks of the continent's terminus. The lodge sits on the southern edge of the massive Valle de Tierra Mayor which runs east-west and seems to be an old, shallow lake bed. Trails start at the lodge, cross the valley, and weave in and out of the forest below the barren peaks north of the valley. The *hostería* is the most modern lodge in the Ushuaia area, and 20 rooms should be ready for rental by the 1991 season.

Tierra Mayor is run by Gustavo Giró and his large family who all share in the duties of operation. Anna, the oldest daughter, directs the Ski School, while Gustavo, Alejandro, and María help where needed. Other activities at the resort include snowmobile rides on 340cc Lynx machines, dog-sled trips behind stocky huskies, and "wind skiing" in the spring. On a recent return trip from the Antarctic season, their three snowcats were lost in the treacherous depths of the Drake Passage.

There are four principle trails at Tierra Mayor. The Pista Valle/Bosque more or less circumnavigates a section of the valley, weaving in and out of the trees for 5km. Dique de Castores crosses the road to make a 6km loop southeast of the valley. A 13km loop located west of and then behind the lodge is used for training purposes. The last trail is the circuit to the small **Refugio Cerro Bonete** and the frozen Laguna Perdida (10km). The cozy *refugio*, 8km from the *hostería*, can sleep six. Overnight arrangements can be made in the main lodge.

Prices for the 1990 season were US$4 for the use of their well-maintained rental equipment. Lessons are provided by several qualified racers. Prices range from US$5 for a one-hour group lesson to US$18 for a one-hour private. Classical, skating, and biathlon techniques are taught to classes of any level. Snowmobile tours can be arranged with rates starting at US$6. A guide accompanies all trips to keep snowmobilers apart from skiers and their tracks. The new hotel rooms will be priced around US$35. Use of the ski area's trails was free in 1990.

Francisco Jerman

The CAU opened this nordic ski area in 1980 on a broad ledge above its alpine run at 165m (541ft) above sea level. Named for Argentina's greatest cross-country skier who passed away before seeing its completion, the trail network at Francisco Jerman provides 15km of skiing on six well-marked routes with a total vertical change of about 50m (165ft). FIS homologated trails of 3km, 5km, and 7.5km are complemented by 1km, 2.5km, and 4km routes. The trails alternate through the forested glades and open clearings, and sturdy wooden bridges cross the countless brooks that flow through. All the trails are well-signed with color codes keeping skiers on the correct route and skier silhouettes demonstrating the proper technique.

The small *refugio* is located at the start of the trail network 5km (3 miles) from the center of Ushuaia and 1km below the Glacier Martial alpine area. A small amount of rental equipment is available for US$3/day. Ticket prices in 1990 were US$2/day. Be sure to check at the club's office before going up.

Las Cotorras

Las Cotorras is an old ranch which lies 26km (16 miles) northeast of Ushuaia and 5km (3 miles) past Tierra Mayor. Most of the 30km of trails are cut through the forest, but many cross open clearings as well. A homey restaurant is located inside the roadside lodge where nordic equipment can be rented. Snowmobiles and sleds are also available for non-skiing adventures. There is no public transportation to this ski center, but it would be possible to ski here from Tierra Mayor when snow levels permit.

Getting There

From Ushuaia

To Wolfgang Wallner:
Taxi: 5min, US$2.
Bus service from Club Andino: check at office.
To Glacier Martial:
Van service: from Rumbo Sur, 4-14/day depending on snow, 10min, US$2rt.
To Tierra Mayor:
40 passenger bus: 10.00am and 2.00pm from hotels Antartida, Cabo de Hornos, Beagle, and Albatross, returns 1.00pm and 6.00pm, 30min, US$6rt.
To Francisco Jerman:
Bus service from Club Andino: check at office.

To Las Cotorras:
Private auto: Hwy3, 26km (16 miles), 30min, unpaved, chains required.

Further Information
Las Cotorras
Km26, (9410) Ushuaia.
Glacier Martial
Hotel Maitén, 1406 12 de Octubre, (9410) Ushuaia. Tel: (0901) 92745.
Tierra Mayor
638 San Martín, Loc 14, (9410) Ushuaia. Tel: (0901) 21073.
Wolfgang Wallner, Francisco Jerman
Club Andino de Ushuaia, 58 Juana Fadúl, (9410) Ushuaia.

USHUAIA

Ushuaia, at 55 degrees south latitude, is the southernmost city on earth. It sits on the south end of the island of Tierra del Fuego on the northern shore of the Beagle Channel. In spite of its maritime location, the city's port facility is important only as a small naval station. The city stretches along the coast on a gently sloping and wooded bench below Cerro Martial and the impressive Monte Olivia. The city was founded in 1880 and has about 25,000 inhabitants. Important regional industries are timber harvesting, sheep ranching, fishing, trapping, and tourism. Ushuaia is still administered from Buenos Aires, but locals hope to have their own government by 1992.

Ushuaia has a well-developed and modern tourist infrastructure, but it is Argentina's most expensive city. Winter rates at the wide variety of hotels are generally half of the summer rates though, and reservations are never needed in the off-season. The city is similar to a small Bariloche with the main streets paralleling the coast and steep, icy secondary streets linking the sea to the mountains. The main street is **San Martín** with the two blocks (or months?) between 9 de Julio and 25 de Mayo reserved for pedestrians. The city is duty-free which is of great benefit to the sport of skiing in the region as all ski-related equipment can be cheaply imported.

Several days will be needed in Ushuaia to fully enjoy all of its winter activities. In addition to the five surrounding ski areas, there is good ice skating in the 250m-wide Bahía Encerada in front of the city (skate rentals are available in the office of the CAU). There is a good museum which has displays of the region's interesting Indian and pioneer histories. The best souvenirs from the region, fungi-laced wood knot deformations called *nudos*, are available everywhere. Summer visitors should bring heavy spinning tackle because the trout and salmon in the area's lakes and rivers are the fattest of South America's fresh fish monsters.

Transportation
Ushuaia has a good airport on an island in the bay 2km south of the city (with a good view of Ushuaia and its ski runs). Construction on a major new international airport has been slowed due to economic difficulties. It is possible to walk from the airport to town without much luggage. Taxis are overwhelmed when the flights arrive, so share (US$2 to any hotel). Only Los Carlos operates a bus to Ushuaia. The scenery is spectacular but the trip is slow and cold. There are no direct connections to Punta Arenas, yet (see *Chapter 6*). Drivers must carry chains whose use is usually obligatory in winter outside of the city.

From Río Grande
Via Private Auto:
Hwy3: 229km (142 miles), 3hr, unpaved, chains required.
Via Bus:
Transportes Los Carlos: daily, 5hr, US$14.
Via Air:
LADE: daily, 30min, US$20.

From Buenos Aires
Via Air:
Aerolíneas Argentinas: daily via Bahía Blanca, Trelew, and Río Gallegos (US$47), 6hr, US$252; from Bariloche via Trelew, US$257.

Hotels
First Class:
Canal Beagle (ACA): Maipú w/25 de Mayo, Sgl:US$31, Dbl:US$34, waterfront, great restaurant, best in Ushuaia.
Albatross: 505 Maipú, Sgl:US$14, Dbl:US$27, best value, waterfront.
Cabo de Hornos: San Martín w/Triunvirato, Sgl:US$16, Dbl:US$19, central, good.
Moderate:
Antártida: 1600 San Martín, Sgl:US$11, Dbl:US$18, on hill overlooking city, long walk to center, best restaurant, disco.

Mustapic: 230 Piedra Buena, Sgl:US$11, Dbl:US$14, cheaper rooms w/shared bath, good.
Monte Cervantes: San Martín w/Sarmiento, Dbl:US$12, homey and nice.
Hostal Malvinas: 615 Deloqui, Dbl:US$19, overpriced, poor, noisy.
Budget:
Capri: 120 San Martín, Sgl:US$7, Dbl:US$10, less with shared bath.
César: 753 San Martín, Sgl:US$9, Dbl:US$11, very central, simple.
Maitén: 1406 12 de Octubre, English speaking, west side of town.

Restaurants
Typical:
Tante Elvira: 232 San Martín, best in Ushuaia.
Quick: 140 San Martín, good, typical menu.
Budget:
Ideal: San Martín w/Roca, great *empanadas*.

Important Addresses
Foreign Exchange: Banco del Sud, 116 Roca, poor rates and high commissions; better in tourist office.
Post Office: San Martín w/Godoy.
Telephone: 154 Roca.
Hospital: 12 de Octubre w/Malvinas Argentinas.
Tourist Office: 505 Maipú, in lobby of Albatross.
Travel Agents: Rumbo Sur, 342 San Martín; Tiempo Libre, 154 San Martín; Onas, 50 25 de Mayo.
Museum: Museo Territorial, 177 Maipú, good natural and Indian histories.
Consulate: Chile, Malvinas Argentinas w/Kuanip.
Airlines: Aerolíneas, 505 Maipú, in lobby of Albatross; LADE, 542 San Martín; Austral, 564 San Martín.
Car Rental: Avis, in Albatross; Austral, 1022 Paz; Autograd, 368 Deloqui.
Bus Terminal: Los Carlos, 85 Triunvirato.
Newsstand: Kiosko Avenida, 749 San Martín, English language periodicals and *Buenos Aires Herald*.
Laundromat: 139 Rosas.
Ski Shop: Popper, 740 San Martín, outstanding store and repair shop, huge selection, alpine and nordic.
Ski Area Offices:
Club Andino Ushuaia: 58 Fadúl (ex-Solis).
Cerro Martial: in Hostería Maiten, 1406 12 de Octubre.
Tierra Mayor: Antartur, 638 San Martín, Loc 14.

Part IV

THE NORTHERN ANDES AND ANTARCTICA

The story of skiing in South America certainly does not end with Chile and Argentina. Indeed, the Andes extend north into Venezuela, and many high peaks and volcanoes dot the entire length of the range. Snow quality and quantity in the northern Andes is generally poor due to the equatorial latitudes in spite of high elevations. But, economic and cultural factors are as important as geography for explaining the total absence of ski lifts north of the Uspallata Pass (excepting Chacaltaya).

Each of the northern Andean countries of Bolivia, Peru, Ecuador, Colombia, and Venezuela do have mountains and snowfields that offer skiing. None have native skiers that engage in the sport locally for recreation, and any limited operations found exist for foreign visitors. Only Chacaltaya in Bolivia presently operates a ski lift, although Colombia did have two lifts operating on the Nevado del Ruiz earlier in the century.

The northern Andes differ from the southern Andes in several respects. From northern Chile to Venezuela, the mountains often form two or three distinct *cordilleras* that often boast comparable elevations. As such, the northern Andes never form an international border as they do between Chile and Argentina.

There is no clearly defined ski season in the northern Andes. The tropical wet and dry seasons have little influence in the higher altitudes. Thus, the only consistent skiing is found year-round on the glaciers where good ski conditions are rarely found. Tropical glaciers are receding worldwide however, and skiing prospects in the region are dimming as well.

Only the most proficient and conditioned skiers should attempt to ski at any of the following locations. Crevasses, ice falls, and rapidly changing weather are some of the unique hazards presented on the high (5,000m+), glaciated peaks of the northern Andes. Skiers must bring their own ski equipment, but mountaineering equipment and experienced guides are widely available in each town listed.

Chapter 38

Bolivia

Chacaltaya, the World's Highest Ski Area

Ski Area Facts and Figures

Elevation: Top: 5,420m; 17,785ft
             Bottom: 5,220m; 17,130ft
Vertical Drop: 200m; 655ft.
Season: November through March.
Lifts: 1 Cable Tow
Runs: 1
             100% Intermediate
Ticket Prices, 1990:
  US$3 Adults Full Day.

Introduction

Chacaltaya. The highest ski area in the world. The only ski area in South America outside of Chile and Argentina. The most equatorial ski area in the world. The oldest ski lift in South America. The fastest surface lift in the world. The northernmost ski area in South America. The only ski area in South America with a season that corresponds to that of North America. The most difficult lift to load in the world. Chacaltaya.

Chacaltaya's lift ascends the middle of a year-round snowfield high above the elevated *altiplano* of Bolivia. The top of the mountain is near 5,570m (18,275ft), and the lift ascends to a point perhaps 150m (500ft) below the summit. The slope itself is mostly intermediate, but combine the slope with the rarified air and the ski area rates advanced. When the complexities involved in loading Chacaltaya's antiquated lift are factored in, this ski area is for experts only.

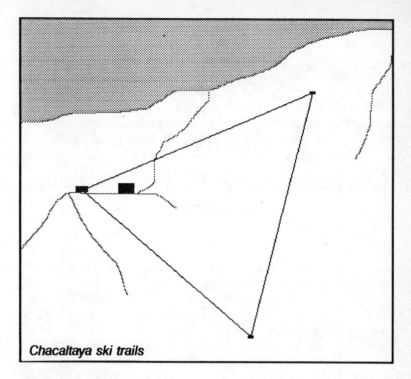
Chacaltaya ski trails

History

Chacaltaya was originally built in the late 1930s by the Club Andino Boliviano which was founded in 1938 by an engineer named Raúl Posnasky. With incredible effort and commitment, the club built a road to the closest permanent snowfield to La Paz. The lift was built with a long cable and an old Ford engine which is sheltered in a stone hut built for the purpose. Raúl made one mistake, however, in the process. He did not inaugurate the project with the traditional Indian *Chaya* ceremony alleged to bring good fortune and success to such undertakings. On July 4 1945, Sr Posnasky and two other club members were caught in an avalanche at Chacaltaya. One victim was able to dig himself out; another was quickly rescued and revived. Raúl Posnasky was found upside-down after an hour of frantic searching. He could not be revived and died of suffocation. The Indian Gods, having finally been appeased, have since permitted skiing to continue at Chacaltaya, but if anyone has plans to develop another,....

Bolivia and Chacaltaya have played an important role in the development of alpine skiing in South America. The Pan American Ski Championships were held there in 1943, and several top international racers developed at the area in the 1940s and 1950s.

The most adept and successful of these racers was René Farwig who competed with top results in Europe. Chacaltaya continues to maintain its racing tradition, and a self-financed team was even sent to the 1988 Calgary Winter Olympics.

Geography

Chacaltaya is located in Bolivia's Cordillera Real. Although it is a year-round snowfield, the lift is generally open only during the rainy season. Skiing can be found as early as mid-September though. During the colder dry season, the snow is too hard and icy for safe skiing. Even in-season, the lift and bus only operate on weekends.

Skiing Tips

The cable tow is a speeding cable that begins its triangular course from the power shed to the bottom of the lift high in the air. It then passes over about seven wooden towers (with old tire rims for sheave support) on its quick trip to the top before descending, again well above the run, back to the power shed. The cable runs at about the same speed as a modern detachable chairlift.

Before attempting to load the lift, skiers must familiarize themselves with the hauling apparatus. This crucial piece of equipment will stay with the skier for the duration of the day. It consists of a bent piece of rebar-type iron tied to a lengthy piece of knotted and frayed rope with a poma-type platter attached to the other end. The whole thing is about 2m (6ft) long and can be wrapped around the skier's waist when descending.

To load, hold the hook over the cable (pointing uphill), and allow the cable to zip freely in the U-shaped groove. When you feel comfortable, lock the hook onto the cable by pulling tension on the rope making sure your fingers are clear. This will not work if the skier is seated on the platter as the length of the rope is too great. As you zoom away, hang on to the rope with your hands, and slowly ease yourself back onto the platter. The key is to maintain constant tension on the rope to sustain its bight on the cable. Whenever this tension is released, the hook will fly off the cable, and the skier will have to try again. Try it without ski poles if experiencing difficulties. To unload, simply flip some slack onto the rope, or just drop it.

The main run is located between the *refugio* and the lift and is called Pista Central Slalon (sic). There are a few little chutes on the other side of the lift for greater challenges. Nearly everyone skis on the left side of the lift. The track can be difficult to cross and is easiest at the top as the cable ascends to the bullwheel. Do not ski below the lift as the snowfield feeds into a cliff. It is possible to hike a bit for a longer run, but rough snow and high altitude make the effort pointless.

Base Facilities

The Club Andino's *refugio* is called the **Cabaña de Las Muchachas** and was constructed of stone in the 1940s. It is located at the midpoint of the main run on the skiers' right. The smaller cabin, precariously perched on the reinforced cliff face, houses the motor of the lift. Visitors who do not arrive on the club's bus may not be allowed into the *refugio*. Tickets and ski rental are obtained in a small room in the lodge. Travellers report that the equipment is for Bolivian-sized skiers. Larger gringos are unlikely to find anything that fits. Since the equipment and lift hooks are in short supply, and the man behind the counter is in no hurry, try to be quick into the lodge to start the process if serious about skiing.

The lift ticket is a flimsy piece of paper which is never checked, but it is not possible to ski without it. That's because the real "ticket" is the tow hook assembly, and skiers should be certain not to lose it while skiing. There is no storage facility, but it is safe to leave shoes and equipment in the lodge. The limited selection of rental equipment is in poor condition, and adequate boots are particularly difficult to find. The cost is about US$10 for the equipment, and a deposit or collateral is required.

The *refugio* serves some food but it is fairly expensive. Most skiers find they have little appetite at the high elevation. The specialty is *té de coca* which is alleged to mitigate some of the effects of the altitude.

Getting There

From La Paz

Via Private Auto:
Take airport road through El Alto and north toward Bolivian Institute of Cosmic Physics and Chacaltaya: 36km (22 miles), 1½hr, unpaved.
Via Bus:
From Club Andino: 8.30am weekends, US$6, 2hr. The bus usually returns early as the high elevation and afternoon rains tend to chase skiers away.

Further Information

Club Andino Boliviano
1638 Calle Mexico, Casilla 1346, La Paz, Bolivia. Tel: 32-4682.

LA PAZ

La Paz, Bolivia's administrative capital, is a unique city. It is the world's highest capital city at 3,650m (11,975ft) above sea level which places it near the top of several of the continent's highest ski resorts. This high elevation seems low for the region though, as La Paz is actually built in a protective hole 440m (1,445ft) below the rim of the blustery *altiplano*. Unlike Santiago where the nicest neighborhoods climb the hillside to view the city, La Paz's best areas are located at the lowest and most sheltered part of the valley.

History

El Hueco, or the "hole" of the gold-filled Choqueyapu River, was discovered by the Spanish expeditionary, Don Juan de Saavedra, in 1535. The city was founded on October 20 1548 by Don Alonso de Mendoza who named it *Nuestra Señora de La Paz*. The site was of geographical importance as a commercial center between the rich silver deposits of Potosí-Sucre and Peru from where the new territory was administered. It was attacked many times by local Indian groups until 1849 when it was declared Bolivia's new capital city. Sucre remains as the legal and judicial capital.

The City

La Paz is one of the world's most culturally and geographically interesting cities and is easily explored by foot. The more than one million *Paceños* are hospitable and view tourists with more disinterest than hostility. Lost street hikers can easily gain their bearings by ascending any of the steep avenues to gain a good view of the clear-aired city. La Paz is neither touristy nor primitive, and visitors can easily assimilate into the urban scene by visiting one of the many markets of the city.

The downtown area of La Paz is filled with beautiful plazas, churches, and markets. It encompasses the area from the Plaza Murillo and the San Francisco church in the north, to the Sheraton La Paz and municipal park to the south and east. The main street runs through the center of the valley from the higher northwest end to lower neighborhoods of Obrajes and Calacoto to the southeast. It is called **Montes** and then **Santa Cruz** when entering the valley from the poorer El Alto neighborhood, and becomes **16 de Julio**, or simply **El Prado**, in the central high-rise area. It then changes to **Villazón** as it passes the San Andres University and finally **Arce** at the lower end of the city.

Things to See and Do

There are many things to do in and around La Paz other than try to hook onto the speeding cable of Chacaltaya. La Paz should be visited as part of a larger tour to the old Inca capital of Cuzco and the 3,790m-high (12,435ft) Lake Titicaca, the world's highest navigable lake. Chacaltaya is the best place for short hikes and for viewing the Cordillera Real although the glacier-riddled slopes of Mt Illimani are visible from most parts of the city. The other "must see" attraction outside of the city is the Valley of the Moon. This geological moonscape of strange erosionary formations is located just a few kilometers southeast of La Paz.

Of all the great markets in La Paz, the most unique is the Witchcraft Market on Linares behind the San Francisco church. The items on display are quite odd but are unavailable for purchase by the amazed *gringos* who would be uninformed and skeptical of the items' true powers. The market found a couple of blocks further up Sagárnaga sells mostly clothing items and seems to continue forever through the narrow backstreets of La Paz. The best general market begins at the north end of the Plaza San Francisco. Work through the huge produce and meat warehouse to the back where proud Indian women in their bowler hats and bulky skirts compete to pump anything into their electric juice machines for thirsty passers-by.

The Plaza Murillo is the heart of the city. Although it is relatively small by South American standards, the square is surrounded by the main cathedral and the executive and legislative government buildings. For entertainment, check for the postings of upcoming shows and concerts around the University. Jazz is particularly popular in La Paz, and there are several good clubs in the nicer neighborhoods.

Transportation

There are many ways to arrive in La Paz, the easiest of which is flying. Air passengers have the disadvantage of arriving suddenly to the lofty city and will need extra time to acclimate. The **El Alto** airport is the world's highest, and visitors need to temper first-day travel ambitions. Several top airlines have connections to La Paz, and there is an inexpensive bus service to and from the airport. For Cuzco, deal with one of the many travel agents for a comfortable trip combining buses and trains with a ferry across Lake Titicaca.

Other overland connections are tedious, dusty, and complex if inexpensive. The train services are generally better, and tracks lead to Arica and Antofagasta in Chile and Tucumán in Argentina.

Hotels

La Paz has many hotels for both business travellers and more economy minded tourists. They are usually booked by large tourist groups in season, and lodging can be difficult to find late in the day. Prices were unavailable for the 1990 season.

First Class:
Plaza: 1789 16 de Julio, newest and nicest, most central.
Sheraton La Paz: Ave Arce, exclusive, modern, complete.
Sucre Palace: 1636 16 de Julio, best classic, overpriced.
Moderate:
Libertador: 1421 Obispo Cardenas, new, central, nice.
Crillón: Plaza Isabel Catolica, warm, friendly, older.
Gloria: 909 Potosi, nice rooms, good value.
Budget:
Residencial Rosario: 704 Illampu, popular, good.
Residencial La Hostería: 138 Bueno, clean, cheap, basic.
Torino: 457 Socabaya, central, clean.

Restaurants

There are all types of restaurants in La Paz the most expensive of which are located on 11 de Julio. The Bolivian *churrasquería* is similar to the Argentine *parrilla*, and many have a peña folklore show. Those with limited budgets can eat well and cheaply in the markets and on the streets if they are acclimated to this rewarding practice.
Typical:
Paso de Los Torres: 664 Buenos Aires, good typical food.
La Estancia: 1559 Mexico, Bolivian *churrasquería*, good for steaks and all types of meat.
Naira: 161 Sagárnaga, good food and shows.
Budget:
Pizza de la Piedra: 6 de Agosto, basic pizzas.
China: 1549 16 de Julio, good cheap Chinese dishes.
Try around the University and markets for good food and prices.

Important Addresses

Foreign Exchange: several on Camacho and Prado.
Post Office: Ayacucho w/Potosí.
Telephone: 267 Ayacucho.
Tourist Office: Mexico w/16 de Julio.
Travel Agencies: Crillon, 1223 Camacho; Transturin, 1321 Camacho.
Consulates: Brazil, 2038 20 de Octubre; Britain, 2732 Arce; Chile, 13 Siles; France, 5390 Siles; Germany, 2395 Arce; USA, 1285 Colón.

Airlines: AeroPeru, 1490 16 de Julio; Lloyd AB, 1460 Camacho.
Car Rental: Imbex, 2303 Arce; International, 1942 Zuazo.
Train Station: Plaza Zalles.
Books: Los Amigos del Libro, 1321 Mercado.
Cinema: Campero, 1495 16 de Julio.
Ski Area Office: Club Andino Boliviano, 1638 Mexico (ring bell).

ALTITUDE SICKNESS

The only serious medical problem cautious skiers are likely to develop is altitude sickness, called *soroche* locally. This is a potentially serious condition that can lead to acute mountain sickness. Common symptoms include weakness, headache, dizziness, disorientation, stomach sickness, and shortness of breath to name just a few. The most likely to be affected are skiers who arrive to La Paz by plane, but any such sudden ascent mandates an unambitious pace in the early parts of a visit. In Chile and Argentina, the elevations at some of the resorts around Santiago and Mendoza are only slightly higher than at major US ski areas. The highest base is at Portillo (2,850m, 9,350ft), and skiers should have little difficulty here or at any other resort in Chile or Argentina.

The best precautions against altitude sickness are to acclimate slowly, drink plenty of sugary fluids like fruit juice, and avoid alcohol and other drugs. Although oxygen and aspirin can mitigate some of the effects, the only cure for *soroche* is a decrease in elevation. From Las Leñas, visit San Rafael or Mendoza for a day, at Portillo or Farellones, return to Santiago and enjoy the sites of this great capital. At Chacaltaya, *coca* tea is the recommended remedy, and it is served in the clubhouse.

Chapter 39

Peru

Pastoruri

The main range of the Andes in Peru is the westernmost. Several subranges lie east of this ridge especially in the south near Cuzco. Peru's highest mountain is Huascarán (6,768m; 22,205ft) north of the capital, Lima. Just south of Huascarán is one of Peru's nicest towns, Huaraz. Huaraz is Peru's climbing and skiing capital, and local guides have an established ski network. The main ski area is a few hours from Huaraz at Pastoruri. Longer expeditions can be organized to several good *refugios* in the region. For further information, seek Jorge Martel in the Casa de Guias in Huaraz.

THE SOUTH AMERICAN EXPLORER'S CLUB

With offices in Quito, Lima and the USA, the club serves the interests of adventurous travellers. Members receive the quarterly magazine *South American Explorer*, have access to libraries and trip reports, can buy, sell or store equipment, talk to experts, and get the most out of South America.

Membership details from the following addresses:

BRITAIN	USA	ECUADOR	PERU
Bradt Publications	126 Indian Creek Rd	Apartado 21-431	Casilla 3714
41 Nortoft Road	Ithaca	Eloy Alfaro	Lima 1000
Chalfont St Peter	NY 14850	Quito	
Bucks SL9 0LA			

Chapter 40

Ecuador
The Avenue of the Volcanoes

Ecuador's Andes are split into two ranges, the Eastern and Western Cordilleras. Between the two, the central valley is divided into several basins with Quito, Ecuador's capital, set at 2,850m (9,350ft) in one. The central valley is often referred to as the Avenue of the Volcanoes because high volcanoes rise to prominence on both sides of the valley. The highest is Chimborazo (6,310m; 20,702ft) in the Western Cordillera whose summit is the furthest point from the center of the earth due to the equatorial bulge. The south slope of Cayambe (5,790m) contains the world's highest point on the Equator (at about 4,600m or 15,090ft). Other important peaks in Ecuador include Antisana (5,704m), Cotopaxi (5,897m), Carihuairazo (5,020m), and Pinchincha (4,794m).

PUCE's Club de Andinismo, Excursionismo, y Esquí

Although there are all sorts of climbing clubs and mountain guides in Ecuador, only the club of Quito's Catholic University has embraced skiing. A French engineer named Thierry Ruf donated about ten pairs of skis to the club and taught skiing to many members. The club introduced skiing to Ecuador with a public demonstration in 1989 which was well covered by the local media. They followed this event with the nation's first ski race on the slopes of Cotopaxi in March of 1990.

Club members report that Antisana probably has the best slopes for skiing although Cotopaxi, Cayambe, and Carihuairazo have had good days as well. Modern *refugios* are located on the slopes of many of the major volcanoes, and ground transportation, mountaineering equipment, and experienced guides are easily found in Quito. All the major peaks have been skied from their summits by a variety of foreigners. There is no real ski season as snow can fall any time of year, but as in the other countries of the region, the old snowfields are receding. For further logistical information, see Rob Rachowiecki's recently updated *Climbing and Hiking in Ecuador* by Bradt Publications. In Quito, talk to Mario Vascones at the Club de Andinismo, Excursionismo, y Esquí located at back of the *Coliseo* at the Catholic University.

Chapter 41

Colombia
Manizales and the Nevado del Ruiz

The Andes are split into three *cordilleras* in Colombia. No peaks in the Western Cordillera reach the snowline; the longest range is the Eastern Cordillera whose highest mountain is Ritacuba Blanca (5,493m; 18,022ft) in the Sierra Nevada de Cocuy. The highest mountain in Colombia is the remote Sierra Nevada de Santa Marta which rises from a coastal plain on the edge of the Caribbean to 5,775m (18,947ft). The glaciers here are nearly inaccessible and too steep and rugged to ski.

The Central Cordillera is the rugged backbone of Colombia, and its highest mountain is the Nevado del Huila (5,750m; 18,865ft). It is here that much of the nation's rich coffee crop is grown.

The only lift operating in the country is an incredibly steep tram which rises from Bogotá, Colombia's capital, to Montserrat, a convent on a ledge of the Eastern Cordillera overlooking the city. Running through the narrow lanes of the complex is a double chairlift, of domestic manufacture, that apparently has not operated in many years. Colombia is, however, the only country in the region that has had lift serviced skiing.

On July 26th and 28th, 1956, the South American Ski Championships were held on the slopes of the Nevado del Ruiz (about 5,300m; 17,390ft) near the picturesque coffee center of Manizales. The Slalom and GS series was part of the annual *Feria de Manizales* and served as an inauguration for the new T-Bar. The championship was eventually won by the Argentine, Luis de Ridder, after a strong challenge by the press favorite, Mario Vera, 17, of Chile.

Skiing had progressed to this point largely because of the efforts of Dr Hernán Jaramillo Duque who had learned how to ski while studying in Santiago, Chile. Several national championships had been held in earlier years under the auspices of the local Club de Ski of which Dr Jaramillo was President. The late '50s were the heyday of skiing in Colombia, and after the initial hype, the motorcycle race from Manizales to the *refugio* became the most popular sporting event of the annual *Feria*.

A second lift was eventually built and led to a point just below the volcano's summit. Although the "season" was December to April, the lifts operated year-round, at any hour, whenever anyone wanted to ski. A good road led to a well-equipped *refugio*, and a beautiful hot springs resort still operates several kilometers below the lifts.

Several factors led to the demise of skiing in Manizales. No locals skied: there were no Colombians in the 1956 races, and no Colombian ever won a "National Championship." Only foreigners skied on the Pista del Ruiz, with Swiss and Germans the most predominant. Consistently poor weather, a receding snowline, the descending glacier, ground warming, and tower instability due to ground movement forced officials to give up the operation several years before the volcano's eruption in November, 1985.

The *refugio* would still be the place to begin a ski excursion, even though the old lift cables now feed directly into a wall of solid glacial ice. The nearby peak of Santa Isabel could also be skied. For assistance in the region, contact Javier Echavarría, a mountain guide who works out of the main tourist office in Manizales' central Parque Bolivar.

Chapter 42

Venezuela

Mérida, The World's Highest Tramway

The Andes arguably begin just southeast of Venezuela's capital, Caracas. The mountains run due west to Barquisimeto from where they form the considerably higher Cordillera de Mérida which extends to the Colombian border. The Andes' first (but neither northernmost nor easternmost) 5,000m peak lies in this range which is the only area in Venezuela that accumulates snow.

When Venezuelans tire of beaches, humidity, and urban blight, they head to Mérida, the country's only mountain resort. The small (pop:150,000), clean town is perched on a grassy ledge above the Chama River. Mérida is dominated by a towering *corona* of peaks including, from east to west, Humboldt (4942m), Bompland (4882m), Bolívar (5,007m; 16,427ft), Toro (4,755m), and León (4,740m). Access to the mountains is greatly facilitated by a tram system which leads to the top of Pico Espejo (4,765m).

The tram ascends 3,188m (10,459ft) from a plaza a few blocks from the center of town. Although it is also alleged to be the longest tram in the world (12,590m; 41,306ft), there are actually four distinct tram lines. Each car holds 40 passengers and equipment, and total ascending time is about 48 minutes plus transfers at three stations. Each station has a restaurant and gift shops, and the top station has great views of the nearby peaks. The trams were constructed by Applevage of Paris in 1958 and are operated by the government tourist company Corporturismo. Backpacks and skis are allowed at no extra charge in the cars (US$5). The tram opens at 7:30am and lines begin to form at 6:00am. Arrive early to avoid long lines and to enjoy clearer mornings. Reservations are required in high season (tel: 074-525-080).

In spite of the skiing image presented in Mérida, very little skiing actually takes place. Skiing is limited due to the lack of enduring snowfields, slope steepness, and the perils of the glaciers. The most skied run lies near the top of the tram, but skiing is not encouraged here as the slope ends in a cliff. Other peaks and glaciers are best reached with technical hikes from the top of the tram. A park permit is required to leave the top station and is obtained at a booth at the base of the tram. The Club Andino Venezolano is now defunct, but a good rescue organization is active in the area. Guides and mountaineering equipment are widely available. For more information, seek the Casa de Guias or Tour de Montaña both located in the plaza at the base of the tram.

SOUTH AMERICAN HANDBOOK

FROM THE DARIEN GAP TO TIERRA DEL FUEGO
"The best guidebook in existence" – Graham Greene

This comprehensive and well researched guidebook, the 'bible' for South America, is massively updated each year. New annual editions come out on the 1st September and are available from good bookshops or direct from the Publishers.

Also available:
The Caribbean Islands Handbook
The Mexico & Central American Handbook

TRADE & TRAVEL PUBLICATIONS
6 Riverside Court, Riverside Road, Bath BA2 3DZ. England

Chapter 43

Antarctica
Marsh Air Force Base

In October of 1988, a ski race was held in Antarctica. The Chilean Air Force and Ski Federation organized the competition to inaugurate a new lift for the residents of the tiny Villa Las Estrellas. A 10km nordic race and a giant slalom were held on a slope called Cerro Franciscano near the Marsh Air Force Base on King George Island. Racers from six countries and Chile were invited including Billy Kidd from the US. The lift is a 200 meter-long Doppelmayr surface tow that was donated, and permanently installed, by the Chilean Ski Federation. With 60 vertical meters, it probably isn't worth the expense of a trip to Antarctica, but if you happen to be in the area.... There are also small lifts in the camps of the New Zealanders and North Americans. The best plan would be to bring cross-country skis, as Antarctica is undoubtedly the world's greatest nordic ski area.

Are you an adventurous traveller?
Send for our catalogue of guide books for places off the beaten track.

Bradt Publications
41 Nortoft Road, Chalfont St Peter, Bucks SL9 OLA

APPENDICES

A. SPANISH SKI VOCABULARY

Verbs
to ski—*esquiar*
to turn—*doblar*
to fall—*caer*
to crash—*chocar*
to jump—*saltar*
to take a run—*bajar, hacer una bajada*
to ride (a lift)—*subir*
to unload (a chairlift)—*bajar* (a surface lift)—*soltar, largarse*
to pack (snow)—*pisar, compactar*
to adjust (bindings)—*ajustar*
to tighten—*apretar*
to loosen—*aflojar, soltar*

Equipment
ski—*ski, tabla, esquí*
  tip—*punta*
  tail—*cola*
  base—*base*
  sidewall—*lado*
  edge—*canto*
snowboard—*tabla (de surf)*
bindings—*fijaciones*
  toe piece—*puntera*
  heel piece—*talonera*
  spring—*resorte (de tensión)*
  wings—*bigotes*
ski brake—*freno, ski stoper*
safety strap, leash—*correa*
slip plate—*teflón, multicontrol*
poles—*bastones*
  grip—*mango, puno*
  basket—*roseta, rodela*
  strap—*correa*
boots—*botas, zapatos de ski*
  buckle—*gancho*
  hinge—*bisagra*

gloves—*guantes*
goggles—*antiparras*
sunglasses—*lentes*
ski hat—*gorro*
hood—*capucha*
helmet—*casco*
visor—*visera, gorinche, jockey*
scarf—*ajete, bufanda*
bandana—*chapelele, panuelo*
neck gator—*ojetuda*
headband—*cintillo*
parka—*parka, campera*
bibs—*jardinera*
one—*piece suit-buzo*
backpack—*mochila*
patch—*cataleja, parche*
pin—*medalla, insignia*
ice skates—*patines*
ice skating—*patinar de hielo*
snowshoes—*raquetas de nieve*

Ski Area
chairlift—*silla, telesilla, aerosilla*
surface lift—*arrastre, poma*
T-Bar-*ancla*
gondola—*teleférico*
tram—*telecabina, cable carríl*
lifts—*medios de elevación, andariveles*
  top—*llegada, cima, retorno*
  bottom—*base, matríz*
lift line—*cola, fila*
ski area—*centro de ski*
ticket—*ticket, boleto, abono, forfait*
snowcat—*pisanieve, snowtrack*
snowmobile—*motonieve, snowcat*
skier—*esquiador*
ski instructor—*profesor, instructor, monitor*

coach—*entrenador*
ski patrolman—*patrulla, pistero, patrullero*
lift operator—*medio de elevación, operador andarivelista*
run—*pista, cancha*
track, trail—*huella, sendero*
bowl—*embudo, anfiteatro*
chute—*canaleta, garganta*
cliff—*precipicio, farellón*
wall, face—*pared, cara, ladera*
summit—*cumbre, cima*
valley—*valle*
canyon—*cajón (Chile), cañón*
gorge—*cañada*
ridge—*filo*
cornice—*cornisa*
tree—*árbol*
forest—*bosque*
hill—*cerro, colina*
mountain—*montaña*
mountain range—*sierra, cordón*
glacier—*ventisquero, glacier*
volcano—*volcán*

Ski Technique
beginner—*novicio, principante, debutante*
intermediate—*intermedio*
advanced—*avanzado*
expert—*experto*
alpine—*alpino*
nordic—*nórdico, ski de fondo, de marcha, de travesía*
traverse—*travesía*
sideslip—*derrape*
snowplow—*cuña*
skate—*patinar*
stride—*paso*
glide—*deslizar*

Racing
slalom—*slalom especial*
giant slalom—*slalom gigante*
downhill—*descenso*
speed ski—*kilómetro lanzado*

starting gate—*partida*
finish line—*meta*
race course—*trazado*
rut—*canaleta*
bib—*número*
gate—*puerta*
bamboo pole—*caña, coligue*
breakaway gate—*pivotante*

Weather and Conditions
season—*temporada, estación*
weather—*tiempo*
clear—*claro, despejado*
cloudy—*cubierto, nublado*
raining—*lluviendo*
snowing—*nevando*
fog—*nublada;* foggy—*nublando*
windy—*mucho viento*
storm—*tormenta*
blizzard—*temporal*
wind chill—*sensación térmica*
snow—*nieve*
conditions—*condiciones*
  hard, icy—*dura, hielo, helada*
  packed powder—*pisada, compactada*
  soft—*blanda*
  slushy—*sopa, húmeda*
  corn—*granulada, nieve primavera*
  crust—*cartón, acortanada*
  powder—*polvo, honda*
  wind slab—*placa de viento*
steepness—*pendiente, inclinación*
steep—*verticál, parada*
flat—*plano, suave*
open—*abierta, habilitada*
closed—*cerrada*
caution—*cuidado, precaución*
danger—*peligro*

Mountaineering
avalanche—*avalancha, alud*
  slab—*lineal, placa*
  point release—*puntual,*

   desprendimiento de punta
crown line—*corona, línea de
   fractura*
sidewall, flank—*laterale, flanco,
   orilla*
snow pillow—*depósito (de nieve)*
avalanche path—*trayectoría,
   recorrido, huella*
snow pit—*hoyo*
snow profile—*perfíl de placa*
snow drift, glacier—*ventisquero*
crevasse—*grieta*
buried—*tapado*
rescue—*salvar, rescatar*
   shovel—*pala*
   rope—*soga, cuerda*
   probe pole—*bastón de sonda*
   avalanche beacon—*radio
   avalancha*
explosive shot—*tiro*
   cap—*fulminante*
   fuse—*mecha*
   det cord—*cordón de
   detonación*
   cache—*contenedor de
   explosivas, polvorín*
climbing skin—*piel de foca*
crampons—*grampones*
ice axe—*piolét*

First Aid

first aid—*primeros auxilios*
frostbite—*hiperlisemia*
hypothermia—*hipotermia*
altitude sickness—*soroche*
injury—*herida*
fracture—*fractura (simple,
   expuesta)*
dislocation—*dislocación*
sprain—*torcedura, esguince*
cut—*lesión*
splint—*férula*
backboard—*tabla*
C—*collar-collarín*
bandage—*venda, vendaje*
band—*aid-curita, parche*
blanket—*manta, frazada*
aspirin—*aspirina*
body—*cuerpo*
   bone—*hueso*
   joint—*juntura, articulación*
   ligament—*ligamento*
   muscle—*muslo, músculo*
   tendon—*tendón*
   spinal cord—*columna espinal*

B. SKI WEEK PRICE COMPARISON

All prices are quoted in US$ for the 1990 season and represent per person rates based on double occupancy unless otherwise indicated.

RESORT	TYPE	HIGH	MID	LOW	INCLUDED
Antillanca		7/7–7/31 9/8–9/24	8/1-9/7 9/25-10/15	5/1-6/28 10/16-10/31	7 Nights 3 Meals/Day
	Single	630	575	485	7 Tickets
	Double	480	440	385	6 Lessons
Chapelco	H.Sol de Andes	6/20-7/7 9/2-9/30	8/5-8/18 8/26-9/1	7/8-7/28 8/19-8/25	7 Nights 6 Tickets
	Single	1,365	1,245	985	2/meals/day
	Double	1,050	965	800	Air fm BA
	Suite	1,316	1,182	961	Transfers
	Htl Ski	645	615	545	Medical Ins
El Colorado		7/13-8/3	7/6-7/13 8/10-9/7	6/15-7/6 9/7-10/12	7 Nights Cleaning
	Double	655	428	218	2meals:$106
	4 pers.	437	286	146	3meals:$275
	6 pers.	437	286	165	
La Hoya		7/15-8/25		8/26-9/20	7 Nights
	Inns	542		514	6 Tickets
	Sol Sur	600		558	6 Lessons
	Thuelche	621		567	Ski Rental
	Cabins	529	for four	502	Air fm BA
La Parva		7/6-8/3	6/29-7/6 8/3-9/7	6/22-6/29 9/7-9/21	Minimum 4 Persons
	no meals	736	550	400	7 Nights
	2 meals	806	620	470	7 Tickets
	3 meals	910	710	545	
Los Penitentes		7/8-8/25	7/1-7/7 8/26-9/15	6/24-6/30 9/16-10/6	7 Nights 7 Tickets
	Hosteria	524	433	365	2 Meals/Day
	Juncal	363	294	365	No Meals
	Portezuelo	408	330	330	No Meals
	Apt Htl	675	555	490	2 Meals/Day

RESORT	TYPE	HIGH	MID	LOW	INCLUDED
Portillo		7/7-8/4	6/30-7/7 8/4-9/15	6/9-6/30 9/15-10/6	
	IncaBunk	413	330	308	7 Nights
	Single	1,197	957	717	4 Meals/Day
	Double	1,072	858	644	8 Tickets
	Suite	1,719	1,375	1,031	
Termas de Chillán		7/7-7/27 9/14-9/18	6/16-7/6 7/28-9/13	5/19-6/15 9/29-10/31	
	Bunk	570	395	285	7 Nights
	Single	1,245	860	620	3 Meals/Day
	DoubleA	900	618	450	7 Tickets
	Suite	1,290	885	645	6 Lessons
Valle de Las Leñas	also low and med-high seasons	7/14-8/3	8/4-8/31	6/23-6/29 9/22-10/6	7 Nights 7 Tickets 2 Meals/Day Air fm BA
	Dormy-Hs	890	750	590	5-8 Persons
	Aprt-Htl	1,200	1,020	720	4 Persons
	Escorpio	1,460	1,220	830	2 Persons
	Pisces	2,790	2,250	1,440	Jr Suite
Valle Nevado		7/13-8/3	7/6-7/13 8/3-9/7	6/15-7/6 7/7-10/14	
	Sol Sgl	1,365	1,071	833	7 Nights
	Nvdo Dbl	1,309	1,015	784	8 Tickets
	Nvdo Ste	1,715	1,309	1,032	3 Meals/Day
	2RmCondo	800	590	370	No Meals
Villarrica-Pucón		8/10-8/18 9/7-9/22	7/6-7/26 8/19-9/6 9/23-10/18	6/1-7/5 7/27-8/2 10/19-11/30	Shuttle Service to Ski Area
	Std Sgl	460	425	330	7 Nights
	Sup Dbl	590	540	405	Half Board
	DblSuite	845	770	560	7 Tickets
	3RmCondo	450	415	330	6 Lessons

C. PROPOSED ITINERARIES

1. One-week:

A. **Santiago Ski Vacation.** Four top ski areas.
   Features: Maximum diversity in skiing, Santiago city life, 4½ days skiing.
   Day 1: Arrive in Santiago am, find hotel, visit city, visit ski area offices, reserve Portillo.
   Day 2: Ski La Parva.
   Day 3: Ski El Colorado.
   Day 4: Ski Valle Nevado
   Day 5: Go to Portillo am, ski half-day.
   Day 6: Ski Portillo
   Day 7: Return Santiago am, leave Chile p.m.

B. **Structured Ski Vacation.** One major ski area.
   Book package with Portillo, Valle Nevado, Las Leñas, or Villarrica-Pucón.
   Features: Maximum skiing, most convenience and ease of travel, least cultural interaction, 6 days skiing.
   Day 1: Arrive in country, travel to ski area, half-day skiing possible with some packages.
   Day 2-6: Ski.
   Day 7: Return to city and fly home.

2. Two-week:

A. **Southern Lakes District Tour.** Two major resorts, three smaller areas.
   Features: Cross Lakes ferry trip, independent and leisurely travel, 6½ days skiing.
   Day 1: Arrive in Santiago, fly to Puerto Montt.
   Day 2: Ski La Burbuja, fresh fish and Chilean wine dinner in Puerto Montt.
   Day 3: Travel (by bus) to Antillanca, ski half-day.
   Day 4: Ski Antillanca.
   Day 5: Travel to Bariloche.
   Day 6-7: Ski Catedral, enjoy Bariloche.
   Day 8: Rent car, drive to San Martín via Limay River.
   Day 9: Ski Chapelco.
   Day 10: Drive to Angostura via Siete Lagos.
   Day 11: Ski Cerro Bayo, return to Bariloche.
   Day 12-13: *Cruce de Lagos* ferry trip to Puerto Montt.
   Day 14: Return to Santiago am, quick visit of downtown area, fly out pm.

B. **Full Chile Tour.** Four major resorts, four smaller areas.
   Features: Maximum cultural interaction, quick visits of 8 of Chile's best towns and cities, high adventure and independence, fast pace, 8-9 days skiing.
   Day 1: Arrive Santiago am, reserve Chillán, Villarica-Pucón, rental car in Los Angeles, visit Santiago.
   Day 2-3: Ski local Santiago areas of choice.
   Day 4: Train to Chillán.
   Day 5: Ski Chillán.
   Day 6: Ski am, return to Chillán mid-day, bus to Los Angeles.
   Day 7: Rent auto, ski Antuco, return to Los Angeles.
   Day 8: Drive to Lonquimay, ski, stay at Manzanar.
   Day 9: Ski at New Llaima, stay in Temuco.
   Day 10:To Pucón, ski half day on Villarrica Volcano.
   Day 11:Ski Villarrica-Pucón.
   Day 12:Drive to Puerto Montt via Valdivia and Puerto Varas, return auto.
   Day 13:Ski La Burbuja using local transportation.
   Day 14:Return to Santiago and fly home.

C. **Tierra del Fuego Tour Adventure.** Nordic and alpine skiing.
   Features: Challenging travel, high costs, unique adventures, high cultural interaction, 6-7 days of skiing.
   Day 1: Arrive Santiago, fly to Punta Arenas.
   Day 2: Ski Mirador.
   Day 3: Ferry to Porvenir, bus to Río Grande.
   Day 4: Bus or fly to Ushuaia.
   Day 5-8: Ski alpine and nordic at five areas.
   Day 9: Fly to Río Gallegos.
   Day 10:Bus to Río Turbio.
   Day 11:Ski Valdelén, bus to Puerto Natales pm.
   Day 12-13:Extra days for visit to Torres del Paine, more skiing around Punta Arenas, or to accommodate lost travel days.
   Day 14:Return to Santiago am., quick visit of downtown, fly out pm.
   Note: due to ferry schedule, the itinerary may need to be juggled or possibly reversed, check ferries immediately after arriving at Punta Arenas.

D. BUENOS AIRES SKI ADDRESSES

Club Argentino de Ski
166 Lavalle, P6, Buenos Aires. Tel: 312-2123

Federación Argentina de Ski y Andinismo
665 Montevideo, P3, 308, (1019), Buenos Aires. Tel: 46-9771

Caviahue:
Parque Caviahue
416 Paraguay, Planta Baja "H", (1057) Buenos Aires. Tel: 312-3227

Chapelco:
Cumbres de Chapelco
233 Suipacha, Loc 20, (1008) Buenos Aires. Tel: 35-0021, FAX: 35-6620, Telex: 02-1611

Catedral:
Gran Catedral
783 Paraguay, P9, "B", (1047) Buenos Aires. Tel: 312-2420

La Hoya:
La Hoya Ski
377 Viamonte, P4, (1053) Buenos Aires. Tel: 311-2164

Penitentes:
Operadores Penitentes
570 Suipacha, P1, "B". Tel: 394-3601

Sol Andino (Ayelen Hotel):
643 Lavalle, P2, "C". Tel: 393-5204

Valle de Las Leñas:
Valle de Las Leñas
707 Arenales, Nivel Jardin, (1061) Buenos Aires. Tel: 313-2121

E. CONVERSION TABLE

Temperature:
C x 9 / 5 + 32 = F
or 1.8C + 32 = F
(F - 32)/1.8 = C

Distance:
1 meter = 3.281 feet or 1.09 yards
1 foot = 0.3048 meters
1 kilometer = 0.62 miles
1 mile = 1.61 kilometers
1 millimeter = .039 inches
1 inch = 25.42 millimeters
1 yard = .9144 meters

Area:
1 hectare = 2.471 acres
1 acre = 0.405 hectares
1 square kilometer = 0.386 square miles
1 square mile = 2.590 square kilometers

Capacity:
1 liter = 0.264 US gallons
1 US gallon = 3.785 liters

Weight:
1 kilogram = 2.205 pounds
1 pound = 4536 grams

INDEX

Aconcagua, 3, 16, 32, 44, 46, 171, 186
Aguas Calientes, 138-9
Alfonsín, Raúl, 170
Alive, 6, 196
Allende, Dr Salvador, 38
altitude sickness, 291
Andes Powder Guides, 16, 55-7, 66, 68
Angelmó, 143, 147-8
Antarctica, 299
Antillanca, 133-9
Antuco, 103-7
Araucano, see Mapuche
araucaria, 7, 111-2, 116
Argentina, 167-70
Atacama Desert, 3, 5, 35
avalanches, 6, 17, 32, 45-6, 72, 77, 171, 197, 285
Ayelen, 176-7, 191
Aylwin, Patricio, 31, 39

Bariloche, see San Carlos de Bariloche
Barrington, Robert, 11
Bolivia, 283-91
Bossoney, Andres, 12, 116
Buenos Aires, 25, 31, 168, 247
buses, 26

Cable Carríl, 15, 233-4
Carabineros de Chile, 29
Caracoles, 13-4, 42-3
Carretera Austral, 148, 151, 154
Casa Blanca, 134
casinos, 128, 193
Caviahue, see Parque Caviahue
Centro Cordillera de Las Condes, 65-6
Cerro Bayo, 223-7, 229
Cerro Campanario, 247
Cerro Catedral, see Gran Catedral
Cerro López, 16, 241
Cerro Martial: see Glacier El Martial
Cerro Mirador, 159-63
Cerro Otto, 11, 13, 233, 240, 247
Chacabuco, 156
Chacaltaya, 284-7
chairlifts, 15
Chapelco, 215-9
Chile, 35-40
Chillán, 99-101
Chiloé, 36, 143, 147, 156, 163
Clark, John and Mathew, 11

Club Argentino de Ski (CAS), 12, 245, 247
Club de Esquí Cruz de Caña, 172, 191
Club Esquí de Los Angeles, 12, 104, 109
coal, 271
colectivo, 26
Colombia, 295-6
Concepción, 38, 106-7
Condor, Andean, 7
Copahue, 16, 207
Coyhaique, 155-8
Cristo Redentor, 42, 44, 48
Cruz de Lagos, 33, 148, 247
Cuerpo de Socorro Andino, 29, 91
Curacautín, 111, 113

Darwin, Charles, 144, 163, 192
De Ridder, Luis, 295
Della Maggiora, Carlos, 116, 124
Diaz, Claudio, 127
DIGEDER, 79, 105, 152, 154, 158
Doppelmayr, 15
driving, 27
DuBois, Eugene, 12

Easter Island, 35-6
Ecuador, 293-4
El Bolsón, 255-7
El Colorado, 59-64
El Fraile, 151-5
El Plomo, 71, 74
Ensenada, 146
Errazuríz, Jaime and Max, 13
Esquel, 203-6

Falklands Islands, see Malvinas
Farellones, 65-8
Federación Argentina de Ski y Andinismo, 13
Federación de Ski y Andinismo de Chile, 13, 91, 299
ferries, 28, 90, 148, 164-5, 289
fishing, 7, 156, 281
Francisco Jerman, 273, 279
Fuerte Bulnes, 161, 163

Garcia, Santiago, 83
gauchos, 169
German Excursion Club, 11, 66

Germans, 37, 124, 134, 139, 169, 246, 296
gifts, 20, 30
Giró, Gustavo, 275, 278
Glacier El Martial, 273, 275-6, 280
Gran Catedral, 231-8
guanaco, 7,
Guiñazú, Francisco, 14, 180-1

Hammersley, Arturo, 13, 93
health, 20, 29
helicopter skiing, 16, 48, 56, 72
Hermundsen, Michel, 10
History
  of Argentina, 167-8
  of Chile, 36-7
  of skiing, 10-14
  of the Chile-Argentina frontier, 30-1
Huaraz, 292
Huife, Termas de, 128, 130

ice skating, 50, 222, 251, 280
Inca, 36, 44, 74
Iñarra, Jorge, 192

Jaramillo, Dr Hernan, 295-6
Jay, John, 5, 13, 42
Jerman, Francisco, 275
Juncal, 14, 32, 42
Junín de los Andes, 130

La Burbuja, 143-47
La Hoya, 259-64
La Parva, 52-7
La Paz, 287-91
La Picada, 134, 144
Lagos del Sur, 216, 233
Laguna Blanca, 7, 212
Laguna de la Laja, 103
Lagunillas, 75-9
LahuenCo, see Los Molles
Langley, Roger, 13
Lanín volcano, 5, 16, 124
Las Cotorras, 273, 275, 279-80
Las Cuevas, 31
Las Leñas, see Valle de las Leñas
Lauryssens, Pedro, 172
Leatherbee, Clifton, 60
Les Arcs, 70, 194
Lindemann, Curt, 13
Lira, Martín, 49, 120
Llaima, 115-9
Lo Valdés, 11

Longitudinal Highway, see Carretera Austral
Lonquimay, 110-4
Los Andes, 32, 144
Los Angeles, 107-9
Los Libertadores, 32, 44, 47, 50
Los Molles, 191, 201-2
Los Penitentes, 171-7
Lowenstein, Ernesto "Tito", 194, 202
Lunn, Arnold, 13
Lynch, Dr Antonio "Tuco", 12-3

Magellan Archipelago, 36
Maipo Canyon, 10-1, 35, 66, 75
Malargüe, 201
Malvinas (Falklands), 31, 163, 167, 170
Manizales, 295
Manzanar, Termas de, 113-4
Mapuches, 36, 112, 120, 246
Marsh Air Force Base, 299
Marte, 15, 202, 196
Matriceria Cuyo, 172
Matthei, Alfredo and Frederico, 134
Meiling, Otto, 11-2, 240
Mendoza, 184-91
Menem, Carlos, 31, 170
Mérida, 297-8
Mina Uno, 267-8

Nahuel Huapi, 33, 225, 228, 246
National Ski Patrol, 13
Neuquén, 25, 27, 32, 168, 210
Nevado del Ruiz, 295
night skiing, 16, 269
Nöbl, Hans, 12, 233

O'Higgins, Bernardo, 36, 99-100
Ojos del Salado, 16
Osorno, 139-41

Palguín, Termas de, 127-8, 131
Pan American Highway, 27, 139
Pan American Ski Championships, 13, 285
Parque Caviahue, 207-8
Pastoruri, 292
Patagonia, 5, 37, 159, 167, 259
Patrullas de Chile, 63, 78, 91, 97, 105, 136
Pelluco, 147, 150
Perito Moreno, 252-5, 257
Perón, Juan Domingo, 12, 169
Peru, 292
Petrinovic, Robert, 56

Petrohue, 33
Peulla, 33, 143
Piedras Blancas, 241, 243
Piltriquitrón, 252-4
Pinochet, Augusto, 37-9
Podesta, Arturo, 13
poma, 15
Pomagalski, Jean, 45
Portillo, 40-51
Porvenir, 34, 164
Posnaski, Raúl, 285
Potrerillos, 183
Primeros Piños, 209-11
Pucón, 129-31
Puente del Inca, 31, 172, 186
Puerto Aisén, 155
Puerto Alegre, 33
Puerto Blest, 11, 33
Puerto Frias, 11
Puerto Montt, 147-50
Puerto Natales, 27, 34, 163, 165, 269-72
Puerto Panuelo, 33
Puerto Varas, 143-4, 146, 149-50
Punta Arenas, 163-6
Punta de Vacas, 31, 172-3
Purcell, David, 43, 54, 83
Purcell, Henry, 43
Purcell, Robert, 43, 54
Puyehue Pass, 32-3, 134, 139, 225
Puyehue, Termas de, 91, 137-9

Quetrupillán, 127

racing, 13
Raemdonck, Jean Pierre, 225
railroads, 25-6, 271-2
remise, 26-7
Ricketts, Ernesto, 11
Río Blanco, 12, 31-2
Río Gallegos, 34, 164, 271-2
Río Grande, 34, 163, 273
Río Turbio, 271-2
Robles, Vicente, 233
Rosenquist, Elmer, 10
Roskenjer, Pablo, 13

San Carlos de Bariloche, 245-51
San Martín de los Andes, 220-2
San Martín, José de, 36, 185, 193
San José de Maipo, 75-9

San Rafael, 203-6
Santiago, 80-91
Sanz, José Luis, 115, 119
Siete Lagos route, 219, 221
Sled City, 271
snowboarding, 17, 72
soroche, see altitude sickness
Stern, Eduardo, 70

Temuco, 120-2
Termas de Chillán, 93-9
Teski Club, 144, 146
Tierra del Fuego, 5, 6, 19, 30-4, 159, 167-8
 see map 274
Tierra Mayor, 273, 278, 280
Todos los Santos Lake, 143
tramway, see Cable Carríl
Trans-Andean railway, 10-1, 42, 44, 172
Tres Mil Cien (3,100), 56-7
Tunuyán, 192
Tupungato, 4

Urzua, Carlos, 116, 124
Ushuaia, 280-2
Uspallata Pass, 10, 12, 17, 31, 172, 174, 186, 283

Va et Vient, 15, 42, 45-7, 126
Valdelen, 267-70
Valdivia, 136
Valdivia, Pedro de, 36, 81-2
Valle de Chall-Huaco, 240-3
Valle de las Leñas, 193-202
Valle Manantiales, 192
Valle Nevado, 69-74
Vallecitos, 179-83
Valparaíso, 10, 31, 38, 85, 116
Varela, Juan Cruz, 233
Venezuela, 297-8
Villa Arelauquen, 242-3
Villa la Angostura, 228-30
Villarrica-Pucón, 123-9
visas, 20

Wallner, Wolfgang, 273, 275-7

Zapala, 212-3
Zinni, Eduardo, 209-10

OTHER BOOKS ON SOUTH AMERICA FROM BRADT PUBLICATIONS

Backpacking in Chile and Argentina
All the best hikes in these two countries, plus best places for viewing wildlife. Emphasis on the astonishingly beautiful scenery of South Patagonia.

Backpacking and Trekking in Peru and Bolivia by Hilary Bradt
Fifth edition (1990) The classic guide for walkers and nature lovers.

No Frills Guide to Venezuela by Hilary Dunsterville Branch
The emphasis is on hiking, but there's plenty of information on remote beaches, uninhabited islands, and national parks, as well as major cities. The No Frills Guide will be replaced by a standard guide in early 1992.

South American River Trips by Tanis and Martin Jordan.
How to explore the rivers of South America in your own boat. Full of anecdote and humour, as well as information.

Backcountry Brazil by Alex Bradbury.
Three areas are covered in depth: Amazonia, the Pantanal, the north-east coast.

Climbing and Hiking in Ecuador (second edition) by Rob Rachowiecki and Betsy Wagenhauser.
New edition updated by the manager of the South American Explorer's Club in Quito.

Plus maps of every Latin American country.

This is just a selection of the books and maps for adventurous travellers that we stock. Send for our latest catalogue.

Bradt Publications, 41 Nortoft Rd, Chalfont St Peter, Bucks SL9 0LA, England. Tel: 02407 3478.